Zumbo

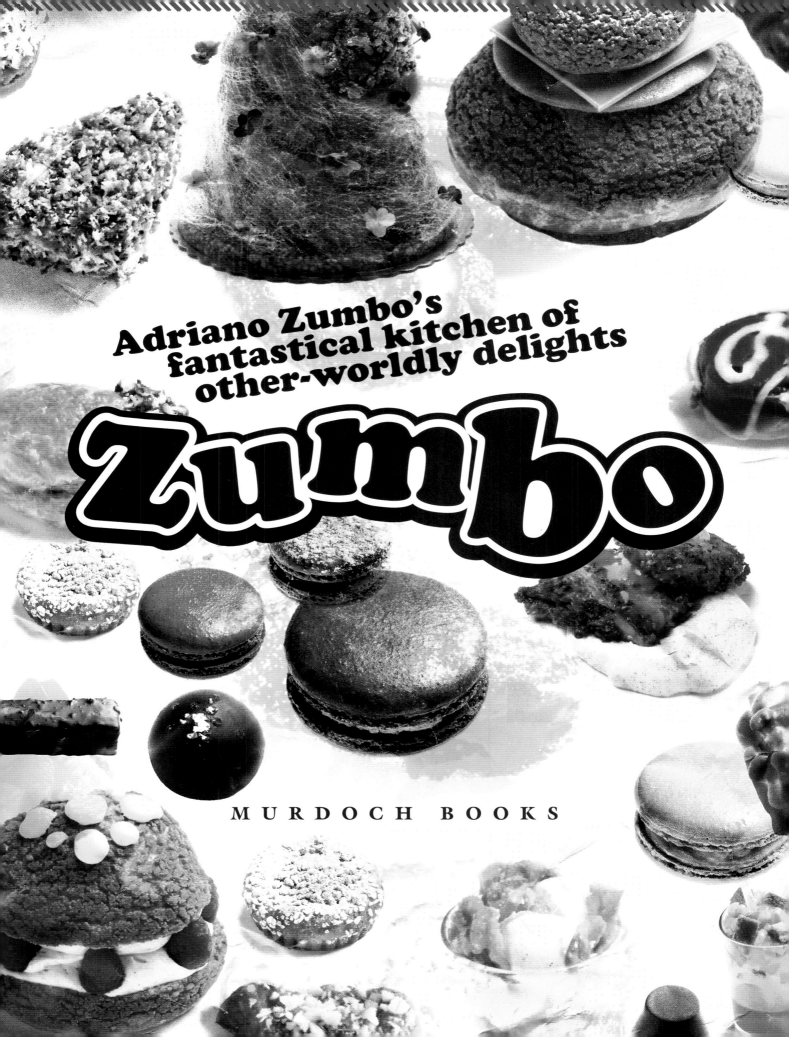

Adriano Zumbo's
fantastical kitchen of
other-worldly delights

Zumbo

MURDOCH BOOKS

I have a great passion for cooking and sweets, and a burning desire to achieve my life goals. But when I'm not madly inventing or perfecting a recipe, I'm a pretty quiet and humble sort of guy, like my dad.

I'm always asked what inspires me, and there's no simple answer. Mostly, my ideas come from within, from my experiences, my childhood and the master of all sweets and lollies, Mr Willy Wonka. I also get ideas from everyday life, friends, family, co-workers and customers — making people happy inspires me a great deal.

My childhood was nothing if not sweet. I was a fussy eater when I was young, and I compensated for this by filling up on junk food instead of the traditional Italian dishes my mother would cook up. But it wasn't such a bad thing, because I built up a pretty accurate and comprehensive sweet palate.

My parents moved to Australia from Reggio, Italy, in the 1960s. They bought a supermarket business at Coonamble, in country New South Wales, and I would hang around there both before and after school because they worked long hours. Little did they know that every morning I'd fill my schoolbag with massive amounts of lollies and chocolate bars to get me through the day, and to share with my schoolmates, of course! I became the 'go to' boy for anything sweet.

Over the years, I worked in all the sections of the supermarket, including the checkout, deli, stacking shelves and the fruit & veg section. School wasn't really my thing — I wasn't particularly academic, though I did well at subjects that involved using my hands, such as metalwork and woodwork, and my experience at the checkout helped with maths. But when my sister Patricia opened a new supermarket with an instore bakery, I found my calling. All she had was one of those frozen dough and premix systems, but I became hooked on pastry.

I wanted to leave school as soon as possible. So when I went to Sydney for a friend's school formal, I looked up the classifieds in the paper, applied for a job and got it. When I returned to Coonamble I applied to leave school, packed my bags and moved to Sydney to live with my sister Rosalba and start my apprenticeship.

It was a big step. I was leaving school and moving from a country town with a population of under 3000 to a city with a population of over three million, and I was only 15 years old. I couldn't drive and I wasn't confident enough to catch the bus in the middle of the night, so for the first 18 months Rosalba got up at two o'clock every morning to drive me to work. (Rosalba, I owe you!) I was so happy to escape school life and head to the big smoke, with no parents watching over me and a chance to find something I could really sink my teeth into.

During my four-year apprenticeship I worked in many establishments, covering all types of pastry, from simple and low-cost to complicated and high-end. I was blessed to work under many talented and encouraging head chefs. I think this makes a big difference in the direction a chef's journey takes.

In 2003 I was chosen to represent Australia at the World Pastry Cup (Coupe du Monde de la Pâtisserie) in Lyon, France. This was a huge honour and a massive eye-opener. It was my first real look at pastry on an international level. When it was over I stayed on in Paris to complete several pastry stages, which are intense learning and working experiences, at various schools and establishments.

I came back from France with a macaron in one hand and a dream in the other. Macarons were an everyday thing in Europe and I wanted to make them equally popular and accessible in Australia.

In the meantime, I needed a job and I was looking for one that would challenge me and let me perfect my new skills. I had now been in charge of a pastry kitchen

for four years, since I was 19, and the downside to this was that I didn't have someone I could look up to and learn from each day. I really had to dig deep and push myself to master new techniques and develop my skills.

By 2005 I needed a change, to get away from it all, so I moved to Cairns to take up a job at a five-star hotel. However, I found the hotel culture creatively stifling — I could no longer make the things I loved because everything had to be cost-effective. I realised that in order to make my dream happen, I needed the opportunities provided by a big city.

When I returned to Sydney I decided it was time to do my own thing and began baking from home. I started supplying a local café, making simple things like biscuits, muffins, a few pastries and some tarts. But although baking from home was satisfying, it didn't provide much of a challenge. The things I was making were pretty basic and people were constantly telling me to open my own shop. I started searching for premises and 10 months later my friend Charlie pointed out a tiny shop for lease on Darling Street in Balmain, in Sydney's inner west. It was just what I was after. Charlie and I spent the next 10 weeks designing and fitting out the shop, but we needed a separate kitchen as the shop was too small to have its own. Fortunately, we found one we could sub-lease in nearby Rozelle. It was a dump, but I needed to cook, so I took it and we opened the Darling Street store in April 2007.

The following November we opened Café Chocolat, just a few doors down in the back of the Balmain Mall arcade. Sadly, we were forced to close it down in early 2010, as it was just too small and out of the way. Instead, we decided to put a café/retail outlet in the newly fitted-out kitchen in Rozelle, where people could come and watch everything being made through viewing windows.

The business has gone from strength to strength over the years, though it has been a steep learning curve for me at times. I have been really fortunate to meet, and work with, many talented and supportive people.

I was given the opportunity to represent Australia again in 2010, at the Asian Pastry Cup. I teamed up with Dean Gibson, one of my bosses from my apprenticeship days, and it was a highlight of the year. I also had the chance to appear on TV several times and hopefully dazzle viewers with my creations. I really want to show Australia what we patissiers can do, and the exposure has done wonders for my career.

I believe a cake or sweet is an experience, starting with the name and the look, progressing with the marrying of flavours and textures, and culminating in the emotions before, during and after eating. It is a whole-body experience resulting in a pleasurable moment in time. I try to achieve this by designing my creations to arouse the senses. To see someone satisfied and happy is the greatest return and something that keeps me motivated each day.

Eat sweet and keep baking!

zumbarons

back row, from left: Vegemite; sticky date; chocolate marshmallow; salted milk chocolate caramel; chocolate salt & vinegar; rice pudding; raspberry beetroot; mandarin & tonka bean
middle row, from left: blackened vanilla bean; chocolate peanut butter & jelly; licorice; kalamata olive; chocolate H_2O; pandan coconut; chocozumbo; chocolate orange; chocolate banana
front row, from left: chocolate mayo; cherry coconut; caramel au beurre salé; salt & vinegar; salted butter popcorn; strawberry bubblegum

I fell in love with macarons on my first trip to France. They weren't popular in Australia back then but I was determined to change that. It took a few years of researching recipes and practising and perfecting the technique before I could produce them successfully on a commercial scale, but now they're one of my favourite products to make. I love everything about them — their versatility, colour, texture and, of course, the endless flavour options.

Every year we have Macaron Day at Zumbo's. It's an idea inspired by the French 'Jour du macaron'. We transform our stores to solely sell macarons for the day and we create around 65 different flavours, both new and old.

We also have larger macarons in most of our collections, which are classified as individual cakes. Their fillings are very different from the smaller ones, being mousses, crème légères, jellies and fresh fruit rather than ganaches and buttercreams.

This selection of Zumbarons includes some of my favourites. I hope you enjoy making them as much as I do.

macarons

makes 100 macaron shells

300 g (10½ oz) almond meal
300 g (10½ oz) pure icing (confectioners') sugar
110 g (3¾ oz) egg whites, at room temperature
300 g (10½ oz) caster (superfine) sugar
75 g (2¾ oz) water
Food colouring, if required (see Note)
2 g (²⁄₂₅ oz) powdered egg white (see Glossary)
110 g (3¾ oz) egg whites, extra, at room temperature

Grease 3 large baking sheets and line with non-stick baking paper or Silpat (see Glossary). Combine the almond meal and icing sugar in a bowl. Use a large spoon to push the mixture through a fine sieve into a large bowl.

Put the egg whites in an electric mixer with a whisk attachment. Put the sugar and water in a small saucepan over low heat and stir until the sugar has dissolved. Use a clean pastry brush to brush down the side of the pan to avoid any crystallisation. Increase the heat and bring to the boil. Add the food colouring (if required) at this stage. Cook until the mixture reaches 118°C (244°F). When it is getting close to this temperature, add the powdered egg white to the egg whites in the mixing bowl and whisk on medium speed until frothy.

Once the sugar syrup is at the right temperature, increase the mixer speed to high and slowly add the sugar syrup in a steady stream down the side of the bowl. Whisk until warm, about 8 minutes. Add the extra egg whites to the dry ingredients, then add the meringue and use a large spatula to fold them through until combined.

Continue to fold the mixture so it begins to loosen. Working the mixture this way will slightly soften the meringue — when the mixture falls slowly off the spatula it is at the right texture. The texture is important for the next stage, which is piping.

Transfer the mixture to a piping (icing) bag with a 13 mm (½ inch) plain nozzle. Holding the piping bag about 1.5 cm (⅝ inch) above a tray, pipe straight down onto the tray to make 4 cm (1½ inch) diameter rounds, leaving a 3 cm (1¼ inch) gap between each macaron. As you finish piping each macaron, move the nozzle from 12 o'clock to 6 o'clock quickly to finish the piping action. If you have the correct texture, the macaron will soften again slightly and the tip on top of the macaron will drop, leaving a smooth top. Some macarons are dusted, using a fine sieve, or sprinkled with a flavour at this stage (refer to specific recipes).

Leave the macarons at room temperature for 30 minutes or until a skin forms. After 10 minutes, preheat the oven to 135°C (275°F/Gas 1). To test if the macarons are ready, gently touch one with your fingertip to check that a light skin has formed — the macarons should not be sticky. On humid days this may take longer. The skin is important as it lifts while the macaron cooks, creating a 'foot' at the base.

Bake the macarons for 16 minutes, until they have a firm outer shell. Remove from the oven and set aside for 2 minutes, then carefully remove one macaron with a spatula to check that the base is also cooked and dry. If it is still slightly sticky, return the macarons to the oven for 2–3 minutes, then check again. Cool the macarons completely on the trays.

note: See specific recipes in this chapter as to whether colouring is necessary. Bear in mind that food colouring brands can vary vastly — some gels will require only 2 or 3 drops to give the desired colour, whereas some liquids will require more than 1 tablespoon to achieve intense colours such as red. You must add the colour as you are making the syrup, because if you add it to the macaron mixture itself it will change the mixture's consistency. Getting the colour right really comes down to practice — you need to make the macarons and see how the colour looks in the sugar syrup and then how that changes when it combines with the other ingredients. If you need to colour the macaron shells with two different colours, you can make two half-quantities, in separate batches, and add a different colour to each.

variation — chocolate macarons
Sift 60 g (2¼ oz) unsweetened cocoa powder with 270 g (9½ oz) almond meal and 270 g (9½ oz) pure icing (confectioners') sugar, then continue as for the basic recipe.

variation — drop-shaped macarons
Hold the piping bag about 1.5 cm (⅝ inch) above a tray and pipe straight down onto the tray to make 4 cm (1½ inch) diameter rounds as before, but as you finish piping each macaron flick the nozzle downwards to form a teardrop shape.

storage
Filled macarons can be stored in an airtight container, layered with sheets of non-stick baking paper, for 3–5 days. Depending on the moisture content of the fillings, they will keep for up to 1 week in the refrigerator. They can be frozen for up to 3 months.

filling the macaron shells
Before you begin making a ganache filling, ensure the butter is chopped into small cubes and left at room temperature for approximately 30 minutes. You don't want it to be too soft as it won't add enough body to the ganache. Before you start piping the filling, it's a good idea to match up likely pairs of macarons to sandwich together.

sticky date

licorice

date purée

90 g (3¼ oz) stoned dates, chopped

2.5 g (²⁄₂₅ oz) bicarbonate of soda (baking soda)

150 g (5½ oz) boiling water

sticky date ganache

250 g (9 oz) white couverture chocolate,
  chopped or buttons

100 g (3½ oz) date purée (see recipe above)

38 g (1⅓ oz) pouring (whipping) cream (35% fat)

30 g (1 oz) date molasses (see Glossary)

80 g (2¾ oz) unsalted butter, chopped and softened

1 quantity macaron shells (see page 16),
  coloured light brown

13 fresh dates, stoned and quartered

To make the date purée, put the dates and bicarbonate of soda in a bowl, pour over the boiling water and set aside for 20 minutes. Pour off the excess water, then purée the dates in a food processor until smooth.

To make the sticky date ganache, melt the chocolate in a heatproof bowl over a saucepan of simmering water or in the microwave on medium (50%) in 30-second bursts, stirring after each burst. Take care not to burn the chocolate as it will become grainy. Add 100 g (3½ oz) of the date purée to the melted chocolate and mix well.

Heat the cream and date molasses in a saucepan over medium heat until hot. Add to the chocolate mixture and stir well, then cool to 50°C (122°F).

When the chocolate mixture is at the right temperature, blitz in the butter with a stick mixer until smooth. Allow the ganache to cool and become firm enough to pipe.

Fill a piping (icing) bag with a 9 mm (⅓ inch) plain nozzle with the ganache. Pipe the ganache on the flat side of half of the macaron shells. Press a piece of date into the centre of the ganache on each macaron. Top with the remaining macaron shells. Put the assembled macarons in the refrigerator to set. Bring to room temperature to serve. **makes 50**

175 g (6 oz) pouring (whipping) cream (35% fat)

45 g (1¾ oz) soft licorice (as fresh as possible), chopped

250 g (9 oz) white couverture chocolate, chopped
  or buttons

80 g (2¾ oz) unsalted butter, chopped and softened

1 quantity macaron shells (see page 16), coloured black

Put the cream and licorice in a saucepan over medium heat and bring to the boil. Blitz the cream and licorice together with a stick mixer until smooth.

Put the chocolate in a bowl. Pour over the hot licorice cream and set aside for 2 minutes. Stir until the mixture is smooth, then cool it to 50°C (122°F).

When the mixture is at the right temperature, blitz in the butter with a stick mixer until smooth. Allow the ganache to cool and become firm enough to pipe.

Fill a piping (icing) bag with a 7 mm (³⁄₈ inch) plain nozzle with the ganache. Pipe the ganache on the flat side of half of the macaron shells, then top with the remaining shells. Put the assembled macarons in the refrigerator to set. Bring to room temperature to serve.
makes 50

salted butter popcorn

buttercream

100 g (3¹/₂ oz) caster (superfine) sugar

38 g (1¹/₃ oz) water

75 g (2³/₄ oz) lightly beaten egg

45 g (1³/₄ oz) egg yolks

200 g (7 oz) unsalted butter, chopped and softened

3 g (¹/₁₀ oz) sea salt flakes

1 bag microwave natural or butter-flavoured popcorn

Melted unsalted butter, for brushing

1 quantity macaron shells (see page 16)

Heat the sugar and water in a saucepan over medium–low heat until the sugar has dissolved. Increase the heat to medium and cook until the syrup reaches 121°C (250°F).

Put the eggs and egg yolks in an electric mixer with a whisk attachment and whisk on medium speed for 2 minutes. With the motor running, pour the hot sugar syrup in a thin, steady stream over the egg and mix until thick and cooled to 50°C (122°F). (Stop the mixer when checking the temperature.)

Slowly add the butter, a cube at a time, mixing well to ensure there are no lumps. Fold through the salt.

Cook the microwave popcorn according to the instructions on the bag. Put half the popcorn in a food processor and blitz to small pieces. Lightly brush the tops of the macarons with melted butter and sprinkle with the blitzed popcorn. Leave for 10 minutes, to allow the butter to set.

Fill a piping (icing) bag with a 9 mm (¹/₃ inch) plain nozzle with the buttercream. Pipe buttercream on the flat side of half of the macaron shells, then top with the remaining shells. Put the assembled macarons in the refrigerator to set. Bring to room temperature to serve.

makes 50

strawberry bubblegum

150 g (5¹/₂ oz) sieved strawberry purée (see Basics)

4 pieces (30 g/1 oz) original flavour Hubba Bubba® bubblegum, chopped

250 g (9 oz) white couverture chocolate, chopped or buttons

80 g (2³/₄ oz) unsalted butter, chopped and softened

25 g (1 oz) cocoa butter (see Glossary), finely chopped, melted and cooled to 32°C (90°F)

poprock insert

20 g (³/₄ oz) cocoa butter, finely chopped, melted and cooled to 32°C (90°F)

50 g (1³/₄ oz) plain poprocks (see Glossary)

1 quantity macaron shells (see page 16), coloured pink

Put the strawberry purée and bubblegum in a saucepan over medium heat and cook until the bubblegum softens, then blitz with a stick mixer until smooth.

Put the chocolate in a bowl. Pour over the hot bubblegum mixture and set aside for 2 minutes. Stir until the mixture is smooth, then cool to 50°C (122°F).

When the chocolate mixture is at the right temperature, blitz in the butter and cocoa butter with a stick mixer until smooth. Allow the ganache to cool and become firm enough to pipe.

Meanwhile, to make the poprock insert, combine the 32°C (90°F) cocoa butter and poprocks in a small bowl. Roll the mixture out between two sheets of non-stick baking paper to about 2–3 mm (¹/₁₆ – ¹/₈ inch) thick, then leave at room temperature to set.

Fill a piping (icing) bag with a 7 mm (³/₈ inch) plain nozzle with the ganache. Pipe the ganache on the flat side of half the macaron shells. Break off a piece of the poprock insert and put it on the ganache. Pipe another small amount of ganache over the poprock insert and top with the remaining macaron shells. Put the assembled macarons in the refrigerator to set. Bring to room temperature to serve. **makes 50**

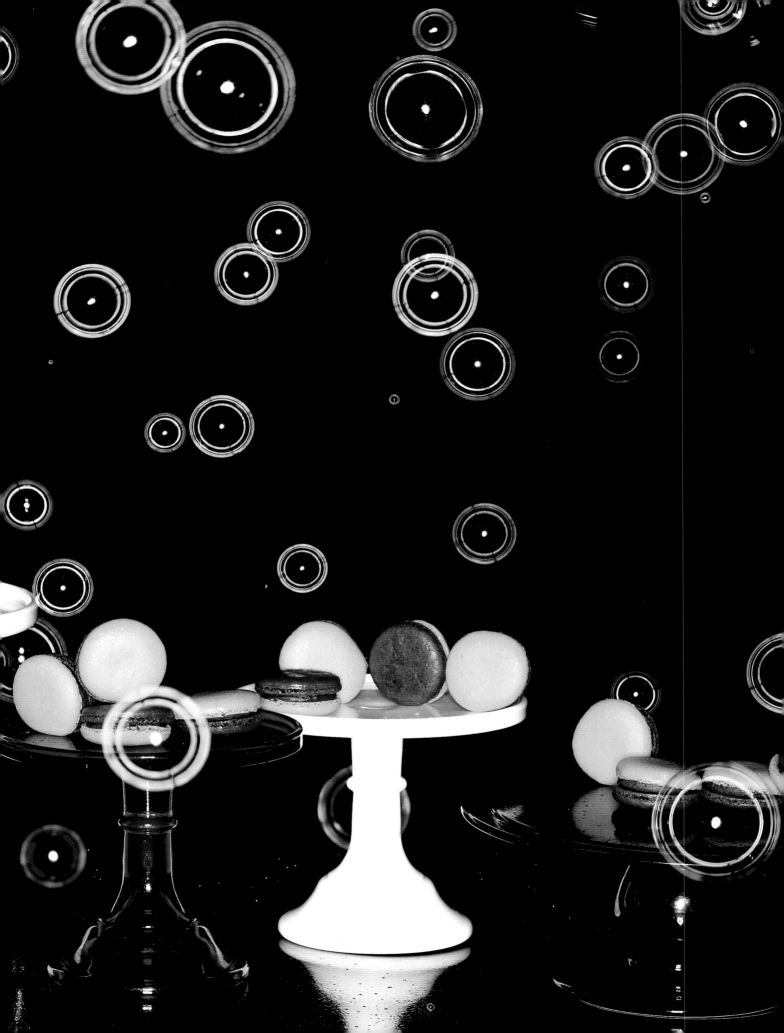

chocolate mayo

mayonnaise suspension

175 g (6 oz) Japanese mayonnaise (see Glossary)
3 g (^{1}/$_{10}$ oz) xanthan gum (see Glossary)

chocolate & mayonnaise ganache

38 g (1^1/$_3$ oz) pouring (whipping) cream (35% fat)
38 g (1^1/$_3$ oz) sieved raspberry purée (see Basics)
225 g (8 oz) dark couverture chocolate (64%),
    chopped or buttons
175 g (6 oz) mayonnaise suspension (see recipe above)
88 g (3^1/$_4$ oz) unsalted butter, chopped and softened

1 quantity chocolate macaron shells (see page 17),
    dusted with edible silver metallic (see Glossary)

To make the mayonnaise suspension, whisk together the mayonnaise and xanthan gum.

Put the cream and raspberry purée in a saucepan over medium heat and bring to the boil. Put the chocolate in a bowl. Pour over the hot cream mixture and set aside for 2 minutes. Stir until the mixture is smooth, then mix in 175 g (6 oz) of the mayonnaise suspension. Cool the mixture to 50°C (122°F).

When the chocolate mixture is at the right temperature, blitz in the butter with a stick mixer until smooth. Allow the ganache to cool and become firm enough to pipe.

Fill a piping (icing) bag with a 7 mm (^{3}/$_8$ inch) plain nozzle with the ganache. Pipe the ganache on the flat side of half of the macaron shells, then top with the remaining shells. Put the assembled macarons in the refrigerator to set. Bring to room temperature to serve.
makes 50

blackened vanilla bean

blackened vanilla bean dust

6 large vanilla beans (30 g/1 oz in total)

blackened vanilla crème

150 g (5^1/$_2$ oz) ground almonds
120 g (4^1/$_4$ oz) unsalted butter, chopped and softened
120 g (4^1/$_4$ oz) pure icing (confectioners') sugar
14 g (^{1}/$_2$ oz) blackened vanilla bean dust
    (see recipe above)
110 g (3^3/$_4$ oz) crème pâtissière, at room temperature
    (see Croque-en-bouche recipe, page 164, make
    ^{1}/$_2$ quantity and use the rest in another recipe)

1 quantity macaron shells (see page 16),
    coloured black

To make the blackened vanilla bean dust, preheat the oven to 200°C (400°F/Gas 6). Put the vanilla beans on a baking tray and bake for approximately 30 minutes, until blackened, dry and crisp. Set aside to cool.

Put the cooled beans in a spice grinder and grind to a fine dust. This will make 15 g (^{1}/$_2$ oz) of dust.

To make the blackened vanilla crème, put the ground almonds in a dry frying pan over medium heat and toast, stirring often, until light golden. Transfer to a bowl; cool.

Put the butter and icing sugar in an electric mixer with a beater attachment. Beat on low speed until combined, then increase the speed to medium and cream the butter and icing sugar until pale and fluffy, approximately 4 minutes. Reduce the speed to low and add the toasted ground almonds and 14 g (^{1}/$_2$ oz) of the blackened vanilla bean dust. Mix until just combined. Remove the bowl from the mixer and use a spatula or spoon to fold through the crème pâtissière.

Fill a piping (icing) bag with a 7 mm (^{3}/$_8$ inch) plain nozzle with the blackened vanilla crème. Pipe the crème on the flat side of half the macaron shells, then top with the remaining shells. Put the assembled macarons in the refrigerator to set. Bring to room temperature to serve.
makes 50

chocolate marshmallow

chocolate orange

32 g (1 oz) hickory chips, for smoking (see Glossary)
61 g (2¼ oz) cocoa mass (see Glossary)
130 g (4½ oz) caster (superfine) sugar
113 g (4 oz) water
60 g (2¼ oz) liquid glucose
80 g (2¾ oz) inverted sugar (see Glossary)
18 g (²⁄₃ oz) gold gelatine leaves
108 g (3¾ oz) cold water, extra
85 g (3 oz) inverted sugar, extra
25 g (⁹⁄₁₀ oz) cocoa butter (see Glossary)

1 quantity chocolate macaron shells (see page 17),
    brushed with edible bronze metallic (see Glossary)
    after baking and cooling completely

Use a kitchen blowtorch to 'burn' the metallic, so you're making the macaron 'toasted'.

Put the hickory chips in a wok lined with a double layer of foil. Put the cocoa mass in a small heatproof bowl on a rack over the hickory. Put the wok over medium heat until it begins to smoke. Cover, reduce the heat to low and cook for 1 minute. Set aside, covered, for 10 minutes.

Put the caster sugar, 113 g (4 oz) water, glucose and 80 g (2¾ oz) inverted sugar in a small saucepan over medium heat and heat to 113°C (235°F).

Meanwhile, cut the gelatine leaves into small squares, put in a bowl with the extra 108 g (3¾ oz) water and set aside to soak. Put the extra 85 g (3 oz) inverted sugar in an electric mixer fitted with a whisk attachment. With the motor running, slowly add the hot sugar mixture. Whisk for 1 minute. Add the gelatine, including any soaking liquid, and whisk until the mixture has cooled.

Melt the cocoa butter and smoked cocoa mass in a small saucepan over low heat, then cool to 45°C (113°F). Add to the sugar mixture and whisk on medium speed until incorporated. Continue to whisk for 8 minutes, or until thick enough to pipe. Put in a piping (icing) bag with a 7 mm (³⁄₈ inch) plain nozzle. Pipe onto the flat side of half of the macaron shells, then top with the remaining shells. Put in the refrigerator to set. Bring to room temperature to serve. **makes 50**

150 g (5½ oz) pouring (whipping) cream (35% fat)
Finely grated zest of 2 oranges
200 g (7 oz) milk couverture chocolate,
    chopped or buttons
60 g (2¼ oz) unsalted butter, chopped and softened

1 quantity macaron shells (see page 16), coloured
    orange and dusted with unsweetened cocoa powder

Put the cream and orange zest in a saucepan over medium heat and bring to the boil. Put the chocolate in a bowl. Pour over the hot cream and set aside for 2 minutes. Stir until smooth, then cool to 50°C (122°F).

When the chocolate mixture is at the right temperature, blitz in the butter with a stick mixer until smooth. Allow the ganache to cool and become firm enough to pipe.

Fill a piping (icing) bag with a 7 mm (³⁄₈ inch) plain nozzle with the ganache. Pipe the ganache on the flat side of half of the macaron shells, then top with the remaining shells. Put the assembled macarons in the refrigerator to set. Bring to room temperature to serve.
makes 50

chocolate h₂o

water bombs

300 g (10½ oz) dark couverture chocolate (64%),
    chopped or buttons
100 g (3½ oz) sparkling mineral water
Seeds scraped from 1 vanilla bean

water ganache

70 g (2½ oz) sparkling mineral water
20 g (¾ oz) inverted sugar (see Glossary)
14 g (½ oz) liquid glucose
240 g (8½ oz) milk couverture chocolate,
    chopped or buttons
0.6 g (¹⁄₅₀ oz) citric acid (see Glossary)
3 g (¹⁄₁₀ oz) bicarbonate of soda (baking soda)
44 g (1¾ oz) cocoa butter (see Glossary),
    finely chopped
36 g (1¼ oz) unsalted butter, chopped and softened
0.5 g (¹⁄₅₀ oz) sea salt flakes

½ quantity drop-shaped macaron shells (see page 17),
    coloured white by mixing a little food colouring
    powder with a tiny bit of water and adding
    to the sugar syrup
½ quantity drop-shaped macaron shells, coloured blue

To make the water bombs, you'll need fifty 2 cm
(¾ inch) diameter demisphere flexipan silicone mould
cavities. Temper the chocolate (see Basics) and use to
fill the mould cavities. Use a wide chocolate spatula to
scrape off any excess from the top of the mould sheets
in one quick, smooth movement. Tap the sheets on the
bench to expel any excess air — you don't want tiny
air bubbles in the chocolate. Then flip each mould
sheet over a clean wide bowl, allowing the excess
chocolate to spill into the bowl. Turn the right way
up and scrape again with the chocolate spatula.

Lay two thin rods (such as chopsticks) parallel on a
silicone mat. Turn a mould sheet upside down over the
mat, laying it on the rods so it doesn't sit directly on the
mat. Leave for 1 minute, then turn the sheet the right
way up and use the spatula one final time to remove the

last remnants of excess chocolate. Allow the chocolate to
dry for 15 minutes. Repeat with the other mould sheet.

Hold the mould sheets up to the light — if there
are any see-through patches you will need to repeat the
whole process again (on top of what you have already
done). Gently reheat the tempered chocolate by directing
a heat gun or hair dryer at the surface of the chocolate,
stirring until it is just liquid again. When you've finished,
put the mould sheets on a baking tray and leave the
chocolate to set for 15 minutes, as before.

Mix the mineral water and vanilla seeds together.
Pour into the chocolate-lined moulds until three-quarters
full (the water will expand when it freezes). Put in the
freezer for 2 hours or until the water is frozen solid.

Heat the remaining tempered chocolate with a heat
gun or hair dryer until liquid again. Remove the mould
sheets from the freezer and fill the top of the moulds with
chocolate, ensuring you seal the chocolate completely or
the water will run out when it defrosts. Scrape the top
with the chocolate spatula, then refrigerate until set.

Pop the chocolates out of the moulds — if they're
sealed properly they shouldn't leak.

To make the water ganache, put the mineral water,
inverted sugar and glucose in a saucepan over medium
heat and bring to the boil. Put the chocolate in a bowl.
Pour over the hot liquid and set aside for 2 minutes.
Stir until the mixture is smooth. Mix the citric acid
and bicarbonate of soda together and stir into the
chocolate mixture.

Melt the cocoa butter in a saucepan over low heat,
then check the temperature and cool it to 32°C (90°F).
Add to the chocolate mixture with the butter and blitz
with a stick mixer until smooth. Allow the ganache to
cool and become firm enough to pipe.

Fill a piping (icing) bag with a 9 mm (⅓ inch) plain
nozzle with the ganache. Pipe the ganache on the flat
side of the white macaron shells, then gently press a
water bomb into the centre of the ganache on each
macaron. Top with the blue macaron shells. Put the
assembled macarons in the refrigerator to set. Bring
to room temperature to serve. **makes 50**

cherry coconut

vegemite

cherry jelly

6 g (¹/₅ oz) gold gelatine leaves

36 g (1¼ oz) cold water

250 g (9 oz) sieved cherry purée (see Basics)

50 g (1¾ oz) caster (superfine) sugar

cherry & coconut ganache

132 g (4²/₃ oz) UHT coconut cream (see Glossary)

180 g (6¼ oz) milk couverture chocolate,
chopped or buttons

48 g (1¾ oz) unsalted butter, chopped and softened

30 g (1 oz) desiccated coconut

1 quantity macaron shells (see page 16), coloured
cherry red and sprinkled with desiccated coconut

To make the cherry jelly, cut the gelatine into small squares, combine with the water and set aside to soak.

Put a quarter of the cherry purée in a saucepan over medium heat, add the sugar and heat to 50°C (122°F). Stir in the gelatine, including any soaking liquid, and stir well to ensure all the gelatine dissolves. Add the remaining cherry purée and mix well.

Pour the jelly mixture into a square 12 cm (4½ inch) container. Put in the refrigerator until set, then cut the jelly into 1.5 cm (⁵/₈ inch) squares.

To make the cherry coconut ganache, put the coconut cream in a saucepan over medium heat and bring to the boil. Put the chocolate in a bowl. Pour over the hot coconut cream and set aside for 2 minutes. Stir until the mixture is smooth, then cool to 50°C (122°F).

When the chocolate mixture is at the right temperature, blitz in the butter with a stick mixer until smooth. Fold through the coconut. Allow the ganache to cool and become firm enough to pipe.

Fill a piping (icing) bag with a 9 mm (¹/₃ inch) plain nozzle with the ganache. Pipe onto the flat side of half the macaron shells, then press a piece of cherry jelly into the centre of each. Top with the remaining macaron shells. Put the assembled macarons in the refrigerator to set. Bring to room temperature to serve. **makes 50**

188 g (6¾ oz) pouring (whipping) cream (35% fat)

225 g (8 oz) white couverture chocolate,
chopped or buttons

40 g (1½ oz) Vegemite™

50 g (1¾ oz) fresh breadcrumbs

125 g (4½ oz) unsalted butter, chopped and softened

1 quantity macaron shells (see page 16), coloured
light brown

Put the cream in a saucepan over medium heat and bring to the boil. Put the chocolate and Vegemite in a bowl. Pour over the hot cream and set aside for 2 minutes. Stir until the mixture is smooth. Stir in the breadcrumbs, then cool the mixture to 50°C (122°F).

When the chocolate mixture is at the right temperature, blitz in the butter with a stick mixer until smooth. Allow the ganache to cool and become firm enough to pipe.

Fill a piping (icing) bag with a 9 mm (¹/₃ inch) plain nozzle with the ganache. Pipe the ganache on the flat side of half of the macaron shells, then top with the remaining shells. Put the assembled macarons in the refrigerator to set. Bring to room temperature to serve.
makes 50

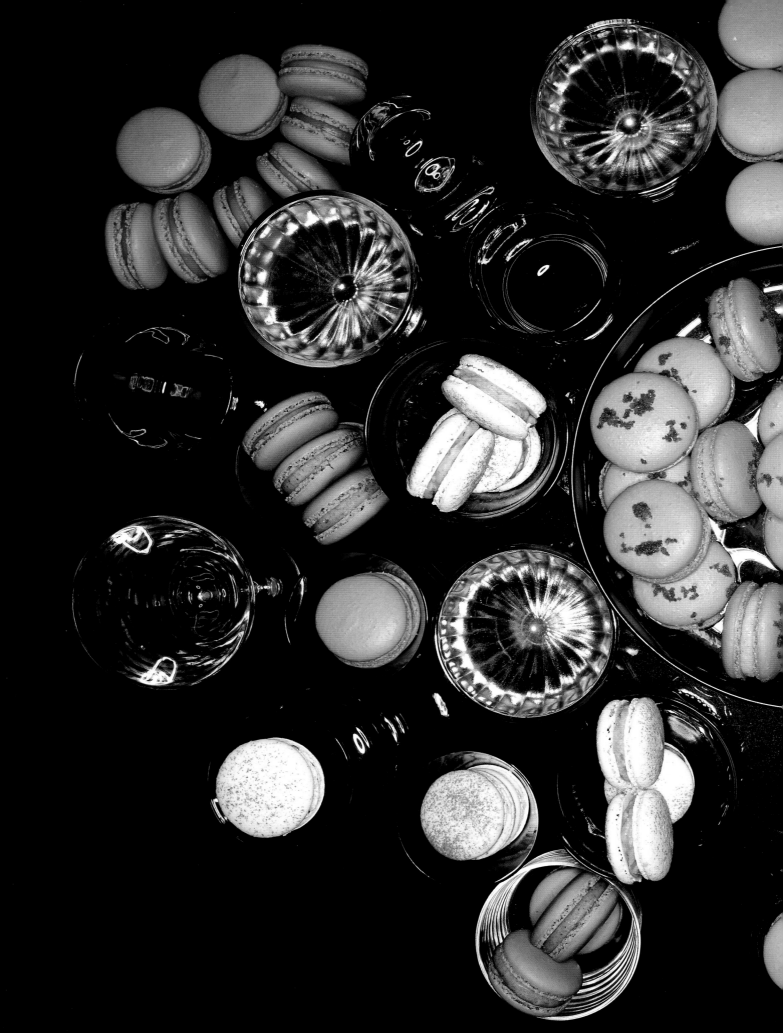

pandan coconut

150 g (5½ oz) UHT coconut cream (see Glossary)
5 g (⅛ oz) pandan extract (see Glossary)
2 pandan leaves (see Glossary)
1 makrut (kaffir lime) leaf, chopped
250 g (9 oz) white couverture chocolate,
    chopped or buttons
80 g (2¾ oz) unsalted butter, chopped and softened
15 g (½ oz) desiccated coconut

1 quantity macaron shells (see page 16), coloured
    white by mixing a little food colouring powder
    with a tiny bit of water and adding to the sugar
    syrup and topped with green shredded coconut
    (see Note)

Put the coconut cream, pandan extract, pandan leaves
and makrut leaf in a saucepan over medium heat and
bring to the boil. Turn off the heat and set aside for
20 minutes to infuse.

Return the coconut cream mixture to the boil. Put
the chocolate in a bowl. Strain the hot coconut cream
over the chocolate and set aside for 2 minutes. Stir until
the mixture is smooth, then cool it to 50°C (122°F).

When the chocolate mixture is at the right
temperature, blitz in the butter with a stick mixer until
smooth. Fold in the desiccated coconut. Allow the
ganache to cool and become firm enough to pipe.

Fill a piping (icing) bag with a 9 mm (⅓ inch) plain
nozzle with the ganache. Pipe the ganache on the flat side
of half the macaron shells, then top with the remaining
shells. Put the assembled macarons in the refrigerator
to set. Bring to room temperature to serve. **makes 50**

note: To colour the coconut, put it in a plastic bag with
a few drops of green food colouring, seal and shake well.

raspberry beetroot

raspberry jelly
3 g (1/10 oz) pectin NH (see Glossary)
1 g (1/25 oz) gellan (see Glossary)
13 g (½ oz) caster (superfine) sugar
125 g (4½ oz) sieved raspberry purée (see Basics)

beetroot buttercream
100 g (3½ oz) caster (superfine) sugar
38 g (1⅓ oz) water
5 g (⅛ oz) freeze-dried beetroot powder (see Glossary)
75 g (2¾ oz) lightly beaten egg
45 g (1¾ oz) egg yolks
200 g (7 oz) unsalted butter, chopped and softened

1 quantity macaron shells (see page 16), coloured red

To make the raspberry jelly, combine the pectin NH,
gellan and sugar in a small bowl. Put the raspberry
purée in a saucepan over medium heat and bring to
50°C (122°F). Add the sugar mixture and mix well.
Bring to the boil, then boil for 1 minute. Pour into a
square 12 cm (4½ inch) container. Refrigerate until set,
then cut into 1.5 cm (⅝ inch) squares.

To make the beetroot buttercream, put the sugar and
water in a small saucepan over medium heat and bring
to the boil. Whisk in the beetroot powder. Boil the sugar
syrup until it reaches 118°C (244°F).

Meanwhile, put the egg and egg yolks in an electric
mixer and whisk on medium speed for 2 minutes. With
the motor running, slowly pour the hot sugar syrup in a
thin stream over the egg. Continue mixing until thick and
cooled to 30°C (86°F). Slowly add the butter, a cube at
a time, mixing well. It may appear curdled, but continue
mixing until it is creamy and thick enough to pipe.

Fill a piping (icing) bag with a 7 mm (⅜ inch) plain
nozzle with the buttercream. Pipe onto the flat side of
half the macaron shells. Press a piece of raspberry jelly
into the centre of each, then top with the remaining
shells. Put the assembled macarons in the refrigerator
to set. Bring to room temperature to serve. **makes 50**

kalamata olive

candied kalamata olive purée
225 g (8 oz) kalamata olives, pitted
375 g (13 oz) caster (superfine) sugar
750 g (1 lb 10 oz) water

lemon candies
195 g (6⁴⁄₅ oz) isomalt (see Glossary)
Finely grated zest of ¹⁄₃ lemon
18 g (²⁄₃ oz) earl grey tea (see Note)
4.5 g (¹⁄₈ oz) bergamot essential oil (see Glossary)

kalamata olive ganache
300 g (10½ oz) white couverture chocolate,
    chopped or buttons
150 g (5½ oz) candied kalamata olive purée
    (see recipe above)
48 g (1¾ oz) unsalted butter, chopped and softened
48 g (1¾ oz) extra virgin olive oil
48 g (1¾ oz) kalamata olives, pitted and finely chopped

1 quantity macaron shells (see page 16),
    coloured maroon

To make the candied kalamata olive purée, fill a medium saucepan three-quarters full of water and bring to the boil. Put the olives in a sieve and rinse them under cool running water. Add to the boiling water, return to the boil and then drain the olives immediately, rinse and drain again. Repeat this process five times.

Heat the sugar and water in a saucepan over low heat until the sugar has dissolved, then increase the heat to medium and bring the sugar syrup to the boil. Add the olives and boil for 20 minutes. Remove from the heat and cool the olives in the syrup.

Drain 150 g (5½ oz) of the candied olives, put in a food processor and blend until smooth.

To make the lemon candies, lightly spray a baking tray with cooking oil and line with non-stick baking paper. Put the tray in the freezer.

Put the isomalt, lemon zest and tea in a heavy-based saucepan and stir occasionally over medium heat until

the isomalt has dissolved. Continue cooking until the mixture reaches 170°C (338°F), then add the bergamot.

Using a heated teaspoon, drop a spoonful (about 2 cm/³⁄₄ inch diameter) of hot isomalt mixture onto the cold tray. Reheat the teaspoon and repeat until all the mixture is used. Allow the candies to cool and harden.

To make the kalamata olive ganache, melt the chocolate in a heatproof bowl over a saucepan of simmering water or in the microwave on medium (50%) in 30-second bursts, stirring after each burst. Take care not to burn the chocolate as it will become grainy.

Put 150 g (5½ oz) of the candied kalamata olive purée in an electric mixer fitted with a whisk attachment. With the motor running on low speed, pour the melted chocolate over the olive purée and whisk for 1 minute.

Slowly add the butter, a cube at a time, continuing to whisk until all the butter has been added and the mixture is smooth. Slowly add the olive oil in a thin stream, whisking until the mixture is homogeneous. Remove the bowl from the mixer and use a spatula or spoon to fold through the chopped olives. Allow the ganache to cool and become firm enough to pipe.

Fill a piping (icing) bag with a 12 mm (½ inch) plain nozzle with the ganache. Pipe ganache on the flat side of half the macaron shells. Press a lemon candy into the centre of the ganache on each macaron. Top with the remaining shells. Put the assembled macarons in the refrigerator to set. Bring to room temperature to serve.
makes 50

note: Make a strong infusion of earl grey tea, then strain and measure out 18 g (²⁄₃ oz) of liquid.

mandarin & tonka bean

75 g (2¾ oz) pouring (whipping) cream (35% fat)

Pinch of seeds scraped from 1 vanilla bean

1 tonka bean (see Glossary), finely grated

75 g (2¾ oz) freshly squeezed and strained mandarin juice

250 g (9 oz) white couverture chocolate, chopped or buttons

60 g (2¼ oz) unsalted butter, chopped and softened

1 quantity macaron shells (see page 16), coloured orange and sprinkled before baking with 100 g (3½ oz) very finely chopped pain d'épices (see Clancy, the rain's a comin' recipe, page 220) mixed with 50 g (1¾ oz) raw (demerara) sugar

Put the cream, vanilla seeds and tonka bean in a saucepan over medium heat and bring to the boil.

Put the mandarin juice in a separate saucepan over medium heat and heat to 50°C (122°F).

Put the chocolate in a bowl. Pour over the hot cream and mandarin juice and set aside for 2 minutes. Stir until smooth, then cool the mixture to 50°C (122°F).

When the chocolate mixture is at the right temperature, blitz in the butter with a stick mixer until smooth. Allow the ganache to cool and become firm enough to pipe.

Fill a piping (icing) bag with a 9 mm (⅓ inch) plain nozzle with the ganache. Pipe the ganache on the flat side of half the macaron shells, then top with the remaining shells. Put the assembled macarons in the refrigerator to set. Bring to room temperature to serve.
makes 50

chocolate peanut butter & jelly

jelly

125 g (4½ oz) sieved redcurrant purée (see Basics)

125 g (4½ oz) sieved raspberry purée (see Basics)

62 g (2¼ oz) caster (superfine) sugar

1 g (1/25 oz) iota (see Glossary)

1.5 g (1/20 oz) gellan (see Glossary)

chocolate & peanut butter ganache

240 g (8½ oz) milk couverture chocolate, chopped or buttons

215 g (7½ oz) crunchy peanut butter

50 g (1¾ oz) unsalted butter, chopped and softened

1 g (1/25 oz) sea salt flakes

½ quantity chocolate macaron shells (see page 17)

½ quantity macaron shells (see page 16), coloured red

To make the jelly, put the redcurrant and raspberry purées, sugar, iota and gellan in a saucepan and blitz with a stick mixer until smooth and thickened slightly. Bring the mixture to the boil over medium heat, then pour into a square 12 cm (4½ inch) container. Refrigerate until set, then cut into 1.5 cm (⅝ inch) squares.

To make the chocolate peanut butter ganache, melt the chocolate in a heatproof bowl over a saucepan of simmering water or in the microwave. Add the peanut butter and mix well, then add the butter and blitz with a stick mixer until smooth. Fold through the sea salt. Allow the ganache to cool and become firm enough to pipe.

Fill a piping (icing) bag with a 9 mm (⅓ inch) plain nozzle with the ganache. Pipe the ganache on the flat side of the chocolate macaron shells, then press a piece of jelly into the centre of the ganache on each macaron. Top with the red macaron shells. Put the assembled macarons in the refrigerator to set. Bring to room temperature to serve. **makes 50**

chocozumbo

barbecued corn purée

2 corn cobs (in their husks)

chocolate & corn ganache

50 g (1¾ oz) milk

150 g (5½ oz) barbecued corn purée (see recipe above)

70 g (2½ oz) dark couverture chocolate (70%), chopped or buttons

250 g (9 oz) white couverture chocolate, chopped or buttons

70 g (2½ oz) unsalted butter, chopped and softened

30 g (1 oz) lightly salted corn kernels (see Glossary)

30 g (1 oz) corn chips

1 quantity chocolate macaron shells (see page 17), dusted before
    baking with 50 g (1¾ oz) each of lightly salted corn kernels
    and corn chips, processed to a coarse dust

To make the barbecued corn purée, preheat a barbecue or griddle plate on high.
Put the corn cobs, still in their husks, in a saucepan of boiling water and cook for
5 minutes. Remove the husks and cook the corn cobs on the barbecue or griddle
plate until lightly blackened. Allow to cool, then cut the kernels away from the cob.
Put the corn kernels in a food processor and process until smooth.

Put the milk and 150 g (5½ oz) of the barbecued corn purée in a saucepan over
medium heat and heat to 70°C (158°F).

Melt the chocolates in a heatproof bowl over a saucepan of simmering water
or in the microwave on medium (50%) in 30-second bursts, stirring after each
burst. Stir the milk mixture into the melted chocolate until combined, then cool the
mixture to 50°C (122°F).

When the chocolate mixture is at the right temperature, blitz in the butter with
a stick mixer until smooth.

Put the corn kernels and corn chips in a food processor and process until the
mixture resembles breadcrumbs. Fold into the ganache, then allow the ganache to
cool and become firm enough to pipe.

Fill a piping (icing) bag with a 12 mm (½ inch) plain nozzle with the ganache.
Pipe the ganache on the flat side of half the macaron shells, then top with the
remaining macaron shells. Put the assembled macarons in the refrigerator to set.
Bring to room temperature to serve. **makes 50**

salt & vinegar

150 g (5½ oz) pouring (whipping) cream (35% fat)
250 g (9 oz) white couverture chocolate,
  chopped or buttons
60 g (2¼ oz) balsamic vinegar
2 g (²⁄₂₅ oz) sea salt flakes

1 quantity macaron shells (see page 16), coloured with
  a little pink and a little purple food colouring

Put the cream in a saucepan over medium heat and
bring to the boil. Put the chocolate in a bowl. Pour over
the hot cream and set aside for 2 minutes. Stir until the
mixture is smooth, then stir in the vinegar. Fold through
the sea salt. Allow the ganache to cool and become firm
enough to pipe.

Fill a piping (icing) bag with a 7 mm (³⁄₈ inch)
plain nozzle with the ganache. Pipe the ganache on
the flat side of half the macaron shells, then top with
the remaining shells. Put the assembled macarons in the
refrigerator to set. Bring to room temperature to serve.
makes 50

chocolate salt & vinegar

70 g (2½ oz) pouring (whipping) cream (35% fat)
65 g (2⅓ oz) liquid glucose
25 g (1 oz) caster (superfine) sugar
30 g (1 oz) dark couverture chocolate (64%),
  chopped or buttons
130 g (4½ oz) milk couverture chocolate,
  chopped or buttons
120 g (4¼ oz) white couverture chocolate,
  chopped or buttons
100 g (3½ oz) balsamic vinegar
25 g (1 oz) cocoa butter (see Glossary), chopped
15 g (½ oz) unsalted butter, chopped and softened
3 g (¹⁄₁₀ oz) sea salt flakes

½ quantity chocolate macaron shells (see page 17)
½ quantity macaron shells (see page 16), coloured purple

Put the cream, glucose and sugar in a saucepan over
medium heat and bring to the boil.

Melt all the chocolates together in a heatproof bowl
over a saucepan of simmering water or in the microwave
on medium (50%) in 30-second bursts, stirring after
each burst. Stir in the hot cream, then the vinegar, until
smooth and well combined.

Put the cocoa butter in a small saucepan over low
heat until melted, then cool to 32°C (90°F).

When the cocoa butter is at the right temperature,
stir it into the chocolate mixture. Cool the mixture
to 50°C (122°F), then blitz in the butter with a stick
mixer until smooth. Fold through the sea salt. Allow
the ganache to cool and become firm enough to pipe.

Fill a piping (icing) bag with a 7 mm (³⁄₈ inch) plain
nozzle with the ganache. Pipe the ganache on the flat
side of the chocolate macaron shells, then top with
the purple shells. Put the assembled macarons in the
refrigerator to set. Bring to room temperature to serve.
makes 50

rice pudding

caramel au beurre salé

rice pudding

188 g (6¾ oz) pouring (whipping) cream (35% fat)
188 g (6¾ oz) milk
70 g (2½ oz) arborio or jasmine rice
50 g (1¾ oz) caster (superfine) sugar
75 g (2¾ oz) brown sugar
6 g (⅕ oz) natural vanilla extract

ganache

58 g (2¼ oz) pouring (whipping) cream (35% fat)
Small pinch of seeds scraped from 1 vanilla bean
Small pinch of ground cinnamon
95 g (3¼ oz) white couverture chocolate,
    chopped or buttons
30 g (1 oz) unsalted butter, chopped and softened

1 quantity macaron shells (see page 16),
    sprinkled with ground cinnamon

To make the rice pudding, put all the ingredients in a saucepan over medium–low heat and cook until the rice is tender. Stir often to prevent sticking on the base of the pan and add small amounts of additional milk if the mixture becomes too dry before the rice is cooked. Remove from the heat and allow to cool completely.

Meanwhile, to make the ganache, put the cream, vanilla seeds and cinnamon in a saucepan over medium heat and bring to the boil.

Put the chocolate in a bowl. Pour over the hot cream and set aside for 2 minutes. Stir until smooth, then cool the mixture to 50°C (122°F).

When the chocolate mixture is at the right temperature, blitz in the butter with a stick mixer until smooth. Set aside to cool.

Put the cooled ganache and rice pudding in a bowl and mix until combined. Fill a piping (icing) bag with a 12 mm (½ inch) plain nozzle with the rice pudding ganache. Pipe the ganache on the flat side of half the macaron shells, then top with the remaining shells. Put the assembled macarons in the refrigerator to set. Bring to room temperature just before serving. **makes 50**

caramel buttercream

150 g (5½ oz) unsalted butter, chopped and softened
300 g (10½ oz) caramel maison (see Basics)
4.5 g (³⁄₂₀ oz) sea salt flakes

1 quantity macaron shells (see page 16), coloured caramel

Put the butter in an electric mixer with a beater attachment. Cream the butter on medium speed until light and fluffy.

Warm the caramel maison in the microwave on medium (50%) until it reaches a pouring consistency (approximately 1 minute, though microwave times may vary between models).

With the electric mixer running, slowly add the warmed caramel maison and continue mixing until thick and creamy. Fold through the sea salt.

Fill a piping (icing) bag with a 7 mm (³⁄₈ inch) plain nozzle with the buttercream. Pipe the buttercream on the flat side of half the macaron shells, then top with the remaining shells. Put the assembled macarons in the refrigerator to set. Bring to room temperature to serve.
makes 50

salted milk chocolate caramel

150 g (5½ oz) pouring (whipping) cream (35% fat)

25 g (1 oz) cocoa butter (see Glossary), finely chopped

125 g (4½ oz) caster (superfine) sugar

250 g (9 oz) milk couverture chocolate,
    chopped or buttons

80 g (2¾ oz) unsalted butter, chopped and softened

1 g (¹/₂₅ oz) sea salt flakes

½ quantity macaron shells (see page 16),
    coloured caramel

½ quantity chocolate macaron shells (see page 17)

Put the cream and cocoa butter in a saucepan over medium heat and bring to the boil.

Put the sugar in a saucepan over medium–low heat, shaking the pan frequently until the sugar has dissolved to ensure it does not burn. Cook the sugar until it is caramelised and dark amber in colour.

Carefully pour the hot cream mixture over the caramelised sugar and stir to combine — watch out, it will bubble up and release steam.

Put the chocolate in a heatproof bowl. Pour over the hot caramel and set aside for 2 minutes. Stir until the mixture is smooth, then cool to 50°C (122°F).

When the chocolate mixture is at the right temperature, blitz in the butter with a stick mixer until smooth. Fold through the sea salt. Allow the ganache to cool and become firm enough to pipe.

Fill a piping (icing) bag with a 7 mm (³/₈ inch) plain nozzle with the ganache. Pipe the ganache on the flat side of the caramel macaron shells, then top with the chocolate shells. Put the assembled macarons in the refrigerator to set. Bring to room temperature to serve.

makes 50

chocolate banana

175 g (6 oz) pouring (whipping) cream (35% fat)

Finely grated zest of ¼ lime

1 g (¹/₂₅ oz) finely grated fresh ginger

½ cinnamon stick

125 g (4½ oz) milk couverture chocolate,
    chopped or buttons

50 g (1¾ oz) dark couverture chocolate (70%),
    chopped or buttons

45 g (1¾ oz) dark couverture chocolate (64%),
    chopped or buttons

10 g (¼ oz) inverted sugar (see Glossary)

20 g (¾ oz) cocoa butter (see Glossary), finely chopped

120 g (4¼ oz) mashed ripe banana

38 g (1⅓ oz) unsalted butter, chopped and softened

½ quantity chocolate macaron shells (see page 17)

½ quantity macaron shells (see page 16),
    coloured yellow

Put the cream, lime zest, ginger and cinnamon in a saucepan over medium heat and bring to the boil. Remove from the heat and strain through a fine sieve.

Put all the chocolate, the inverted sugar and cocoa butter in a bowl. Pour over the hot cream and set aside for 2 minutes. Stir until smooth, mix in the banana and then cool the mixture to 50°C (122°F).

When the chocolate mixture is at the right temperature, blitz in the butter with a stick mixer until smooth. Allow the ganache to cool and become firm enough to pipe.

Fill a piping (icing) bag with a 7 mm (³/₈ inch) plain nozzle with the ganache. Pipe the ganache on the flat side of the chocolate macaron shells, then top with the yellow shells. Put the assembled macarons in the refrigerator to set. Bring to room temperature to serve.

makes 50

chocolates

**zumbo-ball
women's league
state champions**

back row, from left: cherry poppins; rotten egg; chocolate adz; fried egg; peanut chocolate bar **front row, from left:** yuzu stick; red wine cameltoe; salted vanilla caramel; katsudon; vanilla raspberry; blackcurrant violet; mint bubble bar

I adore chocolate. If I'm in France I'll
eat chocolate for breakfast, while here in
Australia I stick to six handfuls of dark
chocolate a day. It's this love of chocolate that
led me to making my own.

You can do practically anything with
chocolate, provided you use the right cocoa
percentage with the right flavours. Like wines,
many chocolates have back-note flavours that
need to be considered. It's also important to get
the right balance of sweetness and bitterness.

For me, inspiration comes daily, through life
itself. Shapes, flavours, colours and textures
start joining together until I can taste and
see the idea in my mind. It's then a matter of
working out what moulds and techniques need
to be achieved, mainly through trial and error.

The original idea will be chopped and changed,
adjusted and tasted until the imagination
comes to life. I particularly enjoy working
on the textures — the crunch of a nut, the ooze
of salted caramel or the cold acidic freshness
of a fruit gel. These hidden surprises are
the perfect final touch.

chocolate adz

caramel ganache

125 g (4½ oz) caster (superfine) sugar
150 g (5½ oz) pouring (whipping) cream (35% fat)
250 g (9 oz) milk couverture chocolate,
    buttons or chopped
25 g (1 oz) cocoa butter (see Glossary), finely chopped
150 g (5½ oz) unsalted butter, chopped and softened
Pinch of sea salt flakes

Put the sugar in a saucepan over medium heat and when the edges start to liquefy, swirl the pan. Keep swirling, but do not stir, until all the sugar has liquefied and it has become a dark-amber caramel and smells like toffee. Remove from the heat.

Meanwhile, bring the cream to the boil in a separate small saucepan, then remove from the heat. Pour it over the toffee and carefully stir it in to deglaze — watch out, it will spit. Allow to cool slightly.

Put the chocolate and cocoa butter in a bowl, pour over the hot caramel and stir until melted and smooth. Cool the mixture to 50°C (122°F), then blitz in the butter with a stick mixer until smooth and thick. Fold through the sea salt. Set aside for several hours in the refrigerator or until the ganache is firm, but spreadable.

hazelnut meringue

50 g (1¾ oz) egg whites
36 g (1¼ oz) caster (superfine) sugar
50 g (1¾ oz) ground hazelnuts
33 g (1¼ oz) pure icing (confectioners') sugar, sifted

Preheat the oven to 125°C (257°F/Gas 1). Line 2 baking trays with non-stick baking paper. Put the egg whites and caster sugar in a bowl and beat with hand-held electric beaters on medium speed for 3–4 minutes, until firm peaks form. Mix together the ground hazelnuts and icing sugar, then fold into the egg whites with a spatula until combined, being careful not to beat out too much air.

Spoon the meringue mixture into a piping (icing) bag with a 9 mm (⅓ inch) plain nozzle. Pipe 2 cm (¾ inch) diameter rounds onto the lined trays, spacing them 1 cm (½ inch) apart. Cook in the preheated oven for 2 hours (this will help dry the meringue out completely). Remove from the oven and cool on the trays.

to assemble

200 g (7 oz) roasted and skinned hazelnuts, chopped
200 g (7 oz) roasted blanched almonds, chopped
500 g (1 lb 2 oz) milk couverture chocolate,
    buttons or chopped, tempered (see Basics)

When the meringues have cooled, fill a piping (icing) bag with a 9 mm (⅓ inch) plain nozzle with the caramel ganache. Pipe down onto each meringue and when the ganache meets the edge of the meringue, pull the piping bag up while gently squeezing to make a cone shape about 4 cm (1½ inches) high. Refrigerate until firm enough to dip.

Combine the chopped nuts and spread out on a baking tray. Holding a ganache meringue cone by the base, dip it in the tempered chocolate until the edge of the meringue is just covered, then lift out and gently shake off any excess chocolate. Immediately roll the cone in the nuts, leaving it on the tray until the chocolate has set. Repeat with the remaining cones. **makes 50**

salted vanilla caramels

165 g (5¾ oz) caster (superfine) sugar

100 g (3½ oz) pouring (whipping) cream (35% fat)

67 g (2⅓ oz) liquid glucose

100 g (3½ oz) unsalted butter, chopped and softened

Seeds scraped from ½ vanilla bean

500 g (1 lb 2 oz) dark couverture chocolate (64%), chopped or buttons
   (or 250 g/9 oz if making squares)

Sea salt flakes, for sprinkling

Put the sugar and cream in a saucepan over medium heat and stir until the sugar has just dissolved. Slowly bring to the boil. Add the glucose, butter and vanilla seeds and stir with a heatproof plastic spatula to just combine. Reduce the heat to medium–low and bring the mixture to 118°C (244°F), then remove from the heat.

If making individual caramels, immediately transfer the mixture to a warmed confectionery funnel and pour into fifty 2 cm (¾ inch) diameter demisphere flexipan silicone mould cavities, placed on a baking tray. If making squares, immediately pour the mixture into a square 15 cm (6 inch) cake tin lined with non-stick baking paper, extending over two opposite sides. Allow the caramel to cool at room temperature for 4 hours. (If your kitchen is cool enough, the caramel will be fully set. If not, you will need to refrigerate it for a few hours, but there will be a slight change in texture.)

Temper the chocolate (see Basics).

Remove the caramels from the moulds. If making squares, remove the caramel from the tin, put on a chopping board and use a sharp knife dipped in hot water and then dried to cut it into 3 cm (1¼ inch) squares.

Carefully drop the pieces of caramel into the tempered chocolate and lift out with a dipping fork (see Glossary), gently agitating the fork and allowing the excess chocolate to drip back into the bowl. Transfer the chocolates to a Silpat (see Glossary) or tray lined with non-stick baking paper and sprinkle with a little sea salt. Repeat until all the chocolates are formed. Allow to set at room temperature for 2–3 hours or until the chocolate is completely dry to the touch.

makes 25 squares or 50 individual chocolates

red wine cameltoes

chocolate casing

500 g (1 lb 2 oz) dark couverture chocolate (64–73%), buttons or chopped
Edible red metallic dust (see Glossary)

Temper the chocolate (see Basics).

Use cotton wool to gently polish the inside of one hundred oval 3.5 cm (1²⁄₅ inch) long polycarbonate mould cavities. (You can also use plain mini Easter egg mould sheets.) This will remove any dust particles and ensure a smooth shiny surface on your chocolates. Use a clean finger to rub the inside of each mould cavity with a little metallic dust.

Completely fill the cavities of the moulds with the tempered chocolate, then use a wide chocolate spatula to scrape off any excess from the top of the mould sheets in one quick, smooth movement. Do not put the excess chocolate back in with the rest of the tempered chocolate. Tap the sheets on the bench to expel any

excess air — you don't want tiny air bubbles in the chocolate. Working with one mould sheet at a time, flip it over a clean wide bowl, allowing the excess chocolate to spill into the bowl. Turn the sheet the right way up and scrape again with the chocolate spatula.

Lay two thin rods (such as chopsticks) parallel on a silicone mat. Turn a mould sheet upside down over the mat, laying it on the rods so it doesn't sit directly on the mat. Leave for 1 minute, then turn the sheet the right way up and use the spatula one final time to remove the last remnants of excess chocolate. Repeat with the other sheets. Allow the chocolate to dry for 15 minutes.

Hold the mould sheets up to the light — if there are any see-through patches you will need to repeat the whole process again (on top of what you have already done). Gently reheat the tempered chocolate by directing a heat gun or hair dryer at the surface, stirring until it is just liquid again. When you've finished, leave the chocolate to set for 15 minutes as before.

red wine caramel

50 g (1¾ oz) liquid glucose

250 g (9 oz) caster (superfine) sugar

145 g (5¼ oz) red wine

1½ pinches of freshly ground black pepper

145 g (5¼ oz) pouring (whipping) cream (35% fat)

Put the glucose, sugar and 120 g (4¼ oz) of the red wine in a deep saucepan over medium–high heat and stir until the sugar has dissolved. Boil for 10–12 minutes or until the caramel reaches 165°C (329°F) and smells like red wine toffee.

Meanwhile, put the remaining red wine, pepper and cream in a separate saucepan, bring just to the boil and then remove from the heat. When the caramel is at the right temperature, remove it from the heat and use a small whisk to slowly whisk in the warm cream mixture until just combined. Be careful when pouring in the cream as the hot caramel will spit and release a lot of steam if you add it too quickly. Pour the mixture into a heatproof bowl and cool to room temperature (approximately 1 hour).

red wine ganache

105 g (3½ oz) red wine

33 g (1¼ oz) liquid glucose

52 g (1¾ oz) unsalted butter, chopped

Pinch of freshly ground black pepper

210 g (7½ oz) small milk couverture chocolate buttons

18 g (⅔ oz) cocoa butter (see Glossary), finely chopped

Put the red wine, glucose, butter and pepper in a small saucepan and bring to the boil over high heat. Put the chocolate in a heatproof bowl, pour the red wine mixture over the top and stir with a small whisk until the chocolate has completely melted and is smooth.

Melt the cocoa butter in a very small saucepan or in the microwave, then cool to 32°C (90°F). Stir into the ganache mixture. Allow the ganache to cool to room temperature and become firm enough to pipe.

to assemble

Take two piping (icing) bags, each fitted with a 3 mm (¹⁄₁₀ inch) plain nozzle, and fill one with the ganache and the other with the red wine caramel. Fill half the mould cavities with caramel and the other half with ganache, to 1 mm (¹⁄₂₅ inch) from the top of each mould.

Gently reheat the remaining tempered chocolate by directing a heat gun or hair dryer at the surface until it is just liquid again. Fill the top of the moulds with chocolate, ensuring you seal the chocolate completely. Scrape the top of the mould with the chocolate spatula to remove the excess in one quick, smooth movement.

Allow the chocolate to set at room temperature for a few hours and then, keeping the mould sheets separate so you don't confuse which filling is inside each, refrigerate for 5 minutes. This will shrink the chocolates a little so they will come out of the moulds easily. Keeping the sheets separate, invert the moulds onto your benchtop and tap firmly on the bench to release the chocolate halves.

Heat a flat baking sheet in a 180°C (350°F/Gas 4) oven for 4 minutes, then put it on the bench.

Take a piece of caramel-filled chocolate and a ganache-filled chocolate and briefly put the flat side of each on the hot baking sheet, then immediately join the flat surfaces together. Put it back in the mould sheet on its side so that the joins are facing up and repeat with the remaining chocolates. Leave for 1 hour at room temperature to set. **makes 50**

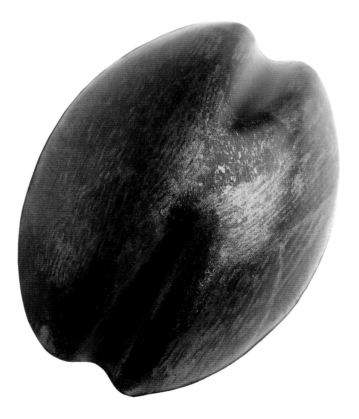

cherry poppins

cherry pâte de fruit

175 g (6 oz) sieved cherry purée (see Basics)
5 g ($^{1}/_{8}$ oz) pectin NH (see Glossary)
20 g ($^{3}/_{4}$ oz) caster (superfine) sugar
135 g ($4^{3}/_{4}$ oz) caster (superfine) sugar, extra
40 g ($1^{1}/_{2}$ oz) liquid glucose
6 g ($^{1}/_{5}$ oz) citric acid solution (see Basics)

Spray a square 15 cm (6 inch) cake tin with cooking oil and line with non-stick baking paper, extending over two opposite sides. Put the cherry purée in a small saucepan over medium heat and bring to 60°C (140°F). Combine the pectin and 20 g ($^{3}/_{4}$ oz) sugar, then add to the cherry purée when it reaches 60°C (140°F). Bring the mixture to the boil and add the extra sugar and glucose. Stir with a whisk until the mixture returns to the boil, then boil for 1 minute. Add the citric acid solution, stir well and pour into the lined tin. Set aside.

coconut & white chocolate ganache

125 g ($4^{1}/_{2}$ oz) coconut cream
15 g ($^{1}/_{2}$ oz) inverted sugar (see Glossary)
Seeds scraped from 1 vanilla bean
25 g (1 oz) cocoa butter (see Glossary), finely chopped
250 g (9 oz) white couverture chocolate,
    chopped or buttons
100 g ($3^{1}/_{2}$ oz) desiccated coconut
50 g ($1^{3}/_{4}$ oz) glacé cherries, finely diced

Put the coconut cream, inverted sugar and vanilla seeds in a small saucepan and bring to the boil over medium heat. Meanwhile, melt the cocoa butter in a small saucepan over medium heat, then cool to 32°C (90°F).

Put the chocolate in a bowl. Pour over the coconut cream, set aside for 10 seconds and then stir gently with a whisk until smooth. Gently fold in the coconut, glacé cherries and 32°C (90°F) cocoa butter. Pour over the pâte de fruit and use a palette knife to smooth out to the edges. Gently tap the tin on the bench and leave overnight to set (if the weather is hot, you may need to use the refrigerator).

chocolate base

50 g ($1^{3}/_{4}$ oz) milk couverture chocolate,
    chopped or buttons

Melt the chocolate in a heatproof bowl over a saucepan of simmering water or in the microwave. Use a crank-handled palette knife to spread a very thin layer of chocolate over the ganache. Allow to set.

Remove from the tin and turn upside down, so the chocolate layer forms the base. Remove the paper and use a ruler and sharp knife to mark out 7.5 x 2.4 cm (3 x 1 inch) bars. Heat the knife by dipping it in hot water and then drying, and use it to cut out the bars.

to finish

800 g (1 lb 12 oz) dark couverture chocolate (70%),
    chopped or buttons
80 g ($2^{3}/_{4}$ oz) plain poprocks (see Glossary)

Line a baking tray with non-stick baking paper or Silpat (see Glossary). Temper the dark chocolate (see Basics), then stir through the poprocks. Use a dipping fork (see Glossary) or ordinary fork to dip each bar in the chocolate coating, agitating it slightly so that the excess chocolate drips back into the bowl. Drag the bottom of each bar over the edge of the bowl to neaten, then put on the lined tray.

If you'd like to create a ripple effect in the chocolate coating, gently point a hair dryer on the cool setting towards the top of each bar. Set aside for 6 hours to set.

makes 12

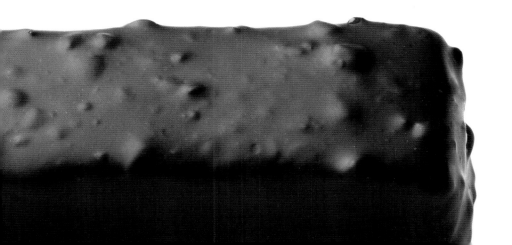

katsudon

katsu jelly

200 g (7 oz) clear apple juice
100 g (3½ oz) tonkatsu sauce (see Glossary)
50 g (1¾ oz) Japanese mayonnaise (see Glossary)
308 g (11 oz) caster (superfine) sugar
12 g (⅖ oz) yellow pectin (see Glossary)
90 g (3¼ oz) liquid glucose
12 g (⅖ oz) citric acid solution (see Basics)

Line a square 20 cm (8 inch) cake tin with non-stick baking paper, extending over two sides. Heat the apple juice, tonkatsu sauce and mayonnaise in a saucepan over low heat until the mixture reaches 80°C (176°F).

Combine 28 g (1 oz) of the sugar with the pectin, sprinkle over the apple juice mixture and stir with a whisk until the sugar has dissolved. Increase the heat to medium and bring to the boil, then add the remaining sugar and glucose and stir just until the sugar has dissolved. Boil for 2 minutes more, or until the mixture forms a gel-like thread that doesn't quite reach the syrup when drizzled from a teaspoon about 15 cm (6 inches) above the pan.

Immediately stir in the citric acid solution. Pour into the tin and set aside for 3–4 hours, until cooled and firm.

yuzu ganache

100 g (3½ oz) pouring (whipping) cream (35% fat)
385 g (13½ oz) dark couverture chocolate (55%), chopped
90 g (3¼ oz) yuzu juice (see Glossary)
82 g (2¾ oz) chilled unsalted butter, chopped

Bring the cream to the boil in a saucepan over medium heat. Put the chocolate in a bowl. Pour over the hot cream and set aside for 2 minutes, then stir until smooth.

Meanwhile, put the yuzu juice in a saucepan and bring to the boil. Remove from the heat and allow the temperature to drop to 50°C (122°F) before stirring it into the melted chocolate mixture. Blitz in the butter with a stick mixer until smooth. Spread the ganache over the set jelly and leave at room temperature for 2 hours or until set.

panko coating

150 g (5½ oz) brioche or croissant, roughly torn
200 g (7 oz) panko breadcrumbs (see Glossary)
50 g (1¾ oz) caster (superfine) sugar
50 g (1¾ oz) unsalted butter, melted
Pinch of ground cinnamon
Seeds scraped from 2 vanilla beans

Process the brioche or croissant in a food processor until it forms coarse crumbs. Put in a bowl, add the remaining ingredients and mix to combine. Heat a non-stick frying pan over medium heat and dry-fry the crumb mixture for 2–3 minutes or until crisp and golden.

to assemble

240 g (8½ oz) cocoa butter (see Glossary), finely chopped
750 g (1 lb 10 oz) white chocolate, tempered (see Basics)

Remove the jelly and yuzu ganache square from the tin. Discard the paper. Cut it into miniature triangular 'chicken breast fillet' shaped pieces, about 3.5 cm (1⅖ inches) long and 2 cm (¾ inch) wide at the widest part. Set aside.

Melt the cocoa butter in a small saucepan over medium heat. Cool to 32°C (90°F), then pour into the tempered chocolate. Carefully drop the 'fillets' into the chocolate mixture, then lift out with a dipping fork (see Glossary), agitating it slightly so that the excess chocolate drips back into the bowl. Roll in the panko coating to cover completely. Set aside for 1 hour or until the chocolate has set and the panko coating has adhered to the chocolate.

makes 100

fried eggs

passionfruit pâte de fruit

400 g (14 oz) sieved passionfruit pulp (see Note)

11.5 g ($^2/_5$ oz) yellow pectin (see Glossary)

342 g (12 oz) caster (superfine) sugar

103 g (3½ oz) liquid glucose

14 g (½ oz) citric acid solution (see Basics)

You'll need fifty 2 cm (¾ inch) diameter demisphere flexipan silicone mould cavities for this recipe. Place the mould sheets on baking trays. Ideally, you would use a warmed confectionery funnel (common in commercial pastry kitchens) to get the pâte de fruits into the mould cavities, as you need to work very quickly. If you can't get hold of one, you can use a warmed metal jug, although this will be slower and you will find the mixture begins to thicken before you're finished. Don't worry too much, the flavour will still be fine.

Put the passionfruit pulp in a small saucepan over medium heat and bring it to 60°C (140°F). Combine the pectin with 35 g (1¼ oz) of the sugar and sprinkle over the warmed passionfruit, stirring with a whisk to dissolve the sugar. Bring to the boil, then add the remaining sugar and the glucose and stir until the sugar has dissolved. Bring to the boil and boil for 2 minutes or until the mixture forms a gel-like thread that doesn't quite reach the syrup when drizzled from a teaspoon about 15 cm (6 inches) above the pan. Remove from the heat, immediately add the citric acid solution and stir to combine.

Quickly transfer the mixture to the warmed confectionery funnel or jug and divide among the mould cavities. You need to work quickly as this mixture does not take long to set. Allow to cool completely.

to assemble

190 g (6¾ oz) desiccated coconut, toasted

930 g (2 lb 1 oz) small white couverture chocolate buttons, tempered (see Basics)

Sea salt flakes and freshly ground black pepper

Stir the coconut into the tempered chocolate. Line a baking tray with Silpat (see Glossary) or non-stick baking paper. Using a mini ice-cream scoop or tablespoon measure, scoop the mixture onto the tray, leaving 3 cm (1¼ inches) between each.

Pop the pâte de fruits out of the mould and put in the centre of each scoop of chocolate, dome side up. Press gently to form a fried egg shape. Sprinkle with a little salt and pepper and leave for 20 minutes, until set and dry to the touch. **makes 50**

note: It is important to use a precise weight of the sieved (seedless) passionfruit pulp. The weight of unsieved pulp, and number of whole passionfruit you will need to start with, will vary from season to season.

variation – rotten eggs

Use 400 g (14 oz) strained blood orange juice instead of the passionfruit pulp. Just after pouring the pâte de fruits mixture into the moulds, add a drop or two of black or brown food colouring to each. Ask someone to help you if you can. Use milk couverture chocolate buttons instead of white, and replace the coconut with 90 g (3¼ oz) puffed plain rice cereal and the finely grated zest of 1 orange.

vanilla raspberry

raspberry coulis

135 g (4¾ oz) sieved puréed raspberries (see Basics)
18 g (⅔ oz) liquid glucose
14 g (½ oz) inverted sugar (see Glossary)
30 g (1 oz) caster (superfine) sugar
3 g (¹/₁₀ oz) pectin NH (see Glossary)

Put the puréed raspberries, glucose and inverted sugar in a saucepan and stir over medium heat until the sugar has dissolved. Bring the mixture to 60°C (140°F).

Combine the caster sugar and pectin NH (always combine pectin with sugar before adding it to a mixture or it will clump together and not dissolve properly). Add to the pan and stir until the sugar has dissolved, then bring just to the boil and remove from the heat. Pour into a clean heatproof bowl and set aside to cool to room temperature (approximately 20 minutes).

vanilla ganache

300 g (10½ oz) pouring (whipping) cream (35% fat)
Seeds scraped from 4 vanilla beans
500 g (1 lb 2 oz) small white couverture
    chocolate buttons
160 g (5¾ oz) unsalted butter, chopped and softened

Put the cream and vanilla seeds in a saucepan over medium heat and bring to the boil. Put the chocolate in a bowl. Pour over the hot vanilla cream and stir until melted and smooth. Cool the mixture to 40–50°C (104–122°F). When the mixture has cooled enough, blitz in the butter with a stick mixer until smooth.

to assemble

600 g (1 lb 5 oz) dark couverture chocolate (64%)

Temper the chocolate (see Basics). Completely fill fifty 2 cm (¾ inch) diameter demisphere flexipan silicone mould cavities with the tempered chocolate, then use a wide chocolate spatula to scrape off any excess from the top of the mould sheets in one quick, smooth movement. Tap the sheets on the bench to expel any excess air — you don't want tiny air bubbles in the chocolate. Working with one mould sheet at a time, flip it over a clean wide bowl, allowing the excess chocolate to spill into the bowl. Turn the sheet the right way up and scrape again with the chocolate spatula.

Lay two thin rods (such as chopsticks) parallel on a silicone mat. Turn a mould sheet upside down over the mat, laying it on the rods so it doesn't sit directly on the mat. Leave for 1 minute, then turn the sheet the right way up and use the chocolate spatula one final time to remove the last remnants of excess chocolate. Repeat with the other sheet/s. Set aside for 15 minutes to dry.

Hold the mould sheets up to the light — if there are any see-through patches you will need to repeat the whole process again (on top of what you have already done). Gently reheat the tempered chocolate by directing a heat gun or hair dryer at the surface of the chocolate, stirring until it is just liquid again. When you've finished, leave the chocolate to set for 15 minutes as before.

When the chocolate moulds are dry, take 2 piping (icing) bags with 3 mm (¹/₁₀ inch) plain nozzles and fill one with the raspberry mixture and the other with the vanilla ganache. Pipe enough raspberry mixture to come halfway up the sides of each mould, then pipe the vanilla ganache into each mould, stopping 2 mm (²/₂₅ inch) from the top edge. Set aside until cooled to room temperature and the filling has set (approximately 8 hours or overnight).

Gently reheat the remaining tempered chocolate by directing a heat gun or hair dryer at the surface until it is just liquid again. Fill the top of the moulds with chocolate, ensuring you seal the chocolate completely. Scrape the top of the mould with the chocolate spatula to remove the excess in one quick, smooth movement. Set aside until cool and the chocolate is dry to the touch.

makes 50

mint
bubble bar

sablé breton

87 g (3 oz) unsalted butter, softened
45 g (1¾ oz) pure icing (confectioners') sugar, sifted
40 g (1½ oz) almond meal
22 g (⁴⁄₅ oz) egg yolk
62 g (2¹⁄₅ oz) plain (all-purpose) flour, sifted
1 g (¹⁄₂₅ oz) sea salt flakes

Preheat the oven to 170°C (325°F/Gas 3). Lightly spray a square 20 cm (8 inch) cake tin with cooking oil. Line the base and sides with non-stick baking paper, extending over two opposite sides.

Cream the butter, icing sugar and almond meal in an electric mixer with a beater attachment until light and fluffy. Add the egg yolk and mix well. Scrape down the bowl with a spatula and mix in the flour and salt on low speed. Lay a sheet of plastic wrap on the bench. Gather up the dough, put it on the plastic wrap, cover and press down to flatten it to a disc approximately 2 cm (¾ inch) thick. Refrigerate for 1 hour or until firm.

Remove the dough from the refrigerator and knead lightly to soften it slightly. Roll it out on a lightly floured surface to a square about 3 mm (¹⁄₁₀ inch) thick. Using

the base of the tin as a template, cut a square 20 cm (8 inch) piece of dough. Discard the remaining dough. Roll the square of dough over a rolling pin, then lower it into the tin to cover the base. Bake for 10 minutes or until the sablé is lightly golden. Remove from the oven.

choc bubbles

500 g (1 lb 2 oz) dark couverture chocolate (64–73%), chopped or buttons
125 g (4½ oz) cocoa butter (see Glossary), finely chopped

While the sablé is cooking, line a square 20 cm (8 inch) cake tin with non-stick baking paper, extending over two opposite sides. Place in the freezer.

Melt the chocolate and cocoa butter in a heatproof bowl over a saucepan of simmering water or in the microwave. Remove from the heat and check the temperature. When it drops to 45°C (113°F), pour the mixture into a 500 ml (17 fl oz) cream canister (see Glossary), charge with two N_2O bulbs and shake for a few seconds. Remove the tin from the freezer. Cover the base of the tin with the chocolate mixture to form a layer 1 cm (½ inch) thick. Put in the freezer for 5 minutes or until set, then move it to the refrigerator.

(You will have more mixture than you need, but the canister won't operate without this quantity of liquid. The piped mixture is delicious eaten as it is or you can fill another cake tin and freeze and refrigerate for later use.)

mint caramel

100 g (3½ oz) pouring (whipping) cream (35% fat)
6 g (⅕ oz) fresh mint leaves
140 g (5 oz) caster (superfine) sugar
55 g (2 oz) unsalted butter, chopped and softened
1 g (¹⁄₂₅ oz) xanthan gum (see Glossary)

Make the mint caramel as soon as you take the sablé out of the oven. Put the cream in a small saucepan with half the mint and bring to the boil. Remove from the heat.

Heat another small saucepan over medium heat and sprinkle over a thin layer of caster sugar. As soon as it liquefies (approximately 2 minutes), sprinkle over another layer and when that liquefies, repeat, until all the sugar is used. Add the remaining mint and continue to cook for 1½ minutes or until the syrup is dark amber and has a strong toffee smell. Add the butter and swirl it around to deglaze, then add the cream mixture, stirring with a whisk to combine. Add the xanthan gum and blitz with a stick mixer for 20 seconds — this will help activate the gum and it will start to thicken the mixture.

Pass through a sieve into a heatproof bowl while it is still hot, then pour it over the sablé in the tin and tilt the tin so it reaches the edges. Heat a crank-handled palette knife by dipping in hot water and then drying, and use to smooth out the caramel to ensure it's an even thickness all over. Allow to set for 30 minutes.

mint ganache

125 g (4½ oz) pouring (whipping) cream (35% fat)
12 g (²⁄₅ oz) liquid glucose
13 g (½ oz) fresh mint leaves
88 g (3¼ oz) dark couverture chocolate (64%), chopped or buttons
100 g (3½ oz) milk couverture chocolate, chopped or buttons
13 g (½ oz) strained lime juice
Finely grated zest of 1 lime
30 g (1 oz) unsalted butter, chopped and softened

Put the cream, glucose and mint in a saucepan and bring to the boil over medium–high heat. Remove from the heat, cover with plastic wrap and leave to infuse for 20 minutes.

Put both the chocolates in a heatproof bowl. Remove the plastic wrap from the cream mixture and return it to the boil. Immediately strain it over the chocolate and stir until the mixture is smooth. Stir through the lime juice and zest, then blitz in the butter with a stick mixer until smooth. Pour the ganache over the caramel layer, tilting the tin so it covers the caramel evenly. Set aside for 3 hours or until the ganache is set and dry to the touch. You may have to refrigerate it, depending on the temperature of the room. Remove from the tin and cut into twenty 2 x 10 cm (¾ x 4 inch) bars.

to finish

500 g (1 lb 2 oz) dark couverture chocolate (64%), chopped or buttons, tempered (see Basics)

Remove the choc bubble mixture from the tin and cut into small pieces. Set aside or refrigerate if the temperature in the kitchen is warm.

Drop a bar into the tempered chocolate, then lift out with a dipping fork (see Glossary), agitating it slightly so that the excess chocolate drips back into the bowl. Place some choc bubble pieces on top, pressing gently to adhere. Repeat with the remaining bars and choc bubble pieces. Put on Silpat (see Glossary) or a baking tray lined with non-stick baking paper and set aside at room temperature for 20 minutes or until the bars are set and dry to the touch. **makes 20 bars**

blackcurrant violet

225 g (8 oz) dark couverture chocolate (64–73%),
   chopped or buttons
225 g (8 oz) milk couverture chocolate, chopped or buttons
292 g (10¼ oz) sieved blackcurrant purée (see Basics)
50 g (1¾ oz) inverted sugar (see Glossary)
45 g (1¾ oz) cocoa butter (see Glossary), finely chopped
60 g (2¼ oz) unsalted butter, chopped and softened
2 g (²/₂₅ oz) natural violet extract or oil (see Glossary)
50 g (1¾ oz) small milk couverture chocolate
   buttons, extra
500 g (1 lb 2 oz) dark couverture chocolate (64–73%),
   extra, chopped or buttons

Lightly spray a square 20 cm (8 inch) cake tin with
cooking oil and line with non-stick baking paper,
extending over two opposite sides.

   Melt the chocolates together in a heatproof
bowl over a saucepan of simmering water or in the
microwave. Remove from the heat. Put the blackcurrant
purée and inverted sugar in a saucepan over medium
heat and bring to 50°C (122°F). Add to the melted
chocolate and stir to combine.

   Meanwhile, melt the cocoa butter in a separate
saucepan and bring to 32°C (90°F). Immediately mix into
the blackcurrant and chocolate mixture. Blitz in the butter
and violet extract with a stick mixer until smooth.

   Pour the ganache into the tin and set aside at room
temperature for 2 hours, until set and dry to the touch.

   Melt the extra milk chocolate in a heatproof
bowl over a saucepan of simmering water or in the
microwave. Pour over the ganache, use a crank-handled
palette knife to smooth it out to cover the ganache evenly
and leave at room temperature for 15 minutes, until set.

   Lift out of the tin using the overhanging paper. Invert
onto a chopping board so the blackcurrant ganache is on
top. Use a sharp, thin-bladed knife dipped in warm water
and then dried to trim 1 cm (½ inch) from the sides and
then cut into 2.5 cm (1 inch) squares.

   Temper the extra dark chocolate (see Basics).

   Carefully drop a piece of ganache into the tempered
chocolate and lift out with a dipping fork (see Glossary),

agitating it slightly so that the excess chocolate drips
back into the bowl. Put on Silpat (see Glossary) or a
baking tray lined with non-stick baking paper. Lay
your decoration (see below) on top. Repeat until all the
chocolates are formed. Allow to set at room temperature
for 2–3 hours or until the chocolate is completely dry
to the touch. (Keep any remaining chocolate decoration
to decorate cakes, or just eat it!)

decoration
100 g (3½ oz) cocoa butter (see Glossary), finely chopped
2 g (²/₂₅ oz) blue lipid-soluble food colouring (see Glossary)
4 g (⁴/₂₅ oz) red lipid-soluble food colouring (see Glossary)
500 g (1 lb 2 oz) white couverture chocolate, chopped
   or buttons, tempered (see Basics)

Melt the cocoa butter in a medium saucepan over low
heat. Pour into a deep straight-sided jug, add the food
colourings and blitz with a stick mixer until all the
colour particles have disappeared. Set aside to cool
to 32°C (90°F).

   Dampen the benchtop slightly with a moist cloth.
Place a 30 x 40 cm (12 x 16 inch) acetate sheet (see
Glossary) on top and use a clean dry cloth to smooth it
out. The moisture will help the acetate sheet stick to the
bench. Use a pastry brush to brush the coloured cocoa
butter onto the acetate sheet in lines, always brushing
in the same direction. Continue brushing on lines until
the cocoa butter begins to harden. Pour the tempered
white chocolate over the brushed cocoa butter and use
a large crank-handled palette knife to smooth the white
chocolate out to about 2 mm (¹/₁₆ inch) thick. Holding
opposite diagonal corners of the acetate sheet, lightly
shake the sheet to smooth out the chocolate. Set aside
until the chocolate is dry to the touch, yet still pliable.

   Use a ruler and paring knife to cut the chocolate into
2.5 cm (1 inch) squares — you will need 49. Cover with
non-stick baking paper, flip over and put a baking tray
on top to stop the chocolate bending as it crystallises
and sets. Leave until set. *makes 49*

yuzu
sticks

vanilla caramel

200 g (7 oz) caster (superfine) sugar
120 g (4¼ oz) pouring (whipping) cream (35% fat)
80 g (2¾ oz) liquid glucose
60 g (2¼ oz) unsalted butter, chopped
Seeds scraped from 1 vanilla bean
Pinch of sea salt flakes

Put the sugar and cream in a small saucepan and bring to the boil over medium heat. Add the glucose, butter and vanilla seeds and gently stir through. Cook until the mixture reaches 118°C (244°F), then remove from the heat and transfer to a small pouring jug. Pour a thin layer of caramel into fourteen 2 x 15 cm (¾ x 6 inch) flexipan silicone mould cavities. Leave for 1 hour to set.

yuzu ganache

65 g (2⅓ oz) pouring (whipping) cream (35% fat)
255 g (9 oz) dark couverture chocolate (55%),
    chopped or buttons
100 g (3½ oz) yuzu juice (see Glossary)
55 g (2 oz) unsalted butter, chopped and softened

Bring the cream to the boil in a small saucepan. Put the chocolate in a bowl. Pour over the hot cream and stir gently until the mixture is smooth. Put the yuzu juice in a small saucepan over medium heat and bring to 50°C (122°F). Slowly pour the yuzu juice into the chocolate mixture in a thin, steady stream and mix well. Blitz in the butter with a stick mixer until smooth. Use the mixture to fill a piping bag with a 7 mm (⅜ inch) plain nozzle and pipe the mixture over the caramel in the moulds to form a layer 4 mm (⅙ inch) thick.

hazelnut crunchy

40 g (1½ oz) milk couverture chocolate,
    chopped or buttons
165 g (5¾ oz) hazelnut praline (see Basics)
85 g (3 oz) pailleté feuilletine (see Glossary)
15 g (½ oz) unsalted butter, melted

Melt the chocolate in a heatproof bowl over a saucepan of simmering water or in the microwave. Stir through the hazelnut praline, then mix in the pailleté feuilletine. Fold through the melted butter. Use a crank-handled palette knife to press the mixture onto the yuzu ganache in the moulds to form another layer 4 mm (⅙ inch) thick. Leave to set for 12 hours at room temperature (if it's hot you may need to use the refrigerator).

yuzu sugar

200 g (7 oz) caster (superfine) sugar
Finely grated zest of 2 limes
1 drop yellow food colouring
2 drops green food colouring
5 g (⅛ oz) citric acid (see Glossary)

Put all the ingredients in a bowl and, wearing disposable gloves, rub together with your hands until even in colour and free of lumps. Line a baking tray with non-stick baking paper and spread out the yuzu sugar in a thin layer. Leave in a warm place for approximately 1 hour to dry. Store in an airtight container once dry.

to finish

500 g (1 lb 2 oz) dark couverture chocolate (70%),
    chopped or buttons

Temper the dark chocolate (see Basics). Pop the sticks out of the moulds. Using your hands, dip each stick in the chocolate and then wipe off the excess chocolate. Roll each stick in the yuzu sugar until coated, using a fork to help you turn them. Leave until set. **makes 14**

peanut chocolate bars

peanut crunch

42 g (1½ oz) dark couverture chocolate (64%),
   chopped or buttons
83 g (3 oz) smooth peanut butter
83 g (3 oz) pailleté feuilletine (see Glossary)
17 g (³/₅ oz) unsalted butter, melted

Line a square 20 cm (8 inch) cake tin with non-stick
baking paper, extending over two opposite sides.

Melt the chocolate in a heatproof bowl over a
saucepan of simmering water or in the microwave.
Remove from the heat and mix in the peanut butter
with a heatproof spatula until well combined, then stir
through the pailleté feuilletine. Fold through the melted
butter until well combined. Spread the mixture evenly
into the lined tin and place in the refrigerator for
15 minutes or until it is just firm.

peanut praline

80 g (2¾ oz) milk couverture chocolate,
   chopped or buttons
72 g (2½ oz) smooth peanut butter
17 g (³/₅ oz) unsalted butter, chopped and softened
0.5 g (¹/₅₀ oz) sea salt flakes

Melt the chocolate in a heatproof bowl over a saucepan
of simmering water or in the microwave. Remove from
the heat and mix in the peanut butter with a heatproof
spatula until well combined. Blitz in the butter with a
stick mixer until smooth, then stir through the salt.

Pour the praline over the peanut crunch in the tin
and spread it out to form an even layer. Set aside for
1 hour or until firm.

salted peanut caramel

150 g (5½ oz) caster (superfine) sugar
60 g (2¼ oz) water
30 g (1 oz) liquid glucose
76 g (2¾ oz) pouring (whipping) cream (35% fat)
60 g (2¼ oz) unsalted butter
1 g (¹⁄₂₅ oz) agar-agar (see Glossary)
3 g (¹⁄₁₀ oz) xanthan gum (see Glossary)
50 g (1¾ oz) finely chopped roasted peanuts
1 g (¹⁄₂₅ oz) sea salt flakes

Put the sugar, water and glucose in a small saucepan over medium heat and stir until the sugar has dissolved. Continue cooking for 2 minutes or until the syrup is a dark-amber caramel. Meanwhile, heat the cream and butter in another small saucepan until the butter has melted, then bring to the boil over medium heat. Add the agar-agar and xanthan gum and blitz with a stick mixer for 20 seconds or until the mixture resembles a béchamel sauce.

When the syrup is a dark-amber caramel, remove from the heat and mix in the thick cream mixture with a small whisk until smooth. Process again briefly with the stick mixer to ensure it is as smooth as possible. Stir in the peanuts and salt. Pour evenly over Silpat (see Glossary) or a baking tray lined with non-stick baking paper. It will easily spread out and cool quickly, so working as fast, but as safely, as you can cut it into twenty 2 x 10 cm (¾ x 4 inch) bars and separate them to cool completely.

nougatine

35 g (1¼ oz) liquid glucose
250 g (9 oz) caster (superfine) sugar
100 g (3½ oz) roasted peanuts, very finely chopped
5 drops lemon juice

Heat the glucose in a saucepan over medium heat until it melts and covers the base of the pan. Sprinkle in the sugar and stir with a heatproof spatula until it has dissolved. Run a pastry brush dipped in water around the inside of the pan, above the liquid sugar, to remove any sugar crystals. Continue to cook for 2 minutes or until the syrup is a dark-amber caramel that smells like well-cooked toffee. Remove from the heat, immediately add the peanuts and lemon juice and stir to combine. Pour out onto Silpat or a baking tray lined with non-stick baking paper (you will get a better result using Silpat).

After a couple of minutes the edges will start to set. Wearing clean disposable gloves, gently tap the set edges back into the soft caramel. Continue tapping, and eventually folding, the set edges in towards the centre until you have one solid mass of even temperature that is still pliable. Use a rolling pin to roll it into a 20 cm (8 inch) square, with a thickness of 3 mm (⅛ inch). Cut into twenty 2 x 10 cm (¾ x 4 inch) bars and separate them to help them cool quickly.

to assemble

80 g (2¾ oz) crunchy peanut butter
300 g (10½ oz) plain puffed rice cereal
1 kg (2 lb 4 oz) milk couverture chocolate, chopped or buttons, tempered (see Basics)

When the nougatine has cooled completely, lift the peanut crunch and praline slab from the tin using the paper as handles. Peel away the paper and cut the slab into twenty 2 x 10 cm (¾ x 4 inch) bars. Smear a little peanut butter over the flat side of each bar and press a piece of nougatine on top. Turn all the bars over, then smear the other side with peanut butter and top with a piece of salted peanut caramel. Set aside.

Stir the puffed rice cereal into the tempered chocolate. Dip each bar in the chocolate mixture, then lift out with a dipping fork (see Glossary), agitating it slightly so that the excess chocolate drips back into the bowl. Put on Silpat or a baking tray lined with non-stick baking paper and set aside at room temperature for 20 minutes or until the chocolate bars are set and dry to the touch. **makes 20 bars**

pastries

zumbo karate
white belt division
regional titles

from left: praline toe bun; apple crumble brioche; orange, pumpkin & saffron risotto snail; chocolate raspberry pepito; zumbo's palmier; balmain bun; pineapple, ginger & pepper danish; sticky mango bun; macadamia croissant; sugar lips

Making pastries is one of the things I began my cooking career with. I find it amazing that butter, flour and water can turn into such a beautiful product. I get excited by the layers, by cutting open a croissant or savouring a sugary palmier that crunches and melts perfectly in my mouth.

Pastries are rustic and I enjoy the free-form type of cooking you can do with them. It takes skill to get even layers of butter laminated, keep the dough at a chilled consistent temperature and get the temperature and size right in the proofing stage. These are all crucial components in simply getting your pastries ready to bake. But don't let this put you off, get into the kitchen and start practising, it's the only way to achieve success.

Custards, almond creams and fruit are all fantastic accompaniments to flaky, buttery pastry. I encourage you to try your own combinations using some of the base pastry recipes and changing the flavour additions. There's no better way to wow your friends and family the next time they drop in.

brioche

480 g (1 lb 1 oz) plain (all-purpose) flour
72 g (2½ oz) brown sugar (caster/superfine sugar can be substituted)
12 g (²⁄₅ oz) salt
9.5 g (¼ oz) fresh yeast (see Glossary)
385 g (13½ oz) lightly beaten egg
430 g (15¼ oz) unsalted butter, chopped and softened

Put the flour, sugar and salt in an electric mixer with a dough hook attachment and mix for 1 minute on low speed to combine. With the motor running, crumble in the yeast and then add half the egg and mix until combined. Add the remaining egg and mix to combine — you should have a wet paste. Increase to medium speed and work the dough for 20 minutes or until it becomes elastic and starts to come away from the side of the bowl.

Reduce the speed to low and, with the motor running, add one-third of the butter and mix until thoroughly incorporated (approximately 6 minutes). Add another third of butter and mix until no lumps are visible. Scrape down the side of the bowl. Add the remaining butter and mix until thoroughly incorporated. By this stage, your dough should be shiny, glossy and smooth, and very soft but still pliable. Transfer the dough to a lightly oiled, large plastic container and loosely cover with plastic wrap. Set aside at room temperature for approximately 1 hour or until the dough has doubled in size.

Knock back the dough (this is done by punching once into the dough to expel the air). Cover the dough again and refrigerate overnight — it will take this long for the whole mixture to become firm enough to handle. If you are short on time, it can be used in about 4–6 hours, but it will be particularly fragile. Use as per the individual recipes.

brioche feuilletée

75 g (2¾ oz) fresh yeast (see Glossary)
375 g (13 oz) chilled water
1 kg (2 lb 4 oz) strong plain (all-purpose) flour
65 g (2⅓ oz) caster (superfine) sugar
55 g (2 oz) full-cream (whole) milk powder
15 g (½ oz) salt
200 g (7 oz) lightly beaten egg
400 g (14 oz) chilled unsalted butter

Put the yeast and a little of the water in a bowl and mash together with the back of a fork until smooth and soft. Add the remaining water and whisk to distribute the yeast evenly.

Put the flour, sugar, milk powder, salt, egg and the yeast mixture in an electric mixer with a dough hook attachment and mix on low speed for 2 minutes to just bring the ingredients together. Increase the speed to medium for 5 minutes or until a soft, slightly sticky but elastic dough is formed.

Gather the dough together, wrap in plastic wrap and pat into an even-shaped block. Refrigerate for 2 hours. Unwrap and roll the dough out to a rectangle approximately 15 x 60 cm (6 x 24 inches), then wrap and refrigerate again.

Meanwhile, put the butter between 2 sheets of plastic wrap and allow it to soften slightly, then beat the top of it with a rolling pin to flatten it, forming a slab of butter about 15 x 20 cm (6 x 8 inches) and 1.5 cm (⅝ inch) thick. It is important to retain an even rectangular shape, so if the sides start to wander as you are beating, tap them back in with the side of the rolling pin to even it up. Chill the butter until firm.

Unwrap the dough and place on a clean benchtop so the short sides are on the left and right — it will be horizontal in front of you. Allow the dough to rest so that it softens slightly.

Put the slab of butter in the centre of the dough so it lines up with the top and base, but is 20 cm (8 inches) in from each side. Fold one side of the exposed dough over the butter, then fold over the opposite side of dough.

Turn the dough seam-side down, with the short, open ends now on the left and right. Take a rolling pin and bash the dough evenly along its length until it is 2–3 cm (¾–1¼ inches) thick all over. This will extend the length to approximately 25 x 35 cm (10 x 14 inches). Roll the dough out until it is an even 1 cm (½ inch) thickness

all over, ensuring you retain the long rectangular shape by tapping in any wandering edges. Always roll in the direction of the open ends of the dough. It should be about 100 cm (39½ inches) long now.

Look down at your dough and imagine it divided into 3 even lengths, from left to right. If it helps, you may like to make two small indents in the pastry. Fold over the left third of the dough. Take the time now to even up any wandering edges so you retain a neat rectangle, with all edges lined up. Fold over the right third of the dough and even up the edges again. This is called a single turn. Put a thumbprint in the top of the dough to help you track how many turns you have done — this is particularly handy when working with multiple doughs. Wrap in plastic wrap and refrigerate for 30 minutes.

Roll the dough out to an even 1 cm (½ inch) thickness and repeat another single turn, making two thumbprints this time, and chill for another 30 minutes.

Repeat the rolling, single turn and chilling process until it has been done four times (i.e., four thumbprints). The dough is now ready to be used. Use as per the individual recipes.

doughnut dough

starter

10 g (¼ oz) fresh yeast (see Glossary)

125 g (4½ oz) water

175 g (6 oz) plain (all-purpose) flour

dough

225 g (8 oz) lightly beaten egg

150 g (5½ oz) milk

700 g (1 lb 9 oz) plain (all-purpose) flour

7.5 g (¼ oz) salt

150 g (5½ oz) caster (superfine) sugar

125 g (4½ oz) chilled unsalted butter, chopped

To make the starter, mash the yeast and water together. Put the yeast mixture and flour in an electric mixer with a beater attachment and mix for 30 seconds, until they just come together. Transfer to an oiled bowl, cover with plastic wrap and put in a warm place for approximately 1 hour or until doubled in size.

Put all the dough ingredients in an electric mixer with a dough hook attachment and mix on low speed for 3 minutes or until a smooth dough forms. Add the starter, increase the speed slightly and work the dough for 5 minutes, until it is smooth and slightly shiny. Transfer to an oiled bowl, cover with plastic wrap and set aside until the dough has doubled in size (up to 2 hours).

Knock back the dough (punch it once to expel the air), cover with plastic wrap and refrigerate overnight. Use as per the individual recipes.

croissants

62 g (2⅕ oz) fresh yeast (see Glossary)
475 g (1 lb 1 oz) chilled water
1 kg (2 lb 4 oz) strong plain (all-purpose) flour
120 g (4¼ oz) caster (superfine) sugar
25 g (1 oz) salt
200 g (7 oz) chilled unsalted butter, chopped
2 x 250 g (9 oz) blocks unsalted butter, extra, chilled
Egg wash (see Basics)

Put the yeast and a little of the water in a bowl and mash together with the back of a fork until smooth and softened. Add the remaining water and whisk to distribute the yeast evenly. Put the flour, sugar, salt, chopped butter and yeast mixture in an electric mixer with a dough hook attachment. Mix on the lowest speed for 3 minutes — the mixture should just start to come together as the butter starts to soften.

Increase the speed to medium and mix for 7–8 minutes or until the mixture forms a nice elastic dough. Gather together and shape into a rectangle, about 20 x 30 cm (8 x 12 inches) and 5 cm (2 inches) thick. Wrap in plastic wrap and freeze for 30 minutes or until the dough is really cold but not frozen solid.

As soon as you put the dough in the freezer, remove the blocks of butter from the refrigerator. Cut each block into thirds lengthways, to make 3 rectangles, and lay them close together on a baking tray lined with non-stick baking paper. They should now form a large rectangular block, 15 x 20 cm (6 x 8 inches) and about 1.5 cm (⅝ inch) thick. Refrigerate until firm.

Unwrap the dough and place on a clean benchtop so the short sides are left and right — it will be horizontal in front of you. Roll the dough out to 15 x 60 cm (6 x 24 inches). Put the slab of butter in the centre of the dough, so it lines up with the top and base, but is 20 cm (8 inches) in from each side. Fold one side of the exposed dough over the butter, then fold over the opposite side of dough. Turn the dough seam-side down, with the short, open ends now left and right. Use a rolling pin to bash the dough evenly along its length until it is 2 cm (¾ inch) thick all over. This will extend its length to approximately 25 x 35 cm (10 x 14 inches).

Use a rolling pin to roll the dough out until it is an even 1 cm (½ inch) thickness all over, ensuring you retain the long rectangular shape by tapping in any wandering edges. Always roll in the direction of the open ends of the dough. The dough should be about 100 cm (39½ inches) long now. Look down at your dough and imagine it divided into 3 even lengths, from left to right. If it helps, you may like to make two small indents in the pastry. Fold over the left third of the dough. Even up any wandering edges so you retain a neat rectangle, with all edges lined up. Fold over the right third of the dough and even up the edges again. This is called a single turn. Put a thumbprint in the top of the dough to help you track how many turns you have done — this is particularly handy when working with multiple doughs. Wrap in plastic wrap and refrigerate for 30 minutes to rest and firm up slightly.

Put the dough on a benchtop, with the open ends on the left and right. Use a rolling pin to roll out the dough to 1 cm (½ inch) thick, rolling in the direction of the open ends. You should end up with a long, even rectangle. Fold in both ends so they almost meet in the middle, with a 2 cm (¾ inch) gap between them. Fold the left side over the right, as though you're closing a book. This is called a book turn. Wrap in plastic wrap and refrigerate for 30 minutes to rest. Unwrap and use as per the individual recipes.

rolling the croissants

Use a rolling pin to roll the dough out on a floured benchtop to a 40 x 60 cm (16 x 24 inch) rectangle, with a thickness of 4 mm ($\frac{1}{6}$ inch). Mark the halfway point of each short side with the tip of a knife. Then, using a ruler as a guide, cut from point to point to make 2 long rectangles of dough. Do not separate them.

Starting at the top left corner of the upper rectangle of dough and working to the right, measure and mark 12 cm (4$\frac{1}{2}$ inch) intervals all the way along. Repeat with the lower rectangle of dough, starting from the bottom left corner. Now, go to the line you cut along the centre to create the two rectangles. Measure and mark the first 6 cm (2$\frac{1}{2}$ inches) towards the right, then mark 12 cm (4$\frac{1}{2}$ inch) intervals the rest of the way along. Using these markings as a guide, cut both rectangles of dough into triangles. Do not separate them, leave them on the benchtop as they are. Make a 1 cm ($\frac{1}{2}$ inch) cut into the base of each triangle, at the centre.

Discard the half-size triangles from the ends of the dough, then brush off any excess flour on the remaining triangles with a pastry brush. Lift a triangle up, holding the base in one hand and taking hold of the tip with your other hand. Pull gently down to stretch the triangle by approximately 2 cm ($\frac{3}{4}$ inch). Put the elongated triangle on the bench so the tip is pointing at you. Fold the base towards you by 5 mm ($\frac{1}{4}$ inch). Form an A-frame with your hands, fingers together and one thumb resting slightly over the top of the other. Keeping your hands in this position, gently roll the folded side of dough towards you until it reaches the tip of the triangle. Repeat to roll all the croissants.

(At this point, the croissants can be frozen for up to 2 weeks. When ready to use, defrost in the refrigerator overnight and then prove.)

proving the croissants

Put the croissants on baking trays lined with non-stick baking paper, spaced 5 cm (2 inches) apart. Put the trays in the oven, but do not turn the oven on. Put a roasting tin of warm water on the bottom shelf and close the door. Allow the dough to prove for 1–2 hours or until it has doubled in size. You may need to replace the water as it cools down — the idea is to keep the oven a consistent, moist heat. Remove all the trays, including the roasting tin, from the oven.

Preheat the oven to 190°C (375°F/Gas 5). Lightly brush the top of each croissant with egg wash and cook for 25 minutes or until crisp and golden.

makes 18 croissants

full puff pastry

1020 g (2 lb 4¾ oz) strong plain (all-purpose) flour
35 g (1¼ oz) salt
545 g (1 lb 3 oz) chilled water
435 g (15¼ oz) strong plain (all-purpose) flour, extra
1455 g (3 lb 4 oz) chilled unsalted butter

Put the flour, salt and chilled water in an electric mixer with a dough hook attachment and mix on low speed for 3 minutes until the ingredients are just combined. Increase the speed of the mixer to medium and mix for a further 6 minutes to develop the gluten — the dough should be slightly elastic.

Gather the dough together, wrap in plastic wrap and pat down into a rectangle. Refrigerate for 30 minutes to firm up a little. Roll out to a 20 cm (8 inch) square and refrigerate again to rest the dough.

Put the extra flour in an electric mixer with a beater attachment. Chop the butter into roughly 2 cm (¾ inch) squares. With the motor running on low speed, add a third of the butter and mix until the edges of the butter start to mash slightly and the mixture begins to cling together. Add another third of the butter and mix as before, then add the remaining butter, again mixing until the mixture just comes together — it will look like a lumpy mass of butter.

Lightly flour your work surface. Gather the butter mixture into a block about 2.5 cm (1 inch) thick and use a rolling pin to tap the edges to bring it into a neat rectangle, approximately 10 x 20 cm (4 x 8 inches) and 2.5 cm (1 inch) thick. Wrap in plastic wrap and refrigerate for 30 minutes to firm up slightly.

Unwrap the dough and place on a clean benchtop. Put the slab of butter mixture in the centre of the dough so it lines up with the sides, but is 5 cm (2 inches) from the top and the base. Fold the exposed dough at the top over the butter, then fold over the exposed dough at the bottom. Pinch the edges of the dough together.

Turn the dough seam-side down. Take a rolling pin and bash the dough evenly along its length until it is about 2 cm (¾ inch) thick all over. This will extend the length to approximately 25 x 35 cm (10 x 14 inches).

Use a rolling pin to roll the dough out to an even 1 cm (½ inch) thickness, tapping in any wandering edges to retain the long rectangular shape. Always roll in the direction of the open ends. The dough should be about 100 cm (39½ inches) long.

Look down at your dough and imagine it divided into 3 even lengths, from left to right. If it helps, you may like to make two small indents in the pastry. Fold over the left third of the dough. Take the time now to even up any wandering edges so you retain a neat rectangle, with all edges lined up. Fold over the right third of the dough and even up the edges again. Roll the dough out once more to 1 cm (½ inch) thick and fold into thirds, as before. This is called a double turn. Put a thumbprint in the top of the dough to help you track how many turns you have done — this is particularly handy when working with multiple doughs. Wrap in plastic wrap and refrigerate for 1 hour.

Repeat the rolling, double turn and chilling process until it has been done three times (i.e., three thumbprints). The pastry is now ready to use. (Alternatively, you can wrap the pastry in plastic wrap and freeze it for later use.)

praline toe buns

zumbotella

125 g (4½ oz) milk couverture chocolate,
    chopped or buttons
125 g (4½ oz) dark couverture chocolate (64%),
    chopped or buttons
250 g (9 oz) hazelnut paste (see Pistachio paste in Basics)
50 g (1¾ oz) vegetable oil
25 g (1 oz) unsweetened cocoa powder

Melt the chocolates in a heatproof bowl over a saucepan
of simmering water. Remove the bowl from the pan,
add the hazelnut paste, oil and cocoa and mix until well
combined. Cool to room temperature and refrigerate for
20–30 minutes or until starting to set, but still spoonable.

crunchy praline

65 g (2⅓ oz) milk couverture chocolate,
    chopped or buttons
227 g (8 oz) hazelnut praline (see Basics)
132 g (4⅔ oz) pailleté feuilletine (see Glossary)
26 g (1 oz) roasted and skinned hazelnuts,
    roughly chopped
26 g (1 oz) unsalted butter, melted

Melt the chocolate in a heatproof bowl over a saucepan
of simmering water. Add the hazelnut praline and fold
through the pailleté feuilletine and chopped hazelnuts.
Remove the bowl from the pan, mix in the melted butter
and set aside to cool to room temperature.

to assemble

1 quantity brioche feuilletée (see page 82)
Egg wash (see Basics)
360 g (12¾ oz) milk couverture chocolate, melted
360 g (12¾ oz) roughly chopped roasted and
    skinned hazelnuts

Cut the brioche feuilletée dough in half and roll out one
portion at a time on a lightly floured benchtop to 4 mm
(⅙ inch) thick, then use a round 12 cm (4½ inch) cutter
to stamp out 24 discs. Spread a tablespoon of crunchy
praline over each disc to about 3 mm (⅛ inch) thick,
leaving an 8 mm (⅜ inch) border. Spoon a tablespoon of
zumbotella over the centre of the praline on each disc.

Dip a pastry brush in egg wash and brush lightly
around the plain dough border. Fold the dough over the
zumbotella and praline to make a half-moon and press
the edges of the dough together to seal well.

(At this point the toe buns can be frozen for up to
2 weeks. When ready to use, defrost in the refrigerator
overnight and then prove, as below.)

Put the toe buns, spaced well apart, on baking trays
lined with non-stick baking paper. Put the trays in the
oven, but do not turn the oven on. Put a roasting tin
of warm water on the bottom shelf and close the door.
Allow the dough to prove for 1–2 hours or until it has
doubled in size. You may need to replace the water as it
cools down — the idea is to keep the oven a consistent,
moist heat. Remove all the trays, including the roasting
tin, from the oven.

Preheat the oven to 190°C (375°F/Gas 5). Brush the
buns lightly with egg wash and bake for 20 minutes, until
golden. Remove from the oven and cool on the trays.

Dip the tip of each pastry in the melted chocolate,
forming a 'toe nail', and allow any excess to drip off.
Dip the chocolate-coated end in the chopped hazelnuts
to cover the chocolate. Transfer to a wire rack and set
aside until the chocolate has set. **makes 24**

balmain buns

licorice cream mousseline

333 g (11¾ oz) milk
33 g (1¼ oz) soft licorice sticks (as fresh as possible),
    chopped
100 g (3½ oz) egg yolks
100 g (3½ oz) caster (superfine) sugar
23 g (⁴⁄₅ oz) cornflour (cornstarch)
40 g (1½ oz) unsalted butter, chopped and softened
200 g (7 oz) unsalted butter, extra, chopped
    and softened

Put the milk and licorice in a small saucepan over
medium–high heat and bring to the boil. Turn off the
heat and set aside for 5 minutes, then blitz with a stick
mixer until smooth.

Put the egg yolks, sugar and cornflour in a bowl
and use a small balloon whisk to whisk until thick and
pale. Strain a quarter of the licorice mixture over the
egg mixture while whisking constantly. Whisk in the
rest of the strained licorice mixture and place in a clean
saucepan over medium heat. Whisk until the mixture
comes to the boil and thickens slightly. Remove from the
heat, cover with plastic wrap and cool to 50°C (122°F),
then mix in the butter until incorporated.

Cool slightly, then cover with plastic wrap, pressing
it onto the surface to prevent a skin forming. Refrigerate
for 2–3 hours or until completely chilled and thick.

Weigh out 400 g (14 oz) of the mousseline and put
in an electric mixer with a paddle attachment. Add the
extra chopped butter and beat until light and fluffy.
Set aside, covered with plastic wrap, until required.

peach, apricot & lavender gel

300 g (10½ oz) sieved puréed peach (see Basics)
300 g (10½ oz) sieved puréed apricot (see Basics)
70 g (2½ oz) lavender sugar (see Basics)
3 g (¹⁄₁₀ oz) iota (see Glossary)

Put all the ingredients in a saucepan and blitz with
a stick mixer until well combined. Stir continuously
over medium heat until the mixture comes to the boil.
Immediately pour it into a bowl and allow to cool
slightly, then cover with plastic wrap and refrigerate
for 2–3 hours or until completely chilled.

to assemble

1 quantity brioche dough (see page 81)
1 quantity pâte sablé a choux (see What a great pear of…
    recipe, page 193, omit the green food colouring)

Use a dough cutter or knife to cut the brioche dough into
90 g (3¼ oz) portions — you should have 15 portions.
Use your hands to roll each portion into a smooth ball.
Put on baking trays lined with non-stick baking paper,
spaced well apart.

Put the trays in the oven, but do not turn the oven
on. Put a roasting tin of warm water on the bottom
shelf and close the door. Allow the dough to prove for
1–2 hours or until it has doubled in size. You may need
to replace the water as it cools down — the idea is to
keep the oven a consistent, moist heat. Remove the trays
and the roasting tin from the oven.

Preheat the oven to 180°C (350°F/Gas 4). Roll out
the pâte sablé a choux on a lightly floured benchtop to
4 mm (¹⁄₆ inch) thick. Use a round 7 cm (2¾ inch) pastry
cutter to stamp out discs. Put a disc on top of each ball
of dough — it will flatten the dough slightly, which is
fine. Bake for 18 minutes or until both the dough and
pâte sablé are golden. Allow to cool on the trays.

When the buns have cooled, cut them in half to
form tops and bases. Take two piping (icing) bags with
9 mm (¹⁄₃ inch) nozzles and fill one with the mousseline
mixture and the other with the gel. Pipe alternating strips
of mousseline and gel onto each bun base. Cover with
the bun tops and serve. **makes 15**

orange, pumpkin & saffron risotto snails

orange, pumpkin & saffron risotto

300 g (10½ oz) peeled pumpkin (winter squash),
    chopped, roasted until golden and tender
10 g (¼ oz) unsalted butter
150 g (5½ oz) arborio rice
500 g (1 lb 2 oz) milk
485 g (1 lb 1 oz) pouring (whipping) cream (35% fat)
Pinch of saffron threads
Finely grated zest of 1 orange
400 g (14 oz) boiled pumpkin (winter squash), puréed
90 g (3¼ oz) caster (superfine) sugar

Set aside 70 g (2½ oz) of roasted pumpkin for a garnish.
Process the remaining roasted pumpkin to a purée.

Melt the butter in a saucepan over medium heat,
add the rice and cook for 2 minutes or until translucent.

Meanwhile, put the milk, cream, saffron, orange
zest, boiled pumpkin purée and sugar in a saucepan.
Stir over medium heat until the sugar has dissolved, then
bring to the boil. Add the hot milk mixture, a ladleful
at a time, to the rice, stirring well after each addition
and making sure the liquid has been absorbed by the
rice before adding more. Continue until all the liquid
has been added and the rice is just tender — this should
take about 25 minutes. Remove from the heat and fold
through the roasted pumpkin purée. Cool completely.

orange & saffron custriano

1 navel orange
500 g (1 lb 2 oz) milk
2 g (²/₂₅ oz) iota (see Glossary)
150 g (5½ oz) caster (superfine) sugar
Pinch of saffron threads
60 g (2¼ oz) unsalted butter, chopped and softened

Put the orange in a saucepan, cover with water and bring
to the boil. Reduce the heat and simmer for 45 minutes
or until very soft, adding more water if needed to keep
the orange covered. Remove the orange and cool a little.

Roughly chop the orange, put in a clean saucepan
with the milk and blitz with a stick mixer until smooth.
Add the iota, sugar and saffron and blitz again until
smooth and thickened slightly. Whisk continuously over

medium heat until the mixture reaches 90°C (194°F). Transfer to a bowl, cover with plastic wrap and cool to 40°C (104°F), then blitz in the butter with the stick mixer until well combined. Cover with plastic wrap again, pressing it onto the surface to prevent a skin forming.

When the risotto and the custriano have cooled, mix together until well combined. Cover with plastic wrap, pressing it onto the surface, and refrigerate until chilled.

to assemble

1 quantity brioche feuilletée (see page 82)

Roll out the dough to a 40 x 97.5 cm (16 x 38²/₅ inch) rectangle, with an even thickness of 4 mm (¹/₆ inch). Line 3–4 large baking trays with non-stick baking paper.

Spread the risotto and custriano mixture over the dough to cover it, making a layer approximately 7 mm (³/₈ inch) thick. Carefully fold the top edge towards you by 1 cm (¹/₂ inch), then keep your hands flat and gently roll the dough from the folded edge one-third of the way towards the opposite edge. With your fingers curled behind the roll of dough for support, use your thumbs to push the roll back away from you, working from left to right where the roll meets the flat dough — this will tighten up the roll. With flattened hands again, roll the dough towards you another third of the way and repeat the pushing back and tightening motion. Roll the dough towards you again until it reaches the edge nearest you, then roll it towards you again slightly so that the seam is underneath. Trim the edges to neaten, then cut the roll into 3 cm (1¹/₄ inch) thick slices. Hold up a slice and you will see there is one loose edge. Tuck this 'tail' underneath and place on a lined tray, tail side down. Repeat with all the slices, spacing them well apart.

(At this point the snails can be frozen for up to 2 weeks. When ready to use, defrost in the refrigerator overnight and then prove, as below.)

Put the trays in the oven, but do not turn the oven on. Put a roasting tin of warm water on the bottom shelf and close the door. Allow the dough to prove for 1–2 hours or until it has doubled in size. You may need to replace the water as it cools down — the idea is to keep the oven a consistent, moist heat. Remove all the trays, including the roasting tin, from the oven.

Preheat the oven to 190°C (375°F/Gas 5). Bake the snails for 20 minutes or until they are crisp on the edges and lightly golden on top. Remove from the oven and set aside to cool slightly.

crème fraîche glaze

250 g (9 oz) crème fraîche
100 g (3¹/₂ oz) unsalted butter, chopped and softened
50 g (1³/₄ oz) pure icing (confectioners') sugar
Seeds scraped from 1 vanilla bean

When the snails are almost cooked, put the crème fraîche, butter, icing sugar and vanilla seeds in an electric mixer with a beater attachment and mix on medium speed for 2–3 minutes or until the mixture just comes together. Use a small palette knife to spread over the warm snails. Cut the reserved pumpkin into 1 cm (¹/₂ inch) squares, sprinkle on top and serve. **makes 29**

variation

You can substitute orange sweet potato for the pumpkin.

sticky mango buns

coconut frangipane

100 g (3½ oz) unsalted butter, well softened

100 g (3½ oz) pure icing (confectioners') sugar

3 g (¹⁄₁₀ oz) cornflour (cornstarch)

100 g (3½ oz) desiccated coconut

100 g (3½ oz) lightly beaten egg, at room temperature

50 g (1¾ oz) crème pâtissiére (see Croque-en-bouche recipe, page 164, make ½ quantity and use the remainder in another recipe)

25 g (1 oz) UHT coconut cream (see Glossary)

Put the butter, icing sugar, cornflour and coconut in an electric mixer with a beater attachment and mix on low speed until just combined. With the motor running, gradually add the egg, mixing well after each addition. The mixture should not look split or curdled — if it does, the butter was not soft enough or the eggs were too cold. If this happens, you may need to sit the mixture over a bain marie briefly to warm up the ingredients and then mix again until it comes together.

Put the crème pâtissiére and coconut cream in a very small saucepan and stir with a whisk over low heat until just warmed through. Remove from the heat, then stir into the egg and butter mixture. Cover with plastic wrap, pressing it onto the surface to prevent a skin forming, and place in the refrigerator for 1½–2 hours or until set.

to assemble

½ quantity brioche feuilletée (see page 82)

500 g (1 lb 2 oz) ripe mango flesh, cut into
        1.5 cm (⅝ inch) squares

90 g (3¼ oz) shredded coconut

Roll out the brioche feuilletée dough on a lightly floured benchtop to a 40 x 80 cm (16 x 31½ inch) rectangle, with a thickness of 4 mm (⅙ inch). Line 3–4 large baking trays with non-stick baking paper.

Work the coconut frangipane mixture to make it smooth again. Use a crank-handled palette knife or spatula to spread the coconut frangipane evenly over the pastry, right to the edges. Sprinkle evenly with the mango and then the coconut.

Fold the top edge towards you by 1 cm (½ inch), then keep your hands flat and gently roll the dough from the folded edge one-third of the way towards the opposite edge. With your fingers curled behind the roll of dough for support, use your thumbs to push the roll back away from you, working from left to right where the roll meets the flat dough — this will tighten up the roll. With flattened hands again, roll the dough towards you another third of the way and repeat the pushing back and tightening motion. Roll the dough towards you again until it reaches the edge nearest you and then roll it towards you again slightly so that the seam is underneath.

Trim the edges to neaten, then cut the roll into 3 cm (1¼ inch) thick slices. Hold up a slice and you will see there is one loose edge — tuck this 'tail' underneath and place on a lined tray, tail side down. Repeat with all the slices, spacing them well apart on the trays.

(At this point the snails can be frozen for up to 2 weeks. When ready to use, defrost in the refrigerator overnight and then prove, as below.)

Put the trays in the oven, but do not turn the oven on. Put a roasting tin of warm water on the bottom shelf and close the door. Allow the dough to prove for 1–2 hours or until it has doubled in size. You may need to replace the water as it cools down — the idea is to keep the oven a consistent, moist heat. Remove all the trays, including the roasting tin, from the oven.

palm sugar caramel

1050 g (2 lb 5¾ oz) light palm sugar (jaggery), grated

210 g (7½ oz) liquid glucose

3 makrut (kaffir lime) leaves

420 g (15 oz) water

770 g (1 lb 11 oz) UHT coconut cream (see Glossary)

Meanwhile, put the palm sugar, glucose, makrut leaves and water in a deep saucepan over medium heat. Stir until the sugar has dissolved, then bring to the boil and boil, without stirring, for 20–25 minutes or until it forms a dark-amber caramel, around 165°C (329°F).

While the caramel is cooking, bring the coconut cream to the boil in a separate saucepan, then remove from the heat and cover to keep warm.

When the caramel is at the dark-amber stage, remove from the heat and use a balloon whisk to stir the coconut cream into the caramel to deglaze — watch out, it will spit and release a lot of heat. Stir until smooth and well combined, then remove the lime leaves.

Pour a 1 cm (½ inch) layer of palm sugar caramel into 24 texas muffin tin holes (185 ml/6 fl oz/¾ cup capacity). Spray the exposed side of each muffin hole with cooking oil.

Preheat the oven to 180°C (350°F/Gas 4). Invert the buns, one at a time, into the muffin holes, so they are tail-side up. Use your fingers to tuck the outer edges of the buns down into the caramel. Put the muffin tins on baking trays lined with non-stick baking paper in case the caramel flows over the sides.

Cook the buns for 25 minutes or until puffed and golden. Remove from the oven and take the tins off the trays, then immediately turn the buns out onto the lined trays. Allow the buns to cool on the trays until ready to eat. They are great warm or at room temperature.

makes 24

variation — sticky pear buns

Replace the desiccated coconut with 20 g (¾ oz) ground ginger. Replace the mango with 360 g (12¾ oz) peeled and cored ripe beurre bosc pears, cut into 1.5 cm (⅝ inch) squares, and replace the shredded coconut with 230 g (8 oz) roughly chopped macadamia nuts.

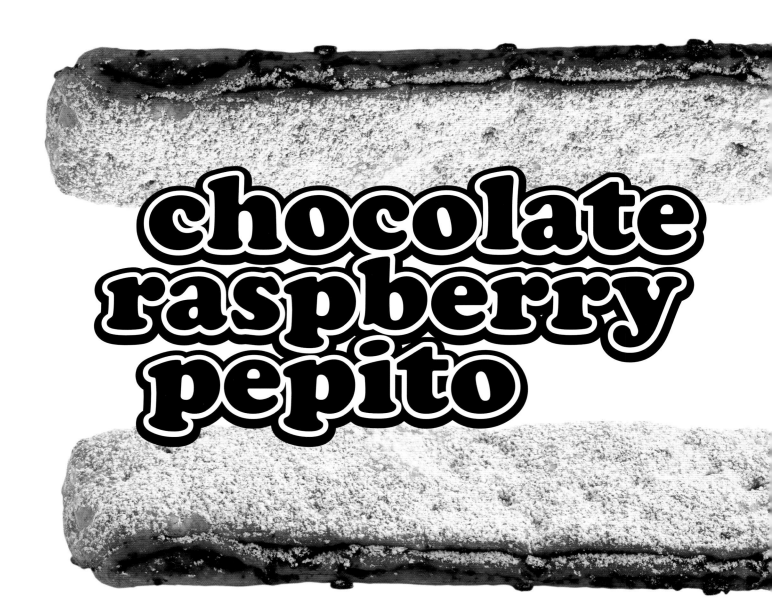

chocolate raspberry pepito

raspberry gel

500 g (1 lb 2 oz) sieved raspberry purée (see Basics)

50 g (1¾ oz) caster (superfine) sugar

2.5 g (²/₂₅ oz) iota (see Glossary)

Put all the ingredients in a saucepan, then blitz with a stick mixer until well combined. Put over medium heat and stir constantly until the mixture comes to the boil. Remove from the heat, pour into a bowl and cool to room temperature.

to assemble

1 quantity brioche feuilletée (see page 82)

500 g (1 lb 2 oz) dark couverture chocolate (70%), processed to
    roughly 2–3 mm (¹/₁₆–⅛ inch) pieces

20 g (¾ oz) freeze-dried raspberry powder (see Glossary)

60 g (2¼ oz) pure icing (confectioners') sugar, sifted

Roll out the brioche feuilletée dough on a lightly floured benchtop to a 40 x 93 cm (16 x 36²/₅ inch) rectangle, with an even thickness of 3 mm (⅛ inch).

Use a crank-handled palette knife to spread the raspberry gel evenly over the dough. Imagine the dough divided into 3 long, equal strips and cover the middle strip with half the chopped chocolate. Fold the top strip over the chocolate to cover it. Sprinkle the remaining chocolate over the folded strip, then fold the bottom strip up and over the chocolate to cover it. Press down lightly, just to help adhere the layers, don't squash them. You should have a long rectangle about 13 cm (5 inches) high.

Measure out the halfway point along the length, then cut in half with a sharp knife and separate the portions of dough. Roll out one portion at a time, ensuring the longer closed edge is facing your body. Roll out in the direction of the opposite edge until 54 cm (21½ inches) long and 22 cm (8½ inches) wide. It should be about 3–4 mm (⅛–¹/₆ inch) thick.

Mark 6 cm (2½ inch) lengths along the dough from left to right and cut them out to form nine 6 x 22 cm (2½ x 8½ inch) strips. Repeat with the remaining portion of dough so you have 18 strips in total.

(At this point the pepitos can be frozen for up to 2 weeks. When ready to use, defrost in the refrigerator overnight and then prove, as below.)

Put the pepitos on baking trays lined with non-stick baking paper, spaced well apart. Put the trays in the oven, but do not turn the oven on. Put a roasting tin of warm water on the bottom shelf and close the door. Allow the dough to prove for 1–2 hours or until it has doubled in size. You may need to replace the water as it cools down — the idea is to keep the oven a consistent, moist heat. Remove all the trays, including the roasting tin, from the oven.

Preheat the oven to 190°C (375°F/Gas 5). Cook the pepitos for 15 minutes or until golden, then remove and cool on the trays.

Combine the raspberry powder and icing sugar and sift over the top of the cooled pepitos before serving. **makes 18**

crumble mix

100 g (3½ oz) chilled unsalted butter, chopped
100 g (3½ oz) brown sugar
100 g (3½ oz) almond meal
100 g (3½ oz) plain (all-purpose) flour

While the dough is proving, put the butter, sugar, almond meal and flour in an electric mixer with a beater attachment and mix on low speed until a paste just forms. Wrap in plastic wrap and refrigerate for 1½ hours or until it is firm.

Preheat the oven to 180°C (350°F/Gas 4). Line a baking tray with non-stick baking paper.

Grate the crumble mix evenly over the lined tray and bake for 15 minutes or until it is crisp and light golden. Set aside to cool to room temperature.

apple filling

500 g (1 lb 2 oz) granny smith apples
50 g (1¾ oz) butter
70 g (2½ oz) caster (superfine) sugar
5 g (⅛ oz) ground cinnamon

Meanwhile, peel and core the apples, then cut them into 1.5 cm (⅝ inch) squares. Melt the butter in a frying pan over high heat, add the apple and shake the pan until the apple is well coated in butter. Sprinkle over the sugar and cinnamon and cook for a further 30 seconds, then transfer to a bowl to cool completely.

dough

1 quantity brioche dough (see page 81)

Cut the brioche dough into fifteen 90 g (3¼ oz) portions. Use your hands to roll each portion into a smooth ball. Lightly spray fifteen 10 cm (4 inch) diameter loose-based, fluted flan (tart) tins with cooking oil.

Use a rolling pin to roll each ball of dough out on a lightly floured benchtop to a 4 mm (⅙ inch) thick disc, approximately 12 cm (4½ inches) in diameter. Brush off any excess flour with a pastry brush. Roll over the outside edge of each disc just 1 cm (½ inch) towards the centre to form an even ridge right around. Invert the dough into the tins, ensuring the ridge side is facing down.

Place the tins on baking trays, spaced well apart. Put the trays in the oven, but do not turn the oven on. Put a roasting tin of warm water on the bottom shelf and close the door. Allow the dough to prove for 1–2 hours or until it has doubled in size. You may need to replace the water as it cools down — the idea is to keep the oven a consistent, moist heat. Remove all the trays, including the roasting tin, from the oven.

to assemble

Egg wash (see Basics), to glaze
Pearl sugar (see Glossary), for sprinkling
525 g (1 lb 3 oz) crème pâtissiére (see Croque-en-bouche recipe, page 164, make ½ quantity and use the remainder in another recipe)
Pure icing (confectioners') sugar, sifted

Preheat the oven to 180°C (350°F/Gas 4).

When the brioche dough is ready, brush the raised edges of each round with egg wash and sprinkle evenly with pearl sugar. Pipe an amount of crème pâtissiére the size of a golf ball into the centre of each round. There is no need to spread it out. Divide the apple filling among the rounds, on top of the crème pâtissiére. Sprinkle the crumble mix evenly over the top. Put the tart tins on baking trays and bake for 25 minutes or until the brioche dough is lightly golden. Just before serving, dust the apple crumble brioche with sifted icing sugar. **makes 15**

variation — berry, rhubarb & almond brioche

Replace the apple filling with 45 pieces of roasted rhubarb (see Basics), 225 g (8 oz) fresh raspberries and 225 g (8 oz) fresh blueberries. Replace the crumble mix with 300 g (10½ oz) flaked almonds, scattered over the fruit before baking (there's no need to toast them first).

apple crumble brioche

sugar lips

blackcurrant filling

500 g (1 lb 2 oz) sieved blackcurrant purée (see Basics)
50 g (1¾ oz) caster (superfine) sugar
9 g (⅓ oz) pectin NH (see Glossary)

Put the blackcurrant purée in a saucepan over medium heat and when it reaches 60°C (140°F) add the combined sugar and pectin and stir with a small whisk until the sugar has dissolved. Bring to the boil, then remove from the heat and set aside to cool to room temperature.

to assemble

1 quantity doughnut dough (see page 83)
25 g (1 oz) freeze-dried blackcurrant powder (see Glossary)
250 g (9 oz) caster (superfine) sugar, to coat
Vegetable oil, for deep-frying

Roll out the doughnut dough to a 40 x 100 cm (16 x 39½ inch) rectangle, with a thickness of 4 mm (⅙ inch). Use an oval 10 x 20 cm (4 x 8 inch) cutter to stamp ovals out of the dough, re-rolling the offcuts to make 12 ovals in total. Fold each oval in half to form a short, half-oval shape. Use your fingers to gently press the edges together all the way around the open sides of the dough.

Put the dough shapes on baking trays lined with non-stick baking paper, spaced well apart. Put the trays in the oven, but do not turn the oven on. Put a roasting tin of warm water on the bottom shelf and close the door. Allow the dough to prove for 1–2 hours or until it has doubled in size. You may need to replace the water as it cools down — the idea is to keep the oven a consistent, moist heat. Remove all the trays, including the roasting tin, from the oven.

Meanwhile, combine the blackcurrant powder and caster sugar and place on a tray. Set aside until ready to use.

Fill a deep-fryer or large, deep saucepan one-third full of oil and heat to 190°C (374°F). Deep-fry 2–3 dough shapes at a time for 1–2 minutes or until puffed and golden. Drain on paper towels and immediately roll in the blackcurrant sugar mixture. Set aside to cool completely.

Fill a piping (icing) bag with a 7 mm (⅜ inch) plain nozzle with blackcurrant filling (or variation below). Poke a finger into the arch of each doughnut and twist it around to form a hollow. Pipe the filling into each hollow and serve. **makes 12**

variation — cinnamon & tonka bean crème pâtissiére filling

Use a nutmeg grater to finely grate 2 tonka beans (see Glossary). Put in a saucepan with 600 g (1 lb 5 oz) milk and 3 toasted cinnamon sticks and bring to the boil over medium heat. Whisk 150 g (5½ oz) egg yolks with 150 g (5½ oz) caster (superfine) sugar and 60 g (2¼ oz) cornflour (cornstarch) in a bowl until pale and creamy. Gradually strain the hot milk mixture over the egg mixture while whisking continuously. Return to the pan and cook, stirring continuously with the whisk, over medium heat for 5–7 minutes or until the mixture comes to the boil. Transfer to a bowl, cover with plastic wrap, pressing it onto the surface to prevent a skin forming, and cool to 50°C (122°F). Whisk in 60 g (2¼ oz) chopped, softened unsalted butter. Cover with plastic wrap, pressing it onto the surface, and refrigerate for 3 hours or until chilled. Once the sugar lips are fried, roll them in sugar only.

pineapple

225 g (8 oz) fresh lime juice
225 g (8 oz) light palm sugar (jaggery), grated
3 makrut (kaffir lime) leaves, bruised
750 g (1 lb 10 oz) pineapple, peeled and
    cut into 1.5 cm (^{5}/8 inch) cubes

Put the lime juice, sugar and makrut leaves in a glass
or ceramic bowl and stir until the sugar has dissolved.
Add the pineapple and toss to coat well, then cover and
refrigerate overnight to macerate.

ginger custriano

500 g (1 lb 2 oz) pouring (whipping) cream (35% fat)
100 g (3½ oz) milk
150 g (5½ oz) caster (superfine) sugar
5 g (⅛ oz) iota (see Glossary)
50 g (1¾ oz) fresh ginger, peeled and roughly chopped
Seeds scraped from 1 vanilla bean
300 g (10½ oz) pouring (whipping) cream
    (35% fat), extra
100 g (3½ oz) milk, extra

Put the cream, milk, sugar and iota in a saucepan and
blitz with a stick mixer until smooth. Add the ginger and
vanilla seeds, place over medium heat and bring to the
boil, stirring constantly. Remove from the heat and set
aside for 10–15 minutes to infuse. Strain into a bowl,
cover with plastic wrap and cool to 40°C (104°F). Pour in
the extra cream and milk and stir until combined. Cover
with plastic wrap, pressing it onto the surface to prevent
a skin forming, and refrigerate for 2–3 hours or until
completely chilled.

to assemble

1 quantity croissant dough (see page 84)
Egg wash (see Basics)
Black pepper, for grinding
50 g (1¾ oz) caster (superfine) sugar
10 g (¼ oz) fresh mint leaves

Roll out the croissant dough on a lightly floured
benchtop to a 35 x 120 cm (14 x 47 inch) rectangle, with
a thickness of 4 mm (⅙ inch). Trim 1 cm (½ inch) from
the edges all around, then cut out thirty 11 cm (4¼ inch)
squares. Fold all four corners evenly into the centre of

each pastry square, pressing the points to secure. Place
the pastries on baking trays lined with non-stick baking
paper, spaced well apart. Put the trays in the oven, but do
not turn the oven on. Put a roasting tin of warm water
on the bottom shelf and close the door. Allow the dough
to prove for 1–2 hours or until it has doubled in size. You
may need to replace the water as it cools down — the
idea is to keep the oven a consistent, moist heat. Remove
all the trays, including the roasting tin, from the oven.

Preheat the oven to 190°C (375°F/Gas 5). Brush
the egg wash over the top of each pastry. Fill a piping
(icing) bag with a 10 mm (½ inch) plain nozzle with the
custriano and pipe an amount the size of a golf ball onto
the centre of each pastry. Lift the pineapple out of the
syrup using a slotted spoon and divide evenly among
the pastries, placing it on top of the custriano and
pressing down to prevent the pastry popping open as it
cooks. Grind a little black pepper over the top of each.

Grind the sugar and mint leaves together using a
mortar and pestle. Sprinkle over the top of each pastry.
Bake the pastries for 20 minutes or until golden. Remove
from the oven and cool on the trays. **makes 30**

pineapple, ginger & pepper danish

zumbo's palmiers

½ quantity full puff pastry (see page 86)
160 g (5⅔ oz) dark brown sugar
325 g (11½ oz) raw (demerara) sugar
25 g (1 oz) ground cinnamon

Preheat the oven to 190°C (375°F/Gas 5). Roll out the puff pastry to a 40 x 55 cm (16 x 22 inch) rectangle, with an even thickness of 6 mm (¼ inch).

Combine the sugars and cinnamon in a bowl. Fill a plastic spray bottle with water and evenly spray the water over the top of the pastry — it should just look wet, but not dripping with water. Liberally sprinkle the sugar mixture over the top of the pastry, just to the point where you can't see the pastry showing through. It should not be more than 2 mm (¹⁄₁₆ inch) thick. Use your hands to gently pat down the sugar to help it adhere to the pastry. Spray the sugar layer with the water until evenly damp all over.

Picture an imaginary line running across the centre of the pastry. Take the top edge of the pastry and fold it towards the imaginary line, stopping about 7 mm (⅜ inch) short. Fold the bottom edge towards the imaginary line, again stopping about 7 mm (⅜ inch) short, so you end up with a gap of about 1.5 cm (⅝ inch) along the middle. Very gently roll a rolling pin along the length of the pastry to flatten it slightly, making it more even.

Spray the pastry again with water until it looks just wet all over, but not so it starts to drip or pool. Liberally scatter another layer of sugar mixture over the top, just until you can no longer see the pastry, then spray again with water.

Fold the top half of the pastry over the bottom half — the edges should line up nicely. Spray the pastry again with water until it looks just wet all over, but not so it starts to drip or pool. Liberally scatter a layer of sugar over the top just until you can no longer see the pastry, then spray again with the water. Turn the pastry over.

Spray the pastry again with water until it looks just wet all over, but not so it starts to drip or pool. Liberally scatter a final layer of sugar mixture over the top, just until you can no longer see the pastry, then spray again with water.

Use a sharp knife to trim the short edges of the pastry, to even them up. Cut the pastry into 2.5 cm (1 inch) slices. (They can be frozen at this point, see Note.)

Transfer the slices, cut side down, onto flat non-stick baking sheets (3 palmiers per sheet). It's important to use baking sheets as they don't have raised sides, so the heat is able to circulate well enough to cook the edges of the pastry. Keep the palmiers well spaced as they will expand dramatically during the cooking process.

Cook for 20–25 minutes or until the palmiers are crisp, golden and aromatic. Use a crank-handled palette knife to transfer to trays lined with non-stick baking paper to cool. The paper makes it easier to remove the palmiers later, by preventing the melted sugar sticking to the trays. **makes 20**

note: If you wish to freeze the palmiers, place them in a sealed plastic container with non-stick baking paper between the layers and freeze for up to 1 month. There is no need to defrost them before cooking, however they will need an extra 5–10 minutes in the oven.

macadamia croissants

macadamia marzipan

400 g (14 oz) macadamia nuts
400 g (14 oz) pure icing (confectioners') sugar

Process both ingredients in a food processor until
the mixture becomes paste-like. Gather the mixture
together, cover with plastic wrap and pat down to
a 1.5 cm (⁵⁄₈ inch) thick block. Set aside.

macadamia custriano

138 g (5 oz) pouring (whipping) cream (35% fat)
28 g (1 oz) milk
83 g (3 oz) caster (superfine) sugar
1.6 g (¹⁄₂₀ oz) iota (see Glossary)
83 g (3 oz) pouring (whipping) cream (35% fat), extra
28 g (1 oz) milk, extra
1 quantity macadamia paste (see Pistachio paste
   in Basics)

Put the cream, milk, sugar and iota in a saucepan and
blitz with a stick mixer until the mixture thickens. Put
over medium heat and stir until the sugar has dissolved.
Heat the mixture to 90°C (194°F), then transfer to a

bowl. Stir regularly until the temperature drops to 40°C
(104°F). Use a small whisk to mix in the extra cream
and milk and 33 g (1¼ oz) of the macadamia paste until
smooth. (Reserve the remaining macadamia paste.) Cover
with plastic wrap, pressing it onto the surface to prevent
a skin forming. Refrigerate for 1½ hours or until chilled.

to assemble

1 quantity croissant dough (see page 84)
Egg wash, to glaze (see Basics)

Roll out the macadamia marzipan between two sheets of
non-stick baking paper to a thickness of 3 mm (⅛ inch).
Cut into triangles, 8 cm (3¼ inches) on the base and
12 cm (4½ inches) on the two long sides.

Roll out the croissant dough on a floured benchtop
to a 40 x 60 cm (16 x 24 inch) rectangle, with an even
thickness of 4 mm (⅙ inch). Mark the halfway point
of each short side with the tip of a knife. Then, using
a ruler as a guide, cut from point to point, forming
2 long rectangles of dough. Do not separate them.
Spread a thin layer of the reserved macadamia paste
over the dough.

pastries

115

Starting at the top left corner of the upper rectangle of dough and working to the right, measure and mark 12 cm (4½ inch) intervals all the way along. Repeat with the lower rectangle of dough, starting from the bottom left corner. Now, go to the line you cut along the centre to create the two rectangles. Measure and mark the first 6 cm (2½ inches) towards the right, then mark 12 cm (4½ inch) intervals the rest of the way along. Using these markings as a guide, cut both rectangles of dough into triangles. Do not separate them, leave them on the benchtop as they are. Make a 1 cm (½ inch) cut into the base of each triangle, at the centre.

Discard the half-size triangles from the ends of the dough. Brush off any excess flour on the remaining triangles with a pastry brush. Lift a triangle up, holding the base in one hand and taking hold of the tip with your other hand. Pull gently down to stretch the triangle by approximately 2 cm (¾ inch). Put the elongated triangle on the bench so the tip is pointing at you.

Put a marzipan triangle on top of the dough so the bases of the triangles are parallel, but with a 2 cm (¾ inch) gap between them. Fill a piping (icing) bag with a 15 mm (⅝ inch) plain nozzle with custriano and pipe an 8 cm (3¼ inch) long tube along the base of the marzipan triangle.

Fold the base of the dough triangle towards you by 5 mm (¼ inch). Form an A-frame with your hands, fingers together and one thumb resting slightly over the other. Keeping your hands in this position, gently roll the dough towards you until it reaches the tip of the triangle. Repeat to roll all the croissants. Put on baking trays lined with non-stick baking paper, 7.5 cm (3 inches) apart.

Put the trays in the oven, but do not turn the oven on. Put a roasting tin of warm water on the bottom shelf and close the door. Allow the dough to prove for 1–2 hours or until it has doubled in size. You may need to replace the water as it cools down — the idea is to keep the oven a consistent, moist heat. Remove all the trays, including the roasting tin, from the oven.

Preheat the oven to 190°C (375°F/Gas 5). Lightly brush the top of each croissant with egg wash and cook for 25 minutes or until crisp and golden. Eat them warm from the oven or cool to room temperature and glaze, if desired. **makes 18**

lemon glaze (optional)
150 g (5½ oz) pure icing (confectioners') sugar
150 g (5½ oz) water
Finely grated lemon zest of 1 lemon
Roasted chopped macadamia nuts, to garnish (optional)

Combine the icing sugar, water and lemon zest until smooth. Brush over the croissants, sprinkle with the macadamias, if desired, and serve.

gateaux de voyage

**zumball
division two
state champions**

back row, from left: attack of the killer tomatoes; toasted lammyjammit;
celia's act; lavender up; oiled up calabrian middle row, from left: chistachio perry;
quince your thirst; blue mondays; it mayo shock u front row, from left:
honey comb-over; sticky tape the date

Gateaux de voyage is a term I came up with to describe these cakes, as they're great travellers. Nearly all of them are in a rectangular bar shape, making them easy to serve and easy to transport. I've been making them since the business opened and they've had a great response from customers.

I guess the idea came from following a lot of my European friends and progressing on their ideas with my own flavours and layers. I love adding jelly, caramels, ganaches and so on to the interior for a surprise and balance with the cake batter itself.

These cakes are commonly served for afternoon tea and are perfect to take as a gift when going to somebody's house to visit. They also make excellent dessert options. Enjoy your journey through this chapter, there's a sweet ending, as always!

toasted lammyjammit

[raspberry/chocolate/coconut]

decoration

250 g (9 oz) dark couverture chocolate (64%), chopped or buttons, tempered (see Basics)

Dampen the benchtop slightly with a moist cloth, put an 10 x 18 cm (4 x 7 inch) acetate sheet (see Glossary) on it and use a clean dry cloth to smooth the sheet out. Use a crank-handled palette knife to spread the tempered chocolate over the acetate sheet until it is 2–3 mm ($\frac{1}{16}$–$\frac{1}{8}$ inch) thick. Holding opposite diagonal corners of the acetate, shake it gently to smooth out the chocolate. Set aside until the chocolate has set and is dry to the touch (it should still be slightly soft). Using a ruler and the back of a paring knife, cut the chocolate into 1.5 x 18 cm ($\frac{5}{8}$ x 7 inch) strips. Cover with baking paper and flip over. Leave for 2–3 hours to crystallise.

raspberry jelly

350 g (12 oz) sieved raspberry purée (see Basics)
35 g ($1\frac{1}{4}$ oz) caster (superfine) sugar
7 g ($\frac{1}{4}$ oz) pectin NH (see Glossary)

Lightly spray two 7.5 x 7.5 x 20 cm (3 x 3 x 8 inch) loaf (bar) tins with cooking oil. Line with a double layer of plastic wrap, extending over the two long sides.

Put the raspberry purée in a saucepan over medium heat and bring to 60°C (140°F). Combine the sugar and pectin, add to the pan and bring to the boil. Remove from the heat and divide the mixture between the tins. Put in the refrigerator to set (approximately 1 hour). Once the jelly has set, carefully lift it out using the plastic wrap. Place on a clean baking tray and cut each jelly in half crossways. Return to the refrigerator until needed.

cake batter

85 g (3 oz) unsalted butter, chopped and softened
340 g (12 oz) dark brown sugar
160 g ($5\frac{2}{3}$ oz) lightly beaten egg
15 g ($\frac{1}{2}$ oz) natural vanilla extract
85 g (3 oz) dark couverture chocolate (64%), chopped or buttons
215 g ($7\frac{1}{2}$ oz) plain (all-purpose) flour, sifted
15 g ($\frac{1}{2}$ oz) bicarbonate of soda (baking soda)
5 g ($\frac{1}{8}$ oz) salt
180 g ($6\frac{1}{4}$ oz) sour cream
180 g ($6\frac{1}{4}$ oz) boiling water

Preheat the oven to 180°C (350°F/Gas 4). Lightly spray two 7.5 x 7.5 x 20 cm (3 x 3 x 8 inch) loaf (bar) tins with cooking oil. Line with non-stick baking paper, extending over the two long sides, and place on a baking tray.

Put the butter and sugar in an electric mixer with a beater attachment and beat on medium speed for 4 minutes or until pale and creamy. Gradually add the combined egg and vanilla, beating well between each addition. Meanwhile, melt the chocolate in a heatproof bowl over a saucepan of simmering water and allow to cool slightly. Beat into the butter and egg mixture. Sift the flour, bicarbonate of soda and salt together and add to the mixer bowl. Add the sour cream and beat on low speed for 2 minutes or until well combined. Add the boiling water and beat until well combined.

Divide half the cake batter between the two tins. Cover with the raspberry jelly, two pieces per tin, then divide the remaining cake batter over the top, filling the tins no more than 1 cm ($\frac{1}{2}$ inch) from the top. Cook for 50–55 minutes or until a skewer inserted into the centre of a cake comes out just a little moist. Cool in the tins.

cocoa coconut

400 g (14 oz) desiccated coconut
100 g ($3\frac{1}{2}$ oz) unsweetened cocoa powder, sifted

Combine the coconut and cocoa in a bowl, then tip the mixture onto a tray and set aside.

chocolate dip

300 g ($10\frac{1}{2}$ oz) pure icing (confectioners') sugar, sifted
40 g ($1\frac{1}{2}$ oz) unsweetened cocoa powder, sifted
20 g ($\frac{3}{4}$ oz) melted butter (still hot)
90 g ($3\frac{1}{4}$ oz) hot water

Remove the cakes from the tins (the jelly may have settled at the bottom, which is fine). Combine the icing sugar and cocoa in a bowl, then stir in the hot melted butter and hot water until smooth. Pour into a shallow rectangular tray just a bit bigger than the cakes. Place a cake in the chocolate dip and carefully turn until coated all over. Remove and allow any excess to drip off, then place on the cocoa coconut, turning to coat and pressing down lightly to help the coating stick. Repeat with the second cake. Place a strip of chocolate on each cake to decorate, and serve. **makes 2 bar cakes**

note: This cake will keep for up to 5 days in an airtight container at room temperature. Undecorated cakes can be stored in the freezer for up to 2 weeks.

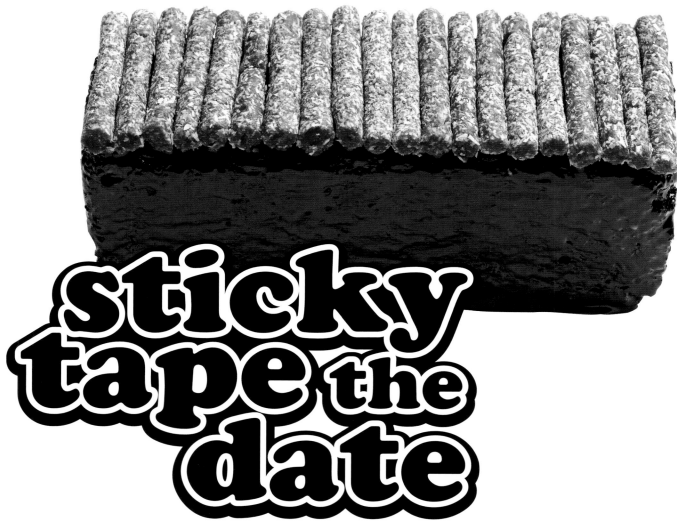

sticky tape the date

[dates/caramel/chocolate]

choc caramel

25 g (1 oz) dark couverture chocolate (70%),
    chopped or buttons

100 g (3½ oz) crème fraîche

100 g (3½ oz) unsalted butter, chopped and softened

50 g (1¾ oz) dark brown sugar

8 g (¼ oz) unsweetened cocoa powder, sifted

Lightly spray two 7.5 x 7.5 x 20 cm (3 x 3 x 8 inch) loaf
(bar) tins with cooking oil. Line with non-stick baking
paper, extending over the two long sides.

    Put all the ingredients in a saucepan over medium
heat and stir until the sugar has dissolved. Bring just to
the boil, then remove from the heat and set aside. Divide
the mixture between the lined tins.

caramel chew

150 g (5½ oz) caster (superfine) sugar

60 g (2¼ oz) water

30 g (1 oz) liquid glucose

60 g (2¼ oz) unsalted butter, chopped and softened

2 g (²⁄₂₅ oz) xanthan gum (see Glossary)

1 g (¹⁄₂₅ oz) iota (see Glossary)

75 g (2¾ oz) pouring (whipping) cream (35% fat)

Put the sugar, water and glucose in a deep saucepan
over medium heat and cook until the caramel becomes
dark amber in colour. Stir in the butter.

    Meanwhile, put the xanthan gum, iota and cream
in a small saucepan and blitz with a stick mixer. Place
the saucepan over medium heat and use a small whisk

to whisk as the mixture thickens and comes to the boil. Carefully stir the hot cream mixture into the caramel — watch out, it will spit and release a lot of heat.

Pour the caramel into a 15 x 22 cm (6 x 8½ inch) baking tray, or similar-sized heatproof container, lined with non-stick baking paper. Set aside to cool, then cut into 4 long strips.

date gel

250 g (9 oz) water
175 g (6 oz) stoned fresh dates
10 g (¼ oz) bicarbonate of soda (baking soda)
5 g (⅛ oz) pectin NH (see Glossary)
40 g (1½ oz) caster (superfine) sugar
6 g (⅕ oz) xanthan gum (see Glossary)
6 g (⅕ oz) lemon juice

Put the water and dates in a saucepan over medium heat and bring to the boil. Remove from the heat, stir in the bicarbonate of soda and allow to sit for 30 minutes.

Blitz the date mixture with a stick mixer until smooth, then return to the heat and bring to 60°C (140°F). Combine the pectin and sugar, add to the date mixture and bring to the boil. Add the xanthan gum and lemon juice and blitz with the stick mixer until well combined. Transfer to a bowl and allow to cool. Fill a piping (icing) bag with an 11 mm (²⁄₅ inch) plain nozzle with the cooled date gel.

cake batter

300 g (10½ oz) water
18 g (⅔ oz) natural vanilla extract
170 g (5¾ oz) stoned dried dates, chopped
135 g (4¾ oz) dried apricots, chopped
18 g (⅔ oz) bicarbonate of soda (baking soda)
180 g (6¼ oz) lightly beaten egg
255 g (9 oz) dark brown sugar
255 g (9 oz) plain (all-purpose) flour, sifted
4.5 g (³⁄₂₀ oz) baking powder, sifted
12 g (²⁄₅ oz) unsweetened cocoa powder, sifted
50 g (1¾ oz) dark couverture chocolate (70%), chopped or buttons
50 g (1¾ oz) unsalted butter

Preheat the oven to 150°C (300°F/Gas 2). Put the water, vanilla, dates and apricots in a saucepan and bring to the boil over medium heat. Stir in the bicarbonate of soda, then remove the pan from the heat and set aside until the mixture has cooled completely.

Combine the egg and sugar in a large bowl. Stir in the sifted dry ingredients. Pour in the cooled date mixture and stir to combine. Melt the chocolate and butter in a heatproof bowl over a saucepan of simmering water or in the microwave, then stir into the cake batter.

Divide one-third of the cake batter between the two tins, spooning it over the caramel. Place a strip of caramel chew along one side of the cake batter (not right against the edge of the tin) and pipe a parallel strip of date gel along the other side of the batter. Repeat for the other cake. Divide another third of the cake batter between the tins, repeat the strips of caramel chew and date gel, then divide the remaining cake batter over the top, filling the tins no more than 1 cm (½ inch) from the top.

Place the tins on a baking tray and cook the cakes for 55–60 minutes or until a skewer inserted into the centre of a cake comes out just a little moist. Cool the cakes in the tins, then invert onto a wire rack.

date & coconut logs

120–175 g (4¼–6 oz) stoned fresh dates, chopped
120 g (4¼ oz) desiccated coconut
60 g (2¼ oz) desiccated coconut, extra

Process 120 g (4¼ oz) dates with 120 g (4¼ oz) coconut in a food processor until a thick paste forms. Turn out onto a clean benchtop, knead the paste a little and see if you can roll it. If not, return the paste to the processor, add 25 g (1 oz) more dates and test again. You may need to use the remaining dates to get it to the right consistency — it all depends on the dates. Roll small amounts of the paste into logs, about 8 mm (³⁄₈ inch) thick and 7.5 cm (3 inches) long, to fit the width of the cakes. (You will need approximately 20 logs per cake.) Roll the logs in the extra coconut to coat.

to finish

1 quantity caramel maison (see Basics)

Gently heat the caramel maison in 10-second bursts in the microwave, until it reaches 35°C (95°F). Pour it over the cakes, then lay the date & coconut logs on top, to cover the cakes from one end to the other. Transfer to a serving plate/s. **makes 2 bar cakes**

note: This cake will keep for up to 1 week in an airtight container in the refrigerator. Undecorated cakes can be stored in the freezer for up to 1 month.

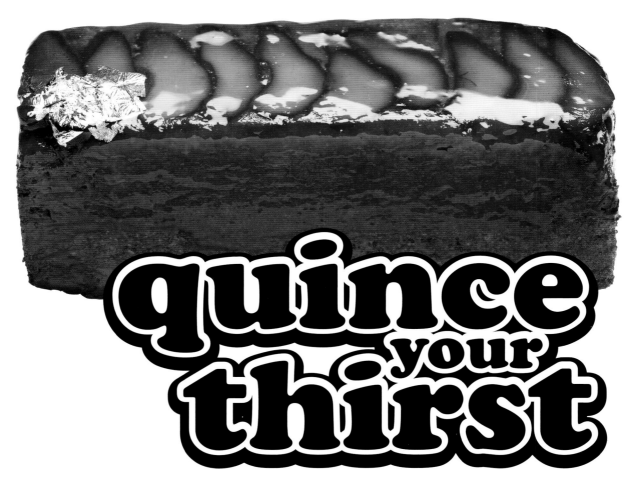

quince your thirst

[quince/caramel/almond]

poached quince

540 g (1 lb 3 oz) quinces
280 g (10 oz) caster (superfine) sugar
800 g (1 lb 12 oz) water
Seeds scraped from 1 vanilla bean
1 cinnamon stick, toasted until fragrant
1 wide strip of orange rind
1 wide strip of lemon rind

Preheat the oven to 160°C (315°F/Gas 2–3). Peel and core the fruit, reserving the skin and cores, then quarter lengthways. Put the sugar, water, vanilla seeds, cinnamon and strips of rind in a saucepan. Stir over medium–high heat until the sugar has dissolved, then bring to the boil. Put the quinces in a small baking tray with the reserved skin and cores, and pour the hot syrup over. Cover with foil and bake for 6–8 hours (the cooking time will depend upon the ripeness of the fruit) or until deep reddish-brown and tender. Cool to room temperature.

muffin mix

25 g (1 oz) desiccated coconut
135 g (4¾ oz) buttermilk
135 g (4¾ oz) self-raising flour
25 g (1 oz) wholemeal (whole-wheat) flour
5 g (⅛ oz) baking powder
68 g (2½ oz) lightly beaten egg
70 g (2½ oz) caster (superfine) sugar
40 g (1½ oz) sugar
135 g (4¾ oz) vegetable oil

Soak the coconut in the buttermilk for 5 minutes. Sift the flours and baking powder together into a bowl. Put the egg, both sugars and the oil in an electric mixer with a beater attachment and mix on medium speed until smooth and well combined. Mix in the dry ingredients, then fold through the buttermilk and coconut mixture. Transfer to a sealed container and refrigerate for 2 hours or until chilled and slightly thickened.

cinnamon crème

300 g (10½ oz) almond crème (see Basics)
7.5 g (¼ oz) ground cinnamon

Mix the almond crème and cinnamon in a bowl until
well combined. Fill a piping (icing) bag with an 11 mm
(²⁄₅ inch) plain nozzle with the cinnamon crème. Line a
baking tray with non-stick baking paper and pipe eight
18 cm (7 inch) long tubes of cinnamon crème. Freeze for
1 hour or until the tubes are frozen through.

caramel cake batter

270 g (9½ oz) unsalted butter
175 g (6 oz) caramel maison (see Basics),
    at room temperature
60 g (2¼ oz) lightly beaten egg
100 g (3½ oz) egg yolks
225 g (8 oz) almond meal, sifted
165 g (5¾ oz) pure icing (confectioners') sugar, sifted
150 g (5½ oz) egg whites
62 g (2⅕ oz) caster (superfine) sugar
135 g (4¾ oz) rice flour, sifted
35 g (1¼ oz) milk

Preheat the oven to 180°C (350°F/Gas 4). Lightly spray
two 7.5 x 7.5 x 20 cm (3 x 3 x 8 inch) loaf (bar) tins with
cooking oil. Line with non-stick baking paper, extending
over the two long sides.

Put the butter and caramel maison in an electric
mixer with a beater attachment and cream together
on medium speed for 5–6 minutes, until light and fluffy.
With the motor running, gradually add the combined
egg and egg yolks, beating well between each addition.
Mix in the almond meal and icing sugar until combined.
Transfer to another bowl and clean the mixer bowl.

Put the egg whites and caster sugar in the clean
mixer bowl and use the whisk attachment to whisk for
4 minutes or until firm peaks form.

Mix a spoonful of the egg white into the cake batter,
then fold through the rest of the egg white, being careful
not to beat out the air. Fold in half the sifted rice flour,
then half the milk, then the remaining rice flour and
then the remaining milk.

to assemble

300 g (10½ oz) clear neutral glaze (see Basics)
Red food colouring
1 sheet edible gold leaf (see Glossary)

Remove the quince quarters from the syrup and slice
each piece in half lengthways. Lay half the pieces
decoratively along the length of the tins, overlapping
slightly. Cover with enough strained poaching liquid to
just come to the top of the quince in each tin.

Fill a piping (icing) bag without a nozzle with caramel
cake batter and pipe a layer over the top of the quince
to a depth of about 3 cm (1¼ inches). Place two tubes
of frozen cinnamon crème in each tin, pressing down
slightly so they sit in the cake batter. Arrange another
layer of quince along the length of each tin. Fill a piping
bag with a 9 mm (²⁄₅ inch) plain nozzle with the chilled
muffin mixture and pipe over the quince in each tin.
Place the remaining tubes of frozen cinnamon crème in
the tins, pressing them down slightly to ensure they are
covered by the muffin mixture. The mixture should be
at least 1 cm (½ inch) from the top of each tin.

Place the tins on a baking tray and cook the cakes
on the middle rack of the oven for 45 minutes or until
a skewer inserted into the centre of a cake comes out
just a little moist. Cool the cakes in the tins.

Heat the clear neutral glaze in a heatproof bowl
over a saucepan of simmering water to 35°C (95°F)
and colour with a drop of red food colouring. Invert
the cooled cakes onto a wire rack and glaze with
the coloured clear neutral glaze. Use a thin, pointed
paintbrush to remove a piece of gold leaf, approximately
3 x 3 cm (1¼ x 1¼ inches), from the sheet. Transfer it
to the corner of one of the cakes and let it rest over the
top — it will naturally fold down to cover the corner.
Repeat with the other cake. Transfer to a serving plate/s.

makes 2 bar cakes

note: This cake will keep for up to 5 days in an airtight
container at room temperature. Undecorated cakes can
be stored in the freezer for up to 2 weeks.

blue mondays

[chocolate/raisin/walnut/blue cheese]

chocolate custard

180 g (6¼ oz) milk

20 g (¾ oz) pouring (whipping) cream (35% fat)

Seeds scraped from 1 vanilla bean

20 g (¾ oz) caster (superfine) sugar

36 g (1¼ oz) egg yolks

10 g (¼ oz) cornflour (cornstarch)

Pinch of sea salt flakes

54 g (2 oz) dark couverture chocolate (70%),
    chopped or buttons

Put the milk, cream and vanilla seeds in a saucepan over medium heat and bring to the boil.

Meanwhile, use a small whisk to whisk together the sugar, egg yolks, cornflour and salt. Pour a little of the hot milk mixture over while whisking continuously, then gradually whisk in the remaining milk mixture until smooth. Return the mixture to the saucepan and stir over medium heat for 1½ minutes or until the mixture thickens and just comes to the boil.

Put the chocolate in a bowl. Pour over the custard, stirring until the chocolate has melted and the mixture is smooth. Cover with plastic wrap, pressing it onto the surface to prevent a skin forming, and set aside. Before using, use a balloon whisk to whisk until smooth.

blue cheese mixture

40 g (1½ oz) stilton or other strong crumbly
    blue cheese, chopped

95 g (3⅓ oz) unsalted butter

95 g (3⅓ oz) pure icing (confectioners') sugar, sifted

90 g (3¼ oz) lightly beaten egg

125 g (4½ oz) plain (all-purpose) flour, sifted

2 g (²⁄₂₅ oz) baking powder

Put the cheese, butter and icing sugar in an electric mixer with a beater attachment and beat on medium speed for 2–3 minutes or until pale and creamy. With the motor running, add the egg gradually, mixing well between each addition. Add the flour and baking powder and mix to combine well. Transfer the mixture to another bowl, cover and set aside. Clean the mixer bowl as you will need to use it again.

chocolate cake batter

65 g (2⅓ oz) dark couverture chocolate (64%), chopped or buttons
50 g (1¾ oz) olive oil
190 g (6¾ oz) unsalted butter, chopped and softened
240 g (8½ oz) pure icing (confectioners') sugar
245 g (9 oz) lightly beaten egg
190 g (6¾ oz) plain (all-purpose) flour
5 g (⅛ oz) baking powder
40 g (1½ oz) unsweetened cocoa powder
110 g (3¾ oz) raisins, soaked in hot water for 15 minutes or until plump, then drained and cooled
100 g (3½ oz) walnut halves, roughly chopped
70 g (2½ oz) dark couverture chocolate (64–74%), extra, chopped or buttons

Preheat the oven to 150°C (300°F/Gas 2). Lightly spray two 7.5 x 7.5 x 20 cm (3 x 3 x 8 inch) loaf (bar) tins with cooking oil. Line with non-stick baking paper, extending over the two long sides.

Melt the chocolate with the olive oil in a heatproof bowl over a saucepan of simmering water, then remove from the heat. Put the butter and icing sugar in an electric mixer with a beater attachment and beat on medium speed for 2–3 minutes or until pale and creamy. Stir in the chocolate mixture until just combined. With the motor running, gradually add the egg, mixing well between each addition. Sift the dry ingredients together and add to the bowl, mixing to combine well. Remove the bowl from the mixer and fold in the raisins, walnuts and extra chocolate.

to assemble

Take two piping (icing) bags with 11 mm (⅖ inch) plain nozzles and fill one with the chocolate custard and the other with the blue cheese mixture.

Divide a third of the cake batter between the tins and smooth it over to cover the bases evenly. Pipe 2 long straight tubes of blue cheese mixture into each tin, 1 cm (½ inch) in from each long side, and starting and stopping 1 cm (½ inch) in from the short sides. Pipe two long straight tubes of chocolate custard evenly between the tubes of blue cheese mixture, once more starting and stopping 1 cm (½ inch) in from the short sides.

Put half the remaining cake batter in a piping bag without a nozzle and pipe an even layer into each tin, ensuring you cover all the tubes but being careful not to squash them.

Repeat the piping with the blue cheese mixture and chocolate custard, to make the same series of tubes as before. Refill the other piping bag with the remaining cake batter and pipe it over the top, again ensuring the tubes are covered but not squashed, and filling the tins no more than 1 cm (½ inch) from the top.

Place the tins on a baking tray and cook the cakes for 45 minutes or until a skewer inserted into the centre of a cake comes out just a little moist. Remove from the oven and leave the cakes in the tins to cool.

blue cheese syrup

250 g (9 oz) caster (superfine) sugar
250 g (9 oz) water
25 g (1 oz) stilton or other strong crumbly blue cheese, chopped

While the cakes are cooling, combine the sugar and water in a saucepan and stir over medium heat until the sugar has dissolved. Bring to the boil, then add the cheese and blitz with a stick mixer until smooth. Divide the syrup between the warm cakes, then leave them in the tins to cool completely.

to finish

400 g (14 oz) chocolate mirror glaze (see Basics)
Stilton or other strong crumbly blue cheese, cut into small wedges, to garnish
Walnut halves, roughly chopped, to garnish
85 g (3 oz) raisins, soaked in hot water for 15 minutes or until plump, then drained and cooled, to garnish

Heat the mirror glaze in the microwave on medium (50%) for 15 seconds, then mix well and check the temperature. Continue this process until the glaze reaches 35°C (95°F).

Turn the cakes out onto a wire rack, then turn right way up and pour over the chocolate mirror glaze. Garnish with the cheese, walnuts and raisins. Transfer to a serving plate/s and serve. **makes 2 bar cakes**

note: Store this cake in the refrigerator in an airtight container for up to 7 days.

orange pulp

2 navel oranges

Put the oranges in a saucepan and cover completely with cold water. Bring to the boil, then reduce the heat and simmer for 2 hours or until they are very soft and the skin just starts to split. The oranges should always be below the water level, so top up as necessary. Remove using a slotted spoon and cool to room temperature. Roughly chop, remove any white pith and seeds, and purée in a food processor. Weigh out 400 g (14 oz).

orange gel wedges

250 g (9 oz) freshly squeezed and strained orange juice
65 g (2⅓ oz) caster (superfine) sugar
1.5 g (¹⁄₂₀ oz) gellan (see Glossary)
1 g (¹⁄₂₅ oz) iota (see Glossary)

Put the orange juice, sugar, gellan and iota in a small saucepan over medium heat and bring to the boil, stirring continuously. Divide the mixture evenly among 3 teacups or similar-shaped containers and place in the refrigerator to set. Working with one teacup at a time, dip the base briefly in hot water, then invert to remove the orange gel. Cut into 4 wedges each.

candied orange strips

1 orange
100 g (3½ oz) water
100 g (3½ oz) caster (superfine) sugar

Use a vegetable peeler or small paring knife to remove the rind from the orange. Remove any white pith remaining on the orange and discard. Finely julienne the rind. Put the water, sugar and strips of rind in a small saucepan over medium heat and bring to the boil. Remove from the heat and cool the strips of rind in the syrup. Store in the refrigerator until required.

flourless almond & orange cake

300 g (10½ oz) lightly beaten egg
460 g (1 lb ¼ oz) caster (superfine) sugar
400 g (14 oz) orange pulp (see recipe above)
510 g (1 lb 2¼ oz) ground almonds
6 g (¹⁄₅ oz) baking powder

Preheat the oven to 150°C (300°F/Gas 2). Lightly spray two 7.5 x 7.5 x 20 cm (3 x 3 x 8 inch) loaf (bar) tins with cooking oil. Line with non-stick baking paper, extending over the two long sides.

Put the eggs and sugar in an electric mixer with a whisk attachment and whisk for 3–4 minutes or until thick and pale. Mix through the orange pulp. Add the combined ground almonds and sifted baking powder and fold through until well combined.

Divide half the cake batter between the two tins. Place 3 orange gel wedges along the cake batter in each tin, then divide the remaining batter between the tins, filling the tins no more than 1 cm (½ inch) from the top. Place the tins on a baking tray and cook for 45 minutes or until a skewer inserted into the centre of a cake comes out just a little moist. Cool the cakes in the tins.

saffron glaze

75 g (2¾ oz) water
Pinch of saffron threads
400 g (14 oz) pure icing (confectioners') sugar

Bring the water and saffron to the boil in a small saucepan. Remove from the heat and cool completely.

Invert the cakes onto a wire rack, so the bases are now the tops. Put the sifted icing sugar in a bowl. Stir in the saffron water, mixing until smooth and runny, then immediately pour evenly over the cakes. Leave for 5 minutes to set, then garnish each cake with 3 orange gel wedges and drained candied orange strips. Transfer to a serving plate/s. **makes 2 bar cakes**

note: This cake will keep for up to 5 days in an airtight container at room temperature. Undecorated cakes can be stored in the freezer for 2 weeks.

celia's act

[almond/orange/saffron]

it mayo shock u

[mayonnaise/chocolate/raspberry]

291 g (10¼ oz) Japanese mayonnaise (see Glossary)
210 g (7½ oz) caster (superfine) sugar
6 g (⅕ oz) natural vanilla extract
300 g (10½ oz) plain (all-purpose) flour, sifted
6 g (⅕ oz) baking powder
5 g (⅛ oz) bicarbonate of soda (baking soda)
65 g (2⅓ oz) unsweetened cocoa powder
285 g (10 oz) water
165 g (5¾ oz) fresh raspberries

Preheat the oven to 170°C (325°F/Gas 3). Lightly spray two 7.5 x 7.5 x 20 cm (3 x 3 x 8 inch) loaf (bar) tins with cooking oil. Line with non-stick baking paper, extending over the two long sides.

Put the mayonnaise, sugar and vanilla in an electric mixer with a whisk attachment and whisk on medium speed for 3–5 minutes, until the sugar starts to dissolve.

Sift together all the dry ingredients, add to the mixer bowl and mix on low speed to combine. With the motor running, pour in the water and mix until combined. Remove the bowl from the mixer and carefully fold through the raspberries.

Divide the cake batter between the two tins. Place the tins on a baking tray and cook for 45 minutes or until a skewer inserted into the centre of a cake comes out just a little moist. Cool the cakes in the tins. Turn out onto a wire rack, then turn right way up.

decoration

100 g (3½ oz) cocoa butter (see Glossary), finely chopped
3 g (⅒ oz) lipid-soluble pink food colouring (see Glossary)
3 g (⅒ oz) lipid-soluble white food colouring
500 g (1 lb 2 oz) dark couverture chocolate (70%), tempered (see Basics)
400 g (14 oz) chocolate mirror glaze (see Basics)
12 fresh raspberries

Melt the cocoa butter in a medium saucepan over low heat. Divide among 2 narrow containers, add the pink food colouring to one and the white food colouring to the other and blitz each mixture with a stick mixer, cleaning it in between, until all the colour particles have disappeared. Set aside to cool to 32°C (90°F).

Dampen the benchtop slightly with a moist cloth. Place a 30 x 40 cm (12 x 16 inch) acetate sheet (see Glossary) on top and use a clean dry cloth to smooth it out. The moisture will help the acetate sheet stick to the bench. Use a teaspoon to drizzle the pink cocoa butter onto the acetate sheet, flicking it back and forth. Set aside until it begins to harden. Repeat with the white cocoa butter and set aside to harden. Pour the tempered dark chocolate over the drizzled cocoa butter and use a large crank-handled palette knife to smooth the chocolate out to about 2–3 mm (¹⁄₁₆–⅛ inch) thick. Holding opposite diagonal corners of the acetate sheet, lightly shake it to smooth out the chocolate. Set aside until the chocolate is dry to the touch, yet still pliable.

Use a ruler and paring knife to cut the chocolate into 5 cm (2 inch) squares. Cover with non-stick baking paper, flip over and put a baking tray on top to stop it bending as it crystallises. Leave until set.

Warm the mirror glaze in a heatproof bowl over a saucepan of simmering water until it reaches 35°C (95°F), then pour it evenly over the cooled cakes. Tap the wire rack lightly at the sides to help the glaze settle and allow any excess to drip off. Transfer to a serving plate/s and top with the chocolate squares and raspberries. (Keep any leftover chocolate decoration to decorate other cakes, or just eat it!) **makes 2 bar cakes**

note: This cake will keep for up to 5 days in an airtight container at room temperature. Undecorated cakes can be stored in the freezer for up to 2 weeks.

caramel

300 g (10½ oz) caster (superfine) sugar
120 g (4¼ oz) water
60 g (2¼ oz) liquid glucose
220 g (7¾ oz) UHT coconut cream (see Glossary)

Lightly spray two 7.5 x 7.5 x 20 cm (3 x 3 x 8 inch) loaf (bar) tins with cooking oil. Line with non-stick baking paper, extending over the two long sides.

Put the sugar, water and glucose in a small, deep saucepan over medium heat and stir until the sugar has dissolved. Bring to the boil and cook until the caramel is dark amber in colour.

Meanwhile, bring the coconut cream to the boil in another saucepan and then remove from the heat.

When the caramel has reached the dark-amber stage, carefully stir in the warm coconut cream to deglaze — watch out, the caramel will rise and spit, releasing a lot of heat. Divide the caramel between the tins.

poached pears

950 g (2 lb 2 oz) (about 4) just ripe, but still firm,
    beurre bosc pears
2.5 kg (5 lb 8 oz) simple sugar syrup (see Basics,
    make 5 quantities)
Seeds scraped from 1 vanilla bean
Small pinch of saffron threads

200 g (7 oz) fresh blueberries

Peel and core the pears and cut each into two even halves. Put the pears, syrup, vanilla seeds and saffron in a saucepan and cover with a cartouche (a round of baking paper cut to just fit over the contents of the pan). Bring to the boil over medium heat, then reduce the heat to low and simmer for 15–20 minutes or until the pears are tender but not mushy. Transfer to a bowl to cool completely.

Cut each piece of pear in half lengthways, then into three wedges. Arrange the pear pieces randomly over the top of the caramel in the tins. Scatter over the blueberries to fill in the gaps between the pears.

cake batter

150 g (5½ oz) unsalted butter
240 g (8½ oz) light palm sugar (jaggery), grated
180 g (6¼ oz) lightly beaten egg
310 g (11 oz) plain (all-purpose) flour
5 g (⅛ oz) baking powder
75 g (2¾ oz) cornflour (cornstarch)
50 g (1¾ oz) lavender sugar (see Basics)
120 g (4¼ oz) desiccated coconut
100 g (3½ oz) crème fraîche
150 g (5½ oz) UHT coconut cream (see Glossary)
Finely grated zest and juice of 1 orange
Finely grated zest and juice of 1 lemon

Preheat the oven to 160°C (315°F/Gas 2–3). Cream the butter and sugar in an electric mixer with a beater attachment on medium speed for 3 minutes or until pale and fluffy. Gradually add the egg, mixing well between each addition. Mix in the sifted flour, baking powder and cornflour. Mix in the combined lavender sugar and desiccated coconut. Remove the bowl from the mixer and stir in the crème fraîche, coconut cream and all the zest and juice, mixing until well combined.

Divide the mixture between the two tins, filling them no more than 1 cm (½ inch) from the top, and place on a baking tray. Cook for 45 minutes or until a skewer inserted into the centre of a cake comes out just a little moist. Cool the cakes in the tins and then carefully invert onto a wire rack.

to finish

200 g (7 oz) clear neutral glaze (see Basics)

Heat the clear neutral glaze in a heatproof bowl over a saucepan of simmering water until it reaches 35°C (95°F) and then pour over the cakes. Transfer to a serving plate/s. **makes 2 bar cakes**

note: This cake will keep for up to 5 days in an airtight container at room temperature. Undecorated cakes can be stored in the freezer for up to 2 weeks.

lavender up

[pear/blueberry/lavender/coconut]

chistachio perry

[cherry/raspberry/pistachio]

cherry jelly

125 g (4½ oz) sieved cherry purée (see Basics)
125 g (4½ oz) sieved raspberry purée (see Basics)
20 g (¾ oz) caster (superfine) sugar
4.5 g (³/₂₀ oz) pectin NH (see Glossary)
75 g (2¾ oz) caster (superfine) sugar, extra
45 g (1¾ oz) liquid glucose

Put the cherry and raspberry purées in a small saucepan over medium heat and bring to 60°C (140°F). Combine the sugar and pectin, add to the purées and bring to the boil. Add the extra sugar and glucose and return to the boil. Boil for 1 minute. Pour into a 18 x 22 cm (7 x 8½ inch) baking tray, or similar-sized heatproof container, lined with plastic wrap. Refrigerate for approximately 1 hour, until the jelly has set. Remove from the tin and cut into four 7.5 x 10 cm (3 x 4 inch) pieces. Refrigerate until required.

pistachio nougatine

125 g (4½ oz) unsalted butter, chopped and softened
50 g (1¾ oz) liquid glucose
150 g (5½ oz) caster (superfine) sugar
2.5 g (²/₂₅ oz) yellow pectin (see Glossary)
90 g (3¼ oz) finely chopped pistachio nuts

Preheat the oven to 190°C (375°F/Gas 5). Put the butter and glucose in a small saucepan over medium heat and bring to 60°C (140°F). Combine the sugar and pectin, add to the pan and mix well to emulsify the butter. Add the pistachios. Spread over a baking tray lined with non-stick baking paper to form a layer about 2–3 mm (¹/₁₆–¹/₈ inch) thick. Bake for 10–12 minutes or until the nougatine is golden.

Remove from the oven and allow to cool for a few minutes. While the nougatine is still warm, cut it into two 7.5 x 20 cm (3 x 8 inch) strips. Set aside.

cake batter

215 g (7½ oz) unsalted butter, chopped and softened

190 g (6¾ oz) caster (superfine) sugar

Finely grated zest of 1 lemon

170 g (5¾ oz) lightly beaten egg

42 g (1½ oz) pouring (whipping) cream (35% fat)

6 g (⅕ oz) baking powder

Pinch of salt

42 g (1½ oz) ground almonds

350 g (12 oz) ground pistachio nuts

35 g (1¼ oz) pistachio paste (see Basics)

128 g (4½ oz) egg whites

53 g (2 oz) caster (superfine) sugar, extra

128 g (4½ oz) plain (all-purpose) flour, sifted

215 g (7½ oz) pitted fresh cherries

Preheat the oven to 180°C (350°F/Gas 4). Lightly spray two 7.5 x 7.5 x 20 cm (3 x 3 x 8 inch) loaf (bar) tins with cooking oil. Line with non-stick baking paper, extending over the two long sides.

Put the butter, sugar and lemon zest in an electric mixer with a beater attachment and beat on medium speed for 4 minutes or until pale and creamy. Gradually beat in the combined egg and cream until they are well incorporated. Scrape down the side of the bowl and mix in the sifted baking powder and salt, and the ground almonds and pistachios until combined. Mix in the pistachio paste, then transfer the mixture to a clean bowl. Clean the mixer bowl and dry it thoroughly as you will need to use it for the next step.

Put the egg whites and extra sugar in the clean mixer bowl and use the whisk attachment to whisk for 6 minutes on medium speed or until firm peaks form.

Use a rubber spatula to fold half the egg whites through the cake batter, then half the sifted flour. Fold in the remaining egg whites, then the remaining flour. Fold through the cherries.

Divide half the cake batter between the lined tins, then cover with 2 pieces of cherry jelly per tin. Cover with the remaining cake batter, filling the tins no more than 1 cm (½ inch) from the top. Put the tins on a baking tray and cook for 1 hour or until a skewer inserted into the centre of a cake comes out just a little moist. Cool the cakes in the tins.

to assemble

250 g (9 oz) white ready-to-roll icing (frosting) (see Glossary)

Pure icing (confectioners') sugar, to dust

100 g (3½ oz) pure icing (confectioners') sugar, extra, sifted

20 g (¾ oz) egg white

Yellow food colouring

Green food colouring

2 macarons (see page 16, optional), coloured white by mixing a little white food colouring powder with a tiny bit of water and adding to the sugar syrup

Roll out 100 g (3½ oz) of the icing on a surface lightly dusted with icing sugar to 2 mm (1/16 inch) thick. Use a fluted round 4 cm (1½ inch) cutter to stamp out 2 circles. Use a fluted round 3 cm (1¼ inch) cutter to stamp out 2 more circles. Use a fluted round 2 cm (¾ inch) cutter to stamp out the last 2 circles. Place the largest circles on non-stick baking paper, dab the centre of each with a small amount of water and place the middle-sized circles on top. Dab the centre of each with water, then place the smallest circles on top. Press down firmly in the centre to make the edges rise up like flowers. Combine the extra icing sugar and egg white, then colour with a few drops of yellow food colouring. Use a piping (icing) bag with a 2 mm (1/16 inch) nozzle to pipe a small dot in the centre of each flower.

Take the remaining icing and knead in a few drops of green food colouring (wear disposable gloves to prevent your hands turning green). Lightly dust the bench with icing sugar and roll out the icing to 2–3 mm (1/16–1/8 inch) thick. Use a round 4 cm (1½ inch) cutter to stamp out 2 circles and a round 3 cm (1¼ inch) cutter to stamp out 4 circles. Use a fluted round 1 cm (½ inch) cutter to stamp out 4 more circles.

Invert the cakes onto a serving plate, so the bases are now the tops. Lay a strip of nougatine on top of each cake. Arrange the green circles and macarons on top, then place a flower on each of the largest straight-sided green circles. **makes 2 bar cakes**

note: This cake will keep for up to 5 days in an airtight container at room temperature. Undecorated cakes can be stored in the freezer for 2 weeks.

honey comb-over

[honey/golden syrup/coconut]

honeycomb

375 g (13 oz) caster (superfine) sugar

115 g (4 oz) golden syrup

105 g (3½ oz) honey

125 g (4½ oz) water

15 g (½ oz) bicarbonate of soda (baking soda)

Line the base and sides of a standard shoe box with two sheets of baking paper, extending 3 cm (1¼ inches) over the two long sides. (I use a shoe box instead of a metal tray as cardboard does not retain heat — this ensures the honeycomb doesn't continue to cook and burn, and also allows it to cool down faster.)

Put the sugar, golden syrup, honey and water in a large saucepan over medium heat and stir until the sugar has dissolved. Bring to the boil and cook until the mixture reaches 145–150°C (293–302°F). Remove from the heat. Add the bicarbonate of soda and whisk quickly to just combine, then immediately pour the foaming mixture into the prepared shoe box where it will continue to expand rapidly. Leave to cool.

Use the overhanging paper to lift the honeycomb out of the shoe box.

honeycomb buttercream

200 g (7 oz) unsalted butter, chopped and softened

200 g (7 oz) pure icing (confectioners') sugar, sifted

250 g (9 oz) almond meal

175 g (6 oz) crème pâtissiére (see Croque-en-bouche recipe, page 164, make ½ quantity and use the remainder in another recipe)

125 g (4½ oz) honeycomb (see recipe above)

Put the butter and icing sugar in an electric mixer with a beater attachment and beat until pale and creamy.

Add the almond meal to the bowl and mix to combine. Fold through the crème pâtissiére until well combined.

Break off a large corner of the honeycomb slab (you will need 125 g/4½ oz) and finely chop. Fold into the buttercream. Set aside while you cook the cake.

honey cake

248 g (9 oz) honey
43 g (1¾ oz) unsalted butter, chopped and softened
135 g (4¾ oz) plain (all-purpose) flour
2 g (²⁄₂₅ oz) ground cinnamon
2 g (²⁄₂₅ oz) ground ginger
88 g (3¼ oz) lightly beaten egg
4 g (⁴⁄₂₅ oz) bicarbonate of soda (baking soda)
33 g (1¼ oz) boiling water
120 g (4¼ oz) desiccated coconut

Preheat the oven to 180°C (350°F/Gas 4). Line two 1.5 x 25 x 30 cm (⅝ x 10 x 12 inch) baking trays with non-stick baking paper and set aside.

Put the honey and butter in an electric mixer with a beater attachment and beat on medium speed for 3–4 minutes or until just combined and smooth. Sift together the flour, cinnamon and ginger, add to the mixing bowl and beat until combined. With the motor running, gradually add the egg, ensuring the mixture is well combined before each addition.

Dissolve the bicarbonate of soda in the boiling water, then mix into the cake batter until well combined.

Divide the cake batter between the two trays and use a crank-handled palette knife to spread it out evenly to the sides of the trays. Cook the cakes for 9–10 minutes or until the surface springs back when lightly touched. Be careful not to overcook the cakes as they will become difficult to roll.

Lay two clean tea towels (dish towels) on the benchtop and evenly sprinkle half the coconut over each. Invert a cake onto each tea towel and peel away the baking paper. Allow the cakes to cool completely. Gently roll the long edge of one cake over and continue rolling until you have a tube shape. Repeat with the other cake.

Unroll the cakes and divide half the buttercream between the cakes, spreading it out with a palette knife to evenly cover the surface of each. Roll the cakes up again, using the tea towels to pull the rolls towards you, stopping periodically and using your thumbs to tighten the rolls. Place the cakes in the refrigerator for 1 hour to help firm up the buttercream.

to finish

300 g (10½ oz) vanilla glaze (see V8 recipe, page 178)
Yellow and brown food colouring
Edible gold metallic dust (see Glossary), for decorating

Place a sheet of plastic wrap, larger than your cake cooling rack, on the bench. Put the rack on top. Remove the cakes from the refrigerator, unroll from the tea towels and place on the rack. Heat the vanilla glaze in the microwave, in short bursts on medium (50%), until it reaches 25–28°C (77–82°F). Use the yellow and brown food colouring to make it a honeycomb colour. Pour the glaze over the cakes, allowing it to run over the sides, and smooth the surface with a palette knife. Check the sides are fully covered with glaze — if there are spots that remain uncovered, use the palette knife to dab some glaze on. Leave the rolls on the racks for a few minutes to allow the excess glaze to drip off. Transfer to a chopping board and trim approximately 1 cm (½ inch) from the short ends to neaten their appearance.

Smash up the remaining honeycomb so you have small rocks about 4 cm (1½ inches) in diameter and place a line of rocks along the centre of each roll.

Take a large, round make-up brush with soft bristles that are clean and dry, and lightly dip it in the gold metallic dust. Place the brush in front of the honeycomb pieces and exhale a short, sharp breath of air to blow the dust off the brush and onto the honeycomb. Repeat until the honeycomb is lightly coated. Transfer to a serving plate/s. **makes 2 rolls**

note: If you need to make this recipe ahead of time, the undecorated buttercream-filled rolls will keep for up to 4 days in the refrigerator, covered with plastic wrap. Before serving, allow the rolls to sit at room temperature for an hour, then glaze and garnish as above.

raspberry caramel

200 g (7 oz) caster (superfine) sugar
60 g (2¼ oz) water
72 g (2½ oz) liquid glucose
88 g (3¼ oz) pouring (whipping) cream (35% fat)
40 g (1½ oz) sieved raspberry purée (see Basics)
12 g (²⁄₅ oz) extra virgin olive oil
Pinch of freshly cracked black pepper

500 g (1 lb 2 oz) cherry tomatoes

Lightly spray two 7.5 x 7.5 x 20 cm (3 x 3 x 8 inch) loaf (bar) tins with cooking oil. Line with non-stick baking paper, extending over the two long sides.

Put the sugar, water and glucose in a small, deep saucepan over medium heat and stir until the sugar has dissolved. Bring to the boil and cook until the caramel is dark amber in colour.

Meanwhile, put the cream and raspberry purée in another saucepan and bring to the boil over medium heat, then remove from the heat. When the caramel has reached the dark-amber stage, carefully stir in the warm cream mixture with a small whisk — watch out, the caramel will rise and spit, releasing a lot of heat. Stir in the olive oil and pepper.

Divide the caramel between the two tins, to make a layer about 1 cm (½ inch) deep in each. Divide the tomatoes evenly over the caramel in each tin so that the caramel is entirely covered.

raspberry & chocolate cake

200 g (7 oz) caster (superfine) sugar
80 g (2¾ oz) unsalted butter, chopped and softened
60 g (2¼ oz) sieved raspberry purée (see Basics)
300 g (10½ oz) dark couverture chocolate (64%),
    chopped or buttons
92 g (3¼ oz) extra virgin olive oil
250 g (9 oz) lightly beaten egg yolks
92 g (3¼ oz) almond meal
6 g (⅕ oz) baking powder
6 g (⅕ oz) sea salt flakes
200 g (7 oz) egg whites

Preheat the oven to 160°C (315°F/Gas 2–3). Heat a saucepan over medium heat and sprinkle over a thin layer of caster sugar. As soon as it liquefies (approximately 2 minutes), sprinkle over another layer and when that liquefies, repeat, until all the sugar has been added. Bring to the boil and cook for 3 minutes or until the syrup is dark amber and has a strong toffee

smell. Turn off the heat and immediately add the butter, swirling it around to deglaze. When the butter has melted, add the raspberry purée, stirring to combine.

Melt the chocolate in a heatproof bowl over a saucepan of simmering water, then remove from the heat and stir in the raspberry caramel mixture. Stir in the olive oil and mix in the egg yolks until well combined. Sift the almond meal and baking powder through a coarse sieve and stir into the chocolate mixture, along with the sea salt. Put the egg whites in an electric mixer with a whisk attachment and whisk until they just form firm peaks. Mix a spoonful of egg whites into the chocolate mixture, then carefully fold through the remaining egg whites until well combined, being careful not to beat out too much air.

Divide the cake batter between the two tins, filling the tins no more than 1 cm (½ inch) from the top. Place the tins on a baking tray and cook the cakes for 45 minutes or until a skewer inserted into the centre of a cake comes out just a little moist. Cool the cakes in the tins, then invert onto a wire rack.

to finish

200 g (7 oz) clear neutral glaze (see Basics)
1 sheet edible gold leaf (see Glossary)

Warm the glaze in a heatproof bowl over a saucepan of simmering water until it reaches 35°C (95°F), then pour evenly over the top of each cake. Tap the wire rack lightly at the sides to help the glaze settle and to allow any excess to drip off, then transfer to a serving plate/s.

Use a thin, pointed paintbrush to remove a piece of gold leaf, approximately 3 x 3 cm (1¼ x 1¼ inches), from the sheet. Transfer it to the corner of one of the cakes and let it rest over the top — it will naturally fold down to cover the corner. Repeat to decorate the other cake. Serve. **makes 2 bar cakes**

note: This cake will keep for up to 5 days in an airtight container at room temperature. Undecorated cakes can be stored in the freezer for up to 2 weeks.

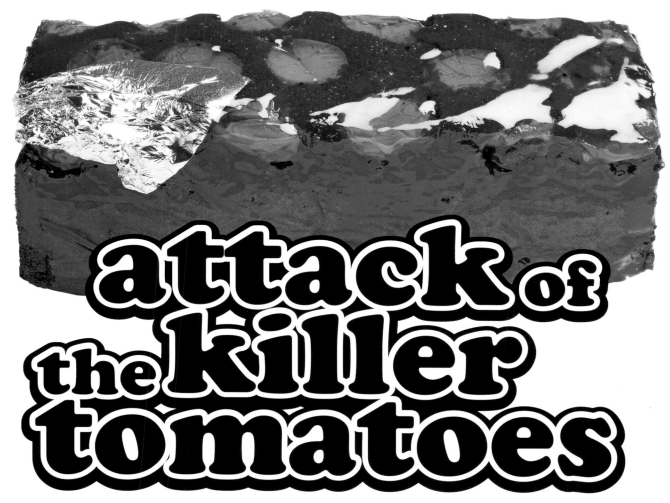

attack of the killer tomatoes

[raspberry/chocolate/tomato]

oiled up calabrian

[strawberry/pistachio/rhubarb/marzipan]

strawberry pâte de fruit

350 g (12 oz) sieved strawberry purée (see Basics)
12 g (²/₅ oz) pectin NH (see Glossary)
280 g (10 oz) caster (superfine) sugar
80 g (2¾ oz) liquid glucose
12 g (²/₅ oz) citric acid solution (see Basics)

Line a square 15 cm (6 inch) cake tin with non-stick baking paper, extending over two sides. Put the strawberry purée in a saucepan over medium heat and bring to 60°C (140°F). Combine the pectin with 40 g (1½ oz) of the sugar, add to the purée and stir with a small whisk until the mixture comes to the boil. Add the remaining sugar and the glucose and stir until the sugar has dissolved. Return to the boil, then immediately remove from the heat and stir in the citric acid solution. Pour into the lined tin. Set aside at room temperature for 2–3 hours to enable the mixture to set and stabilise.

cake batter

153 g (5½ oz) eggs
200 g (7 oz) caster (superfine) sugar
125 g (4½ oz) extra virgin olive oil
100 g (3½ oz) unsalted butter, melted and cooled
50 g (1¾ oz) polenta
200 g (7 oz) ground pistachio nuts
50 g (1¾ oz) rice flour
4 g (⁴/₂₅ oz) baking powder
Juice and finely grated zest of 1 lemon
Juice of 1 orange
300 g (10½ oz) stewed rhubarb (see Basics)

Preheat the oven to 160°C (315°F/Gas 2–3). Lightly spray two 7.5 x 7.5 x 20 cm (3 x 3 x 8 inch) loaf (bar) tins with cooking oil. Line with non-stick baking paper, extending over the two long sides.

Put the eggs and sugar in an electric mixer with a whisk attachment and whisk on medium speed until pale. Gradually add the combined oil and melted butter, mixing well between each addition to ensure they are well incorporated.

Sift the dry ingredients together through a coarse sieve and use a spatula to fold into the egg and sugar mixture. Mix in the lemon zest and lemon and orange juices — the batter will be quite runny at this stage. Refrigerate for a couple of hours to thicken it slightly, or the jellies will sink when you add them instead of being suspended in the batter.

Mix the stewed rhubarb through the cake batter.

to assemble

Fill each lined tin one-third full with cake batter. Cut the strawberry pâte de fruit into 3.5 cm (1²/₅ inch) squares and reserve 2 squares for a garnish.

Place 3 pâte de fruit squares on the cake batter in each tin, running along the centre, and top with another layer of cake batter, bringing it two-thirds of the way up the sides of the tins. Place 3 more pâte de fruit squares on top of each, then divide the remaining cake batter over the top, filling the tins no more than 2 cm (¾ inch) from the top.

Place the tins on a baking tray and cook the cakes for 50–60 minutes or until a skewer inserted into the centre of a cake comes out just a little moist. Cool the cakes in the tins, then invert onto a wire rack.

to finish

350 g (12 oz) marzipan, to decorate
5 drops green food colouring
Pure icing (confectioners') sugar, sifted, for rolling
200 g (7 oz) clear neutral glaze (see Basics)
Caster (superfine) sugar, for rolling
2 strips roasted rhubarb (see Basics), for garnish

Place the marzipan on the benchtop and add the green food colouring. Knead the marzipan until it is a uniform green colour (wear disposable gloves to stop your hands turning green). Lightly dust the benchtop with icing sugar and roll out the marzipan to 3 mm (⅛ inch) thick, then cut into two 7.5 x 20 cm (3 x 8 inch) rectangles.

Heat the clear neutral glaze in a heatproof bowl over a saucepan of simmering water until it reaches 35°C (95°F). Brush each cake with the glaze and place a marzipan rectangle on top of each. Roll the reserved pâte de fruit squares in the extra caster sugar and place one on each cake with a strip of rhubarb. Transfer to a serving plate/s. **makes 2 bar cakes**

note: This cake will keep for up to 5 days in an airtight container at room temperature. Undecorated cakes can be stored in the freezer for 2 weeks.

cakes

**mount zumbo
geological society
general assembly**

back row, from left: tanzanie; v8; cherry cherry; croque-en-bouche;
escape from a colombian rainforest **front row, from left:** barbados; miss marple;
what a great pear of…; a night in the cross; alessia, i like big buns

This chapter is one of the most creative, from the names to the flavours, textures, design and architecture. I believe eating cake should be an experience of the soul and senses, never just eating for the sake of it.

As a patissier, making cakes such as these is my main job. I love the shapes, flavours and shines of glazes. I also enjoy coming up with quirky, humorous names. In my mind, buying a cake should be fun and I get a real kick out of seeing our customers' expressions as they read the names.

The v8 cake was created for Margaret Fulton's 85th birthday party. It was an honour to be asked to make the cake, and I really wanted it to be something special. I was told she likes vanilla, so I decided to do eight textures of vanilla. Hence the v8, which later appeared on *MasterChef Australia*.

I hope these creations catch your eye.

a night in the cross

[pistachio/rose/rhubarb/berries]

pistache pâte sucrée

250 g (9 oz) chilled unsalted butter, chopped

170 g (5¾ oz) pure icing (confectioners') sugar, sifted

50 g (1¾ oz) ground pistachio nuts

Seeds scraped from 2 vanilla beans

102 g (3½ oz) lightly beaten egg

420 g (15 oz) plain (all-purpose) flour, sifted

16 g (½ oz) pistachio paste (see Basics)

Put the butter, icing sugar, ground pistachios and vanilla seeds in an electric mixer with a beater attachment and beat on low speed for 2–3 minutes to soften the butter and combine. Beat for a further 2–3 minutes on medium speed to slightly aerate the mixture. Beat in the egg until combined. Scrape down the bowl, then add the flour and pistachio paste and mix until just combined.

Divide the soft dough evenly between 2 sheets of plastic wrap. Fold the plastic over the top of each and press the dough down to make discs, about 2 cm (¾ inch) thick. Cover and refrigerate for 2 hours or until firm.

Preheat the oven to 180°C (350°F/Gas 4). Put twelve 8 cm (3¼ inch) diameter, 1.5 cm (⅝ inch) deep rings on baking trays lined with non-stick baking paper.

Unwrap a pastry disc and place on a lightly floured bench. Evenly roll out into a square of 4 mm ($^1/_6$ inch) thickness. Repeat with the other pastry disc. Use a round 10 cm (4 inch) cutter to stamp out discs and use to line the rings. Place in the refrigerator for 10 minutes to firm up again slightly.

Place a snug-fitting paper muffin case on top of the pastry in each ring and fill the cases to the level of the rings with baking weights, rice or dried beans. Bake for 18–20 minutes or until the pastry is lightly golden.

Remove from the oven, remove the paper cases and weights and cool to room temperature. Remove the rings.

rose brûlée

532 g (1 lb 3 oz) pouring (whipping) cream (35% fat)
Seeds scraped from 1 vanilla bean
130 g (4$^1/_2$ oz) egg yolks
55 g (2 oz) caster (superfine) sugar
55 g (2 oz) pomegranate molasses (see Glossary)
20 g ($^3/_4$ oz) rosewater

Preheat the oven to 120°C (235°F/Gas $^1/_2$).

Put the cream and vanilla seeds in a saucepan over medium heat and bring to the boil. Meanwhile, put the egg yolks, sugar and pomegranate molasses in a bowl and immediately stir to combine — you should always stir sugar and egg yolk straight away or the sugar will 'burn' the surface of the egg yolk, changing its texture. Stir the rosewater into the egg mixture. Mix in a third of the hot cream to temper the eggs, then mix in the remaining hot cream.

Place twelve 7 cm (2$^3/_4$ inch) diameter, 2 cm ($^3/_4$ inch) deep silicone moulds on a baking tray and fill with the brûlée mixture. Bake for 35–40 minutes or until they are dry to the touch but still wobble slightly when you gently tap the sides of the moulds. Remove from the oven and cool to room temperature. Freeze for 2 hours, until the brûlée is frozen through.

Pop the brûlée discs from the moulds and sit each disc in the centre of a pastry shell (the gap around them will be filled with compote).

rhubarb compote

5 g ($^1/_8$ oz) gold gelatine leaves
30 g (1 oz) cold water
65 g (2$^1/_3$ oz) sieved strawberry purée (see Basics)
75 g (2$^3/_4$ oz) caster (superfine) sugar
265 g (9$^1/_3$ oz) rhubarb purée (see Basics)

Cut the gelatine leaves into small squares, place in a bowl with the cold water and set aside for 10 minutes to soak.

Put the strawberry purée and sugar in a small saucepan over medium heat, stirring until the sugar has dissolved. When the purée reaches 65°C (149°F), add the gelatine mixture and any soaking liquid and stir until the gelatine has completely dissolved. Put the rhubarb purée in a bowl, add the strawberry mixture and stir to combine. Set aside to cool.

Pour the cooled compote over the top of the brûlée discs, filling the gap around them and ensuring there is a light coating over the top of each disc. Refrigerate for 1 hour or until the compote has set.

to finish

250 g (9 oz) fresh raspberries
600 g (1 lb 5 oz) seedless watermelon squares
    (cut slightly larger than the raspberries)
60 g (2$^1/_4$ oz) freeze-dried watermelon powder
    (see Glossary)
24 unsprayed (chemical-free) red rose petals

Remove the cakes from the refrigerator. Arrange the fruit on top of each rhubarb compote layer, alternating raspberries and watermelon until the top of each cake is covered with fruit.

Divide the watermelon powder among 12 square 3 cm (1$^1/_4$ inch) snaplock bags (similar to those that contain spare buttons, or the smallest snaplock bags you can find). Seal and place over the fruit on each cake, then rest 2 rose petals up against each bag. Place on a serving platter or individual plates and serve immediately.

makes 12

note: If you wish to serve the cakes the next day, refrigerate just after the rhubarb compote layer and decorate just before serving.

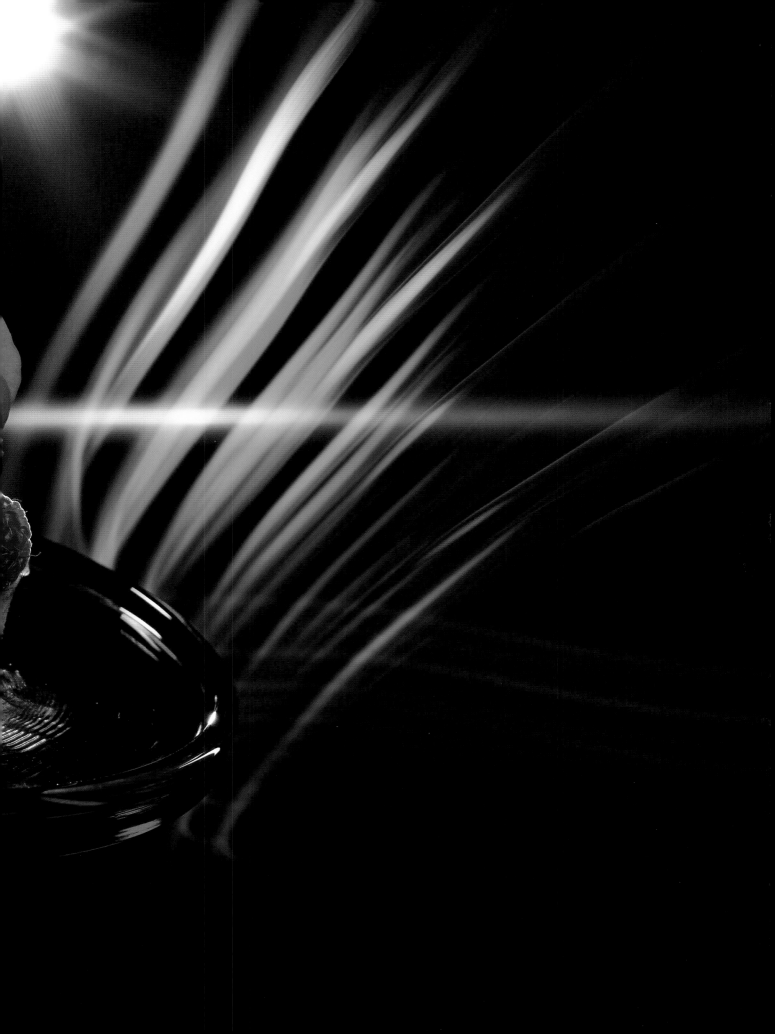

dark crème chantilly

57 g (2 oz) dark couverture chocolate (80%), chopped
    or buttons
250 g (9 oz) pouring (whipping) cream (35% fat)

Put the chocolate and cream in a saucepan over medium heat and stir continuously with a whisk until it comes to the boil. Remove from the heat, transfer to a container and cool to room temperature. Cover and refrigerate overnight. It is important to allow the chantilly to cool at room temperature before refrigerating to avoid any condensation entering the mixture.

cherry jelly

7 g (¼ oz) gold gelatine leaves
42 g (1½ oz) cold water
340 g (12 oz) pitted fresh or frozen cherries
75 g (2¾ oz) caster (superfine) sugar
140 g (5 oz) sieved raspberry purée (see Basics), chilled

Cut the gelatine leaves into small squares, place in a bowl with the cold water and refrigerate until ready to use.

Place the cherries and sugar in a saucepan over medium heat and cook for 5 minutes or until the cherries just start to break down and juice is pooling in the pan. Add the gelatine and any soaking liquid and stir well to combine. Put the raspberry purée in a bowl, pour over the cherry mixture and stir to combine. Set aside for 30 minutes or until the mixture has cooled to room temperature.

You will need twelve 7 cm (2¾ inch) square flexipan silicone mould cavities, placed on a baking tray. Half-fill the cavities with jelly mixture and refrigerate for 2 hours or until set. Freeze for 2 hours or until frozen through.

coconut moisture

205 g (7¼ oz) caster (superfine) sugar
140 g (5 oz) egg whites
7 g (¼ oz) honey
205 g (7¼ oz) desiccated coconut
60 g (2¼ oz) plain (all-purpose) flour, sifted
100 g (3½ oz) red glacé cherries, roughly chopped
205 g (7¼ oz) water

Put all the ingredients in a small saucepan over medium heat and cook, stirring continuously, for about 15 minutes or until three-quarters of the liquid has evaporated. The mixture will look like a thick sludge. Use a crank-handled palette knife to spread it evenly over the frozen jellies, filling them right to the top of each mould cavity. Make sure the tops are as smooth and flat as possible. Return to the freezer for 2 hours or until frozen through.

macarons

½ quantity macaron mixture (see page 16),
    coloured cherry red using red and a little
    bit of black food colouring
Unsweetened cocoa powder, for dusting

Preheat the oven to 135°C (250°F/Gas 1). Fill a piping (icing) bag with a 9 mm (⅓ inch) plain nozzle with the macaron mixture and pipe onto baking trays lined with Silpat (see Glossary) or non-stick baking paper. Holding the bag 1.5 cm (½ inch) above the tray, pipe straight down onto the tray until the mixture is 5 cm (2 inches) in diameter — it will spread to 6 cm (2½ inches) when you stop piping. Repeat, leaving 3 cm (1¼ inches) between each macaron. Dust lightly with cocoa powder through a small sieve and then tap the bottom of the tray a couple of times to eliminate any air bubbles and help flatten the surface of the macarons. Set aside at room temperature for 30 minutes or until a skin forms. To test if the macarons are ready, gently touch one with your fingertip to check that a light skin has formed — they should not be sticky. On humid days this may take longer.

Bake the macarons for 20 minutes or until stable and dry to the touch. Remove from the oven and leave on the trays to cool completely.

to assemble

100 g (3½ oz) shredded coconut

Remove the dark crème chantilly from the refrigerator and place in an electric mixer with a whisk attachment. Whisk carefully on medium speed until soft peaks form.

Use a palette knife to spread a little of the chantilly onto the base of 12 macarons. Pop the frozen jelly and coconut squares from the mould. Using the palette knife, spread chantilly over the sides and surface of each frozen jelly coconut square, forming a 3 mm (⅛ inch) thick layer. Place the shredded coconut on a plate and dip each side of the chantilly-covered coconut jelly squares in it to cover, gently pressing the coconut on. Place the frozen squares on the chantilly-covered macarons. Top with the remaining macarons. Allow to thaw for 25 minutes, place on a serving platter or individual plates and serve.

makes 12

cherry cherry

[chocolate/cherry/raspberry/coconut]

miss marple

[orange/mascarpone/maple]

orange jelly with grand marnier & strawberries

14 g (¹/₂ oz) gold gelatine leaves
84 g (3 oz) cold water
140 g (5 oz) caster (superfine) sugar
700 g (1 lb 9 oz) freshly squeezed and strained
  orange juice
70 g (2¹/₂ oz) Grand Marnier liqueur
6 strawberries, hulled and halved

Cut the gelatine leaves into small squares, place in a bowl with the cold water and refrigerate until ready to use.

Place the sugar and a quarter of the orange juice in a saucepan and heat to 60°C (140°F). Add the gelatine and any soaking liquid and stir until the gelatine has dissolved. Stir through the remaining orange juice and the Grand Marnier. Allow the jelly to cool slightly.

You will need twelve 4 cm (1¹/₂ inch) diameter, 1.5 cm (⁵/₈ inch) deep flexipan silicone mould cavities, placed on a baking tray. Put a strawberry half in each cavity, then half-fill with the jelly mixture. Set aside to cool, then put in the freezer to set, until required.

buttermilk cake

22 g (³/₄ oz) desiccated coconut
135 g (4³/₄ oz) buttermilk
72 g (2¹/₂ oz) caster (superfine) sugar
37 g (1¹/₂ oz) brown sugar
67 g (2¹/₃ oz) lightly beaten egg
135 g (4³/₄ oz) vegetable oil
135 g (4³/₄ oz) self-raising flour, sifted
22 g (³/₄ oz) wholemeal (whole-wheat) flour,
  sifted
5 g (¹/₈ oz) baking powder, sifted

Soak the coconut in the buttermilk for 20 minutes.

Place the sugars, egg and oil in an electric mixer with a beater attachment and mix on medium speed until well combined. Mix in the coconut and buttermilk, then add the dry ingredients and mix until just combined. Cover and place in the refrigerator for 2 hours.

Preheat the oven to 180°C (350°F/Gas 4). Lightly spray a mini muffin tin with cooking oil and half-fill the holes with cake batter. Bake in the oven for 10 minutes or until the cakes spring back when lightly pressed. Cool in the tin, then remove and set aside until required.

crepes

102 g (3¹/₂ oz) lightly beaten egg
10 g (¹/₄ oz) butter, melted, plus extra, for greasing
100 g (3¹/₂ oz) plain (all-purpose) flour, sifted
Seeds scraped from ¹/₂ vanilla bean
2.5 g (²/₂₅ oz) salt
250 g (9 oz) milk
30 g (1 oz) water
15 g (¹/₂ oz) Grand Marnier liqueur

Place all the ingredients, except the extra butter, in a bowl and blitz with a stick mixer until there are no lumps. Pass the mixture through a chinois (cone-shaped sieve). Lightly grease an 18 cm (7 inch) crepe pan with a thin layer of extra butter and place over medium heat.

Pour 40 g (1¹/₂ oz) of the batter into the pan and swirl the pan to make a thin, even crepe. Cook for 30 seconds each side, then transfer to a plate. Continue making crepes, greasing the pan as required, and stacking them on the plate until all the batter has been used. You should have 12 crepes.

maple syrup reduction

500 g (1 lb 2 oz) pure maple syrup

Heat the maple syrup in a saucepan over medium heat until it has reduced by 40% (you should have 300 g/ 10½ oz of maple syrup reduction). Allow to cool to room temperature.

maple syrup & mascarpone mousse

10 g (¼ oz) gold gelatine leaves
60 g (2¼ oz) cold water
300 g (10½ oz) maple syrup reduction
    (see recipe above)
410 g (14½ oz) pouring (whipping) cream (35% fat)
120 g (4¼ oz) egg yolks
590 g (1 lb 4¾ oz) mascarpone cheese
Seeds scraped from 1 vanilla bean

Cut the gelatine leaves into small squares, place in a bowl with the cold water and refrigerate until ready to use.

Put the maple syrup reduction, cream and egg yolks in a saucepan over low heat and whisk until the mixture reaches 85°C (185°F) or until it coats the back of a spoon. Stir through the gelatine and any soaking liquid, then cool the mixture to 35°C (95°F). Place the mascarpone in a bowl and whisk until smooth and free of lumps. Slowly whisk in the maple syrup mixture and vanilla seeds. Set aside until required.

maple soaking syrup

100 g (3½ oz) water
100 g (3½ oz) freshly squeezed and strained
    orange juice
100 g (3½ oz) pure maple syrup

Place all the ingredients in a bowl and blitz with a stick mixer until well combined.

isomalt discs

300 g (10½ oz) isomalt (see Glossary)
30 g (1 oz) water

Preheat the oven to 180°C (350°F/Gas 4). Line 2 large baking trays with Silpat (see Glossary) or non-stick baking paper. Cut a 7 cm (2¾ inch) circle template out of cardboard or plastic.

Put the isomalt and water in a heavy-based saucepan and stir occasionally over medium heat until the isomalt has dissolved. Continue cooking until the isomalt syrup reaches 170°C (338°F), then pour onto a lined tray and set aside to cool completely at room temperature.

Once the isomalt has cooled, break it into smaller pieces and put in a food processor. Process until the mixture resembles a very fine powder.

Place the template on the other lined tray and use a small sieve to dust the isomalt powder so it covers the inside of the template with a thin layer. Lift the template and repeat until 12 discs are made. Carefully lay another Silpat or sheet of non-stick baking paper on top and cover with an empty baking tray to weigh the paper down. Place in the oven for 5–7 minutes. Remove from the oven and allow to cool completely.

to assemble

200 g (7 oz) clear neutral glaze (see Basics)
24 orange segments
18 strawberries, hulled and halved

Line a baking tray with non-stick baking paper. Place twelve 7 cm (2¾ inch) diameter, 4.5 cm (1¾ inch) deep rings on the tray.

Place a crepe in each ring so it lines the ring and is pushed to the bottom. Take care not to damage the crepes and ensure they don't overlap on themselves.

Fill a piping (icing) bag without a nozzle with the mascarpone mousse (take care when filling the bag as the mousse is quite runny at this stage). Pipe a small amount of mascarpone mousse into the bottom of each crepe.

Gently heat the maple soaking syrup until it is just warm, then dip the buttermilk cakes in the syrup and place over the mascarpone mousse in each ring. Pipe another layer of mascarpone mousse, 1 cm (½ inch) thick, on top of each cake. Place an orange jelly in each ring, on top of the mascarpone mousse. Top with a little more mascarpone mousse so it's level with the top of the ring. Place the tray of filled crepes in the refrigerator for 3 hours or until the mascarpone mousse has set.

Heat the clear neutral glaze in a heatproof bowl over a saucepan of simmering water to 35°C (95°F). Place 2 orange segments and 3 strawberry halves on top of each filled crepe. Use a pastry brush to gently coat the fruit with clear neutral glaze. Place an isomalt disc on top of each filled crepe, then place on a serving platter or individual plates and serve. **makes 12**

crème pâtissiére

1.5 kg (3 lb 5 oz) milk
Seeds scraped from 1 vanilla bean
375 g (13 oz) egg yolks
375 g (13 oz) caster (superfine) sugar
150 g (5½ oz) cornflour (cornstarch)
150 g (5½ oz) unsalted butter, chopped and softened slightly

Heat the milk and vanilla seeds in a medium saucepan over medium–low heat until almost boiling. Remove from the heat. Whisk the egg yolks, sugar and cornflour in a bowl until thick and pale. Gradually whisk in the hot milk. Return the mixture to the pan and whisk continuously over medium heat until the custard comes to the boil. Boil for 1 minute. Transfer to a bowl and cover with plastic wrap, pressing it onto the surface to prevent a skin forming. Cool the crème pâtissiére to 50°C (122°F), then use a balloon whisk to whisk in the butter until smooth. Cover with plastic wrap as before and refrigerate to cool completely. Before using, use a balloon whisk to whisk until smooth.

choux pastry

300 g (10½ oz) unsalted butter, chopped
320 g (11¼ oz) water
16 g (½ oz) caster (superfine) sugar
400 g (14 oz) milk
16 g (½ oz) salt
400 g (14 oz) plain (all-purpose) flour, sifted
612 g (1 lb 5½ oz) lightly beaten egg

Preheat the oven to 210°C (415°F/Gas 6–7). Lightly butter 3–4 large baking trays, then wipe off any excess with paper towel.

Combine the butter, water, sugar, milk and salt in a heavy-based saucepan and bring to the boil. Remove from the heat and quickly beat in the flour with a wooden spoon. Return the pan to the heat and continue beating until the mixture comes together and leaves the side of the pan. Beat over low heat for a further 1–2 minutes to cook the flour, then remove from the heat and allow the mixture to cool slightly.

Transfer to an electric mixer with a beater attachment and begin beating the mixture on medium speed to release some of the heat. Gradually add the egg, beating well between each addition, until all of the egg has been added. Beat the mixture for several more minutes, or until it is thick and glossy — a spoon should stand upright in it.

Working in batches, spoon some of the pastry mixture into a piping (icing) bag with a 12–15 mm (½–⅝ inch) plain nozzle. Cover the remaining mixture with plastic wrap. Pipe the pastry onto the greased trays, to make puffs about 2.5 cm (1 inch) in diameter and 2 cm (¾ inch) high, leaving room between each for spreading. Bake, in batches, for 25–30 minutes or until firm and hollow when tapped. Transfer to wire racks to cool completely.

Put the crème pâtissiére in a piping bag with a nozzle less than 10 mm (½ inch). Poke a small hole into the base of each puff and fill with crème pâtissiére.

croque-en-bouche

[crème pâtissiére/
choux pastry/caramel]

caramel

200 g (7 oz) blanched almonds

150 g (5½ oz) water

500 g (1 lb 2 oz) caster (superfine) sugar

200 g (7 oz) liquid glucose

300 g (10½ oz) water, extra

1 kg (2 lb 4 oz) caster (superfine) sugar, extra

400 g (14 oz) liquid glucose, extra

Preheat the oven to 180°C (350°F/Gas 4). Grease a round 25 cm (10 inch) stainless-steel cake frame and place on a baking tray lined with non-stick baking paper.

Line a baking tray with non-stick baking paper. Spread the almonds over the lined tray and roast for 10–12 minutes or until lightly golden. Cool slightly, then roughly chop and set aside in a metal bowl (they should be slightly warm when you add them to the caramel).

Meanwhile, bring the water and sugar to the boil in a saucepan over medium heat. Add the glucose and cook until the syrup is caramel in colour. Remove from the heat and dip the base of the pan in a bowl of cold water to cool slightly. Quickly stir through the nuts and pour into the greased ring. This will form the base for the croque-en-bouche. Set aside to cool completely.

Line 3–4 baking trays with non-stick baking paper or Silpat (see Glossary). Bring the extra water and sugar to the boil in a saucepan over medium heat. Add the extra glucose and cook until the syrup is caramel in colour. Remove from the heat and dip the base of the pan in a bowl of cold water to cool slightly. Hold a choux puff carefully by the base and dip the top in the caramel. Place the dipped puff, caramel side down, on a lined tray. Be very careful when handling the caramel as it is extremely hot. (Keep a bowl of iced water nearby to dip your fingers in if you accidently touch it.) Repeat with the remaining choux puffs.

to assemble

Unsprayed (chemical-free) edible flowers of your
   choice, to decorate

Lightly spray the inside of a 60 cm (24 inch) high croque-en-bouche cone with a 25 cm (10 inch) diameter base with cooking oil and turn it upside down. (If you do not have a croque-en-bouche cone, see Note.) Working one at a time, dip the side of a puff in the hot caramel and place it inside the croque-en-bouche cone, at the tip. Continue adding puffs, always placing the freshly dipped side against another puff to secure and building them up around the cone until it is filled. Set aside to cool.

Remove the caramel base from the frame. Place a small amount of the remaining caramel around the base where the croque-en-bouche will sit to help it adhere. Gently grasp the croque-en-bouche, holding it directly over the caramel base, release it from the cone and place it on the caramel base.

Create the angel hair as close as possible to serving time, as the strands are very thin and melt quickly when exposed to any humidity or moisture. (I do not recommend making angel hair if it is raining or very humid, as it will begin to melt as soon as you make it.)

Lay a long sheet of non-stick baking paper on the benchtop. Place 2 rolling pins, approximately 50 cm (20 inches) apart, parallel on the baking paper to catch the strands. Reheat the caramel remaining in the pan over low heat and dip two forks in it, holding them in one hand, back to back. Raise the forks up as high as you can, tines facing down, and quickly flick them back and forth. Repeat until you have enough angel hair to pick up, then carefully wrap the strands around the croque-en-bouche. Continue until the croque-en-bouche is covered with angel hair. Decorate with the flowers.

serves 20 (makes 60–80 choux puffs)

note: If you do not have a croque-en-bouche cone, you will need to build the croque-en-bouche freehand. Remove the caramel base from the frame. Dip the sides of the puffs in the caramel in the saucepan and stick onto the base in a circle. Continue adding puffs, building them up to form a cone.

tanzanie

[chocolate/vanilla/meringue]

meringue française au chocolat

100 g (3½ oz) egg whites
100 g (3½ oz) caster (superfine) sugar
80 g (2¾ oz) pure icing (confectioners') sugar
20 g (¾ oz) unsweetened cocoa powder

Preheat the oven to 110°C (225°F/Gas ½). Line a baking tray with non-stick baking paper and mark a 24 cm (9½ inch) square, then turn the paper over.

Put the egg whites and 1 tablespoon of the caster sugar in an electric mixer with a whisk attachment and whisk on medium speed for 20 seconds or until the egg whites come halfway up the side of the bowl. With the motor running, gradually add the rest of the sugar until the meringue has formed stiff, glossy peaks (approximately 5 minutes).

Meanwhile, sift the icing sugar and cocoa together onto baking paper. Tip half into the meringue mixture and fold through gently with a spatula. Add the remaining cocoa mixture to the meringue and fold through again until just combined.

Fill a piping (icing) bag with a 10 mm (½ inch) plain nozzle with the meringue mixture. Pipe a long straight line of meringue onto the lined tray, from one edge of the marked square to the opposite edge, then pipe another line directly next to it so they are just touching. Continue to fill the marked square in this manner. Bake for 3 hours to produce a dry, crisp meringue.

vanilla crème brûlée

300 g (10½ oz) pouring (whipping) cream (35% fat)
Seeds scraped from ½ vanilla bean
66 g (2½ oz) egg yolks
60 g (2¼ oz) caster (superfine) sugar

Preheat the oven to 120°C (235°F/Gas ½). Grease a square 24 cm (9½ inch) cake tin.

Put the cream in a saucepan with the vanilla seeds and bring to the boil over medium heat. Put the egg yolks and sugar in a bowl and immediately stir to combine — you should always stir sugar and egg yolk straight away or the sugar will 'burn' the surface of the egg yolk, changing its texture. Mix in a third of the hot cream to temper the egg, then mix in the remaining cream.

Pour into the greased tin and bake for 25–30 minutes or until the brûlée is set to the touch, but still wobbles slightly when you gently tap the side of the tin. Remove from the oven and cool to room temperature. Freeze for 3 hours or until frozen through.

chocolate flourless biscuit

188 g (6¾ oz) butter, chopped and softened
88 g (3¼ oz) pure icing (confectioners') sugar, sifted
13 g (½ oz) unsweetened cocoa powder
125 g (4½ oz) dark couverture chocolate (64%),
    chopped or buttons
75 g (2¾ oz) lightly beaten egg
105 g (3½ oz) egg yolks
338 g (11¾ oz) egg whites
125 g (4½ oz) caster (superfine) sugar
80 g (2¾ oz) dark couverture chocolate (64%), extra

Preheat the oven to 170°C (325°F/Gas 3).

Cream the butter, icing sugar and cocoa in an electric mixer with a beater attachment on medium speed until light and fluffy. Melt the chocolate in a heatproof bowl over a saucepan of simmering water. Cool to 40°C (104°F), then add to the butter mixture and mix to combine. Scrape down the bowl. With the mixer on medium speed, gradually add the egg and egg yolks, mixing until well combined. Transfer the mixture to another bowl, then clean and thoroughly dry the mixer bowl as you will need it for the next step.

Put the egg whites and caster sugar in the clean mixer bowl and use the whisk attachment on medium speed to whisk for 3 minutes or until stiff peaks form. Mix a small spoonful of the meringue through the chocolate mixture, then fold through the remaining meringue, being careful not to beat out all the air.

Line 2 square 35 cm (14 inch) flat baking sheets with Silpat (see Glossary) or non-stick baking paper. Divide the mixture between the trays and use a crank-handled palette knife to smooth out evenly. Bake for 25 minutes or until they feel just set to the touch. Remove from the heat and allow to cool to room temperature.

Cut a 24 cm (9½ inch) square out of each sheet of chocolate flourless biscuit. Melt the extra chocolate in a heatproof bowl over a saucepan of simmering water. Use a crank-handled palette knife to spread a thin layer of chocolate over one of the biscuit squares and allow it to set completely. Invert the biscuit onto a large baking tray lined with non-stick baking paper, chocolate side down.

Place a square 24 cm (9½ inch) stainless-steel cake frame over the biscuit. (You could also use the frame of a square 24 cm/9½ inch spring-form tin.)

chocolate jelly

12 g (²⁄₅ oz) gold gelatine leaves
69 g (2½ oz) cold water
375 g (13 oz) water, extra
75 g (2¾ oz) unsweetened cocoa powder
130 g (4½ oz) dark couverture chocolate (64%),
    chopped or buttons
94 g (3⅓ oz) caster (superfine) sugar

Line a square 24 cm (9½ inch) cake tin with plastic wrap. Cut the gelatine leaves into small squares, place in a bowl with the cold water and set aside for 10 minutes to soak. Meanwhile, put 125 g (4½ oz) of the extra water in a saucepan with the cocoa, chocolate and sugar and stir continuously over medium heat until the sugar has dissolved and the chocolate has melted. Bring to the boil, then remove from the heat and cool to 80°C (176°F). Add the gelatine and any soaking liquid and stir until the gelatine has dissolved. Place the remaining 250 g (9 oz) water in a bowl, add the chocolate mixture and whisk to combine. Pour into the lined tin and refrigerate for 30 minutes or until the jelly has set. Place in the freezer for 3 hours or until frozen solid.

salted chocolate flakes

80 g (2¾ oz) dark couverture chocolate (64%),
    chopped or buttons, tempered (see Basics)
1 g (¹⁄₂₅ oz) sea salt flakes

Line a baking tray with non-stick baking paper. Use a crank-handled palette knife to spread the tempered chocolate over the lined tray to a thickness of 2 mm (¹⁄₁₆ inch). Sprinkle with the salt. Allow to set at room temperature for 15 minutes. (If it's a hot day you may need to use the refrigerator.)

Working quickly to avoid the chocolate melting, pick up the chocolate-lined paper and smash it over a bench, catching any stray pieces of chocolate. Keep doing this until all the chocolate ends up in pieces approximately 3–5 mm (⅛–¼ inch). Put in a bowl and set aside.

chocolate tanzanie ganache

137 g (4¾ oz) pouring (whipping) cream (35% fat)
Seeds scraped from ½ vanilla bean
12 g (²⁄₅ oz) inverted sugar (see Glossary)
112 g (3¾ oz) dark couverture chocolate Tanzanie
    (75%) (see Glossary), chopped or buttons
44 g (1¾ oz) butter, chopped and softened
Salted chocolate flakes (see recipe above)

Bring the cream and vanilla seeds just to the boil in a small saucepan over medium heat. Remove from the heat and allow to infuse for 10 minutes. Add the inverted sugar and stir over medium heat until the sugar has dissolved, then return to the boil. Put the chocolate in a bowl. Pour over the hot cream mixture and stir until completely melted and smooth. Check the temperature and cool to 50°C (122°F), then blitz in the butter with a stick mixer until thick and smooth. Fold through the salted chocolate flakes.

Spread the ganache over the chocolate biscuit layer in the cake frame. Top this with the remaining chocolate biscuit square and press down lightly to ensure it is flat against the ganache.

Lift the frozen chocolate jelly out of the tin and lay it over the biscuit. Trim the very edges of the meringue, just to neaten the square, then lay the meringue over the jelly. Pop the frozen crème brûlée out of the tin and lay it over the top of the jelly.

chocolate sabayon mousse

338 g (11¾ oz) pouring (whipping) cream (35% fat)
165 g (5¾ oz) dark couverture chocolate Tanzanie
    (75%), chopped or buttons
75 g (2¾ oz) egg yolks
49 g (1¾ oz) caster (superfine) sugar
75 g (2¾ oz) pouring (whipping) cream (35% fat), extra

Whip the cream to soft peaks, then cover and refrigerate. Melt the chocolate in a heatproof bowl over a saucepan of simmering water and allow it to cool to 45°C (113°F). It is important the chocolate is at this temperature before it is added to the cold cream or it will either set too quickly (if cooler) or melt the cream (if too hot).

Meanwhile, put the egg yolks, sugar and extra cream in a heatproof bowl over a saucepan of simmering water and whisk constantly until the mixture reaches 82°C (180°F) and is aerated and thickened. Immediately transfer to an electric mixer with a whisk attachment and whisk for 3 minutes or until cool.

Working very quickly, add all the chocolate to the cold cream and immediately whisk to combine — it needs to look like a soft chocolate whipped cream with an even colour. Fold through the cooled sabayon.

Spread a 1 cm (½ inch) thick layer of mousse over the brûlée, smoothing the surface with a crank-handled palette knife and finishing off with a thin plastic ruler to get a really smooth, even surface. Freeze for 4–6 hours to ensure it is frozen through.

chocolate decoration

400 g (14 oz) dark couverture chocolate (70%), tempered (see Basics)

Dampen the benchtop slightly with a moist cloth, place a 12 x 40 cm (4½ x 16 inch) acetate sheet (see Glossary) on it and use a clean dry cloth to smooth the sheet out. Use a crank-handled palette knife to spread the tempered chocolate over the acetate sheet until it is 2–3 mm (¹⁄₁₆–⅛ inch) thick. Holding opposite diagonal corners of the acetate, shake it gently to smooth out the chocolate. Set aside until the chocolate has set and is dry to the touch (it should still be slightly soft).

Using a ruler and the back of a paring knife, cut the chocolate into 2 x 12 cm (¾ x 4½ inch) strips. Working quickly, cover the strips with non-stick baking paper, then flip over and wrap one end of the strips over the handle of a broomstick, about 1.5 cm (⅝ inch) in diameter, laid across two chairs. Set aside to crystallise. The strips will set in the shape of a hook at one end.

to finish

1 quantity chocolate mirror glaze (see Basics)

Heat the mirror glaze in the microwave on medium (50%) for 15 seconds, then mix well and check the temperature. Continue this process until the glaze reaches 35°C (95°F).

Remove the cake from the freezer. (If you used a spring-form frame or the cake is not the same height as the frame, remove the frame now — see below for technique.) Pour the glaze onto the cake, then use a palette knife to quickly spread it over the cake, ensuring it covers the top of the cake evenly. Don't worry if some of the glaze drips down the sides of the cake, as the cake will need to be trimmed anyway. Freeze the cake again to set the glaze.

Soak a kitchen cloth in hot water and wring it out. Keeping the cake flat on the benchtop, rub the cloth in circular motions around the edge of the cake frame in order to melt the cake slightly so you can carefully slide the frame up and off. You can freeze the cake again at this stage, until the glaze is firm — this will make it easier to slice the cake cleanly and precisely.

Dip a long, sharp knife in a jug of hot water, then dry off carefully with a tea towel (dish towel) and trim about 1 cm (½ inch) from each side of the cake.

Dip the knife in the hot water and dry it off again, then mark ten 4 x 10 cm (1½ x 4 inch) rectangles over the top of the cake. Carefully cut along the lines to cut the cake into portions. Refrigerate for approximately 2 hours to defrost. Place on a serving platter or individual plates, top each with a chocolate decoration and serve.

makes 10

pineapple cubes

100 g (3½ oz) trimmed fresh pineapple,
    cut into 1 cm (½ inch) cubes
1 makrut (kaffir lime) leaf, very finely shredded
40 g (1½ oz) light palm sugar (jaggery), grated

Toss all the ingredients together in a glass or ceramic bowl until they are well combined. Cover with plastic wrap and refrigerate overnight.

coconut rice mousse

1 g (¹/₂₅ oz) gold gelatine leaves
6 g (¹/₅ oz) water
70 g (2½ oz) jasmine rice
185 g (6½ oz) pouring (whipping) cream (35% fat)
185 g (6½ oz) milk
75 g (2¾ oz) light palm sugar (jaggery), grated
50 g (1¾ oz) caster (superfine) sugar
2½ makrut (kaffir lime) leaves
25 g (1 oz) coconut milk powder (see Glossary)
185 g (6½ oz) pouring (whipping) cream (35% fat),
    extra, whipped to soft peaks

Cut the gelatine leaves into small squares, place in a bowl with the water and set aside to soak. Line a square 20 cm (8 inch) cake tin with non-stick baking paper.

Rinse the rice under cold running water and drain well. Put the rice, cream, milk, sugars, makrut leaves and coconut milk powder in a saucepan over medium heat and bring to a simmer. Reduce the heat to medium–low and simmer for 20–25 minutes, stirring occasionally at the start and continuously as it nears the end of the cooking time and has absorbed most of the liquid. The rice should still have a tiny bit of bite to it. Remove from the heat and stir in the gelatine and any soaking liquid.

Cool the mixture to 28°C (82°F), then fold through the lightly whipped cream. Pour into the lined tin and smooth the surface. Freeze for 3 hours or until frozen.

palm sugar mousse

6 g (¹/₅ oz) gold gelatine leaves
36 g (1¼ oz) cold water
220 g (7¾ oz) light palm sugar (jaggery), grated
205 g (7¼ oz) pouring (whipping) cream (35% fat)
40 g (1½ oz) simple sugar syrup (see Basics)
45 g (1¾ oz) egg yolks
210 g (7½ oz) pouring (whipping) cream (35% fat),
    extra, whipped to soft peaks

Cut the gelatine leaves into small squares, place in a bowl with the cold water and refrigerate until ready to use.

To make the caramel, put the sugar in a medium saucepan over medium heat and cook for 1 minute or until the edges start to liquefy. Cook, swirling the pan continuously, for 3 minutes or until all the sugar has liquefied. Do not stir. Continue to cook for 4 minutes or until the caramel reaches 165°C (329°F) and starts to smell like toffee.

Meanwhile, bring the cream to the boil in a small saucepan over medium heat, then remove from the heat.

When the caramel is at the right temperature, remove from the heat and stir in the hot cream mixture — watch out, it will spit and release a lot of heat.

Bring the simple sugar syrup to the boil in another small saucepan. Place the egg yolks in a bowl and beat with hand-held electric beaters on medium speed. With the beaters running, gradually pour the hot sugar syrup down the side of the bowl, mixing until it is thick and foamy, about 3 minutes. Continue beating until the egg mixture has cooled.

Heat the gelatine mixture in a heatproof bowl in the microwave for 5–10 seconds on high (100%) until liquefied (you can also do this in a heatproof bowl over a saucepan of simmering water). Add a third of the caramel, stirring until smooth, then stir this mixture into the remaining caramel until smooth.

Fold the cooled egg mixture into the extra whipped cream. Stir a spoonful of the cream and egg mixture through the caramel mixture to lighten it slightly. Then, fold the caramel mixture into the cream and egg mixture until well combined. Pour the mixture into eight rectangular (9 x 4.5 cm/3½ x 1¾ inch) flexipan silicone moulds, placed on a baking tray, and freeze for 3 hours or until frozen through.

barbados

[pineapple/coconut/palm sugar/mango]

coconut jelly

5 g (1/8 oz) gold gelatine leaves
30 g (1 oz) cold water
120 g (4¼ oz) good-quality coconut milk
50 g (1¾ oz) caster (superfine) sugar
120 g (4¼ oz) UHT coconut cream (see Glossary)

Line a square 20 cm (8 inch) cake tin with plastic wrap, extending over each side. Cut the gelatine leaves into small squares, place in a bowl with the cold water and set aside to soak.

Put half the coconut milk and all the sugar in a saucepan over medium heat and stir until the sugar has dissolved. Remove from the heat, add the gelatine and any soaking liquid and stir until dissolved. Put the coconut cream and remaining coconut milk in a bowl and add the coconut gelatine mixture, stirring to combine. Pour into the lined tin and place in the refrigerator for 1–2 hours, until set.

mango jelly

5 g (1/8 oz) gold gelatine leaves
30 g (1 oz) cold water
250 g (9 oz) sieved mango purée (see Basics)
60 g (2¼ oz) caster (superfine) sugar

When the coconut jelly has set, make the mango jelly. Cut the gelatine leaves into small squares, place in a bowl with the cold water and set aside to soak.

Heat a third of the mango purée and all the sugar in a saucepan over medium heat, stirring until the sugar has dissolved. Remove from the heat, add the gelatine and any soaking liquid and stir until dissolved. Add the rest of the mango purée and stir until well combined. Chill the mixture in the refrigerator, checking it regularly as you don't want it to set. When chilled, pour over the set coconut jelly. Drain the pineapple cubes, sprinkle over the top and refrigerate for 2½ hours or until set.

sablé breton

90 g (3¼ oz) pure icing (confectioners') sugar, sifted
80 g (2¾ oz) almond meal
175 g (6 oz) unsalted butter, chopped and softened
50 g (1¾ oz) egg yolks
125 g (4½ oz) plain (all-purpose) flour, sifted
2 g (2/25 oz) sea salt flakes

Preheat the oven to 170°C (325°F/Gas 3).

Put the icing sugar, almond meal and butter in an electric mixer with a beater attachment and beat on medium speed for 2–3 minutes or until light and fluffy. Gradually add the egg yolks, beating well between each addition. Beat in the flour and salt until just combined. Gather the dough together and place on a sheet of plastic wrap, then flatten to approximately 2 cm (¾ inch) thick. Wrap in the plastic wrap and place in the refrigerator for 2 hours or until the dough has firmed up.

Line a square 35 cm (14 inch) flat baking sheet with non-stick baking paper. Roll the pastry out on the lined tray to 6 mm (¼ inch) thick. Bake for 15–20 minutes or until the pastry is lightly golden.

Remove from the oven and cool for 3–5 minutes, then use a serrated knife to cut out eight 9 cm (3½ inch) squares and transfer to a wire rack to cool completely. (The sablé must be cut soon after it is removed from the oven, as it hardens upon cooling and may otherwise break up when cut.)

to assemble

Place the sablé squares on the benchtop. Remove both the jelly and the rice mousse from their tins and cut eight 4.5 x 9 cm (1¾ x 3½ inch) rectangles from each. Place a piece of jelly and a piece of rice mousse next to each other on each sablé square. Pop the palm sugar mousse rectangles out of the moulds and sit them on top of the rice mousse rectangles. Set aside at room temperature for 45–60 minutes or until the palm sugar mousse has defrosted, then place on a serving platter or individual plates and serve. **makes 8**

[vanilla/chocolate/almond]

vanilla glaze

10 g (¼ oz) gold gelatine leaves

60 g (2¼ oz) cold water

40 g (1½ oz) liquid glucose

35 g (1¼ oz) water, extra

250 g (9 oz) caster (superfine) sugar

400 g (14 oz) pouring (whipping) cream (35% fat)

Seeds scraped from 1 vanilla bean

150 g (5½ oz) clear neutral glaze (see Basics),
    at room temperature

8 g (¼ oz) titanium dioxide (see Glossary)

Cut the gelatine leaves into small squares, place in a bowl with the cold water and set aside to soak.

Put the glucose, extra water and sugar in a deep saucepan over medium heat and bring to the boil. Boil until the mixture reaches 165°C (329°F), but don't let it colour. Meanwhile, put the cream and vanilla seeds in another saucepan and bring to the boil. Carefully stir the hot cream into the sugar syrup — it will spit and release a lot of heat. Mix well, then cool to 70°C (158°F).

Mix in the gelatine and any soaking liquid. Blitz in the clear neutral glaze and titanium dioxide with a stick mixer. Strain into a heatproof bowl and cool to room temperature. Cover and refrigerate overnight to set.

vanilla crème chantilly

4 g (⁴⁄₂₅ oz) gold gelatine leaves

24 g (⁹⁄₁₀ oz) cold water

590 g (1 lb 4¾ oz) pouring (whipping) cream (35% fat)

Seeds scraped from 1 vanilla bean

175 g (6 oz) caster (superfine) sugar

Cut the gelatine leaves into small squares, place in a bowl with the cold water and set aside to soak.

Put the cream, vanilla seeds and sugar in a saucepan over medium heat and bring to the boil. Remove from the heat and cool to 70–80°C (158–176°F). Add the gelatine and any soaking liquid and mix to combine. Place in a container and cool to room temperature, then cover and refrigerate overnight.

vanilla water gel

125 g (4$\frac{1}{2}$ oz) caster (superfine) sugar
250 g (9 oz) water
1.6 g ($\frac{1}{20}$ oz) gellan (see Glossary)
Seeds scraped from 1 vanilla bean

Line a square 18 cm (7 inch) cake tin with plastic wrap. Put all the ingredients in a saucepan over medium heat and whisk continuously until the mixture comes to the boil. Pour into the lined tin and place in the refrigerator to set. Once set, place in the freezer to set hard.

toasted vanilla brûlée

66 g (2$\frac{1}{2}$ oz) egg yolks
50 g (1$\frac{3}{4}$ oz) dark brown sugar
250 g (9 oz) pouring (whipping) cream (35% fat)
Seeds scraped from 1 vanilla bean
14 g ($\frac{1}{2}$ oz) natural vanilla extract

Preheat the oven to 160°C (315°F/Gas 2–3).

Put the egg yolks and sugar in a bowl and mix until just combined. Put the cream and vanilla seeds in a saucepan over medium heat and bring to the boil. Remove from the heat and pour a third of the hot cream into the egg mixture. Mix well, then pour in the remaining hot cream and mix again. Blitz with a stick mixer to spread the vanilla seeds through the mixture.

Pour into a 15 x 20 cm (6 x 8 inch) baking dish and bake for 13 minutes or until just set. Increase the oven temperature to 200°C (400°F/Gas 6) and bake for a further 5 minutes or until there is a golden-brown crust on top. Remove from the oven and cool completely.

Scrape the cooled brûlée into a bowl, then blitz with a stick mixer until smooth and glossy. Cover and place in the refrigerator until required.

vanilla ganache

185 g (6$\frac{1}{2}$ oz) pouring (whipping) cream (35% fat)
Seeds scraped from 1 vanilla bean
14 g ($\frac{1}{2}$ oz) natural vanilla extract
300 g (10$\frac{1}{2}$ oz) white couverture chocolate, chopped
95 g (3$\frac{1}{3}$ oz) unsalted butter, chopped and softened

Put the cream, vanilla seeds and vanilla extract in a saucepan over medium heat and bring to the boil. Put the chocolate in a bowl. Pour over the hot cream and set aside for 2 minutes. Stir until the mixture is smooth, then cool to 50°C (122°F). Blitz in the butter using a stick mixer until smooth. Allow to cool.

vanilla syrup

62 g (2$\frac{1}{5}$ oz) caster (superfine) sugar
125 g (4$\frac{1}{2}$ oz) water
Seeds scraped from $\frac{1}{4}$ vanilla bean
3.5 g ($\frac{1}{8}$ oz) natural vanilla extract

Put all the ingredients in a small saucepan over medium heat and bring to the boil. Remove from the heat. Cool.

vanilla macaron

52 g (1$\frac{3}{4}$ oz) egg whites
50 g (1$\frac{3}{4}$ oz) pure icing (confectioners') sugar, sifted
75 g (2$\frac{3}{4}$ oz) pure icing (confectioners') sugar, extra, sifted
Seeds scraped from $\frac{1}{2}$ vanilla bean
75 g (2$\frac{3}{4}$ oz) ground almonds, sifted

Line a baking tray with non-stick baking paper. Put the egg whites in an electric mixer with a whisk attachment and whisk on medium speed until soft peaks form. Gradually add the 50 g (1$\frac{3}{4}$ oz) of icing sugar, whisking well between each addition. Continue whisking until the meringue has formed stiff, glossy peaks. Mix the extra icing sugar, vanilla seeds and ground almonds together, then gently fold into the meringue. Spread out on the lined tray to an 18 cm (7 inch) square. Set aside at room temperature for 30 minutes or until a skin forms. After 10 minutes, preheat the oven to 160°C (315°F/Gas 2–3). Bake the macaron for 12 minutes, until golden. Remove from the oven and leave on the tray to cool completely.

vanilla dacquoise

60 g (2$\frac{1}{4}$ oz) egg whites
42 g (1$\frac{1}{2}$ oz) caster (superfine) sugar
65 g (2$\frac{1}{3}$ oz) ground almonds
40 g (1$\frac{1}{2}$ oz) pure icing (confectioners') sugar
Seeds scraped from 1 vanilla bean
1.5 g ($\frac{1}{20}$ oz) natural vanilla extract
10 g ($\frac{1}{4}$ oz) pure icing (confectioners') sugar, extra, for dusting

Preheat the oven to 180°C (350°F/Gas 4). Line a baking tray with non-stick baking paper and mark an 18 cm (7 inch) square, then turn the paper over.

Put the egg whites in an electric mixer fitted with a whisk attachment and whisk on medium speed until soft peaks form. Gradually add the caster sugar, mixing well between each addition. Continue mixing until the meringue has formed stiff, glossy peaks. Sift the ground

almonds and icing sugar together, then gently fold through the meringue. Fold the vanilla seeds and vanilla extract through the meringue. Fill a piping (icing) bag with a 7 mm ($^3/_8$ inch) plain nozzle with the dacquoise and, using the marked square as a guide, pipe long strips onto the lined tray, with each strip touching the next so the dacquoise completely covers the square on the baking paper. Dust with extra icing sugar and set aside for 2 minutes. Dust again and bake for 10–12 minutes or until golden. Set aside on the tray to cool completely.

brown sugar crumble

50 g (1$^3/_4$ oz) plain (all-purpose) flour, sifted
50 g (1$^3/_4$ oz) chilled unsalted butter, chopped
50 g (1$^3/_4$ oz) dark brown sugar
50 g (1$^3/_4$ oz) ground almonds
Seeds scraped from $^1/_4$ vanilla bean

Put all the ingredients in an electric mixer with a beater attachment. Mix on low speed until combined, then continue mixing until the mixture resembles a dough. Gather the dough together and wrap in plastic wrap, then refrigerate for 1$^1/_2$ hours or until firm and chilled.

Preheat the oven to 180°C (350°F/Gas 4). Line a baking tray with non-stick baking paper. Use a coarse grater to grate the dough over the lined tray. Bake for 8–10 minutes or until golden. Cool on the tray.

vanilla & almond crunch

2 large vanilla beans
45 g (1$^3/_4$ oz) milk couverture chocolate
90 g (3$^1/_4$ oz) almond praline (see Hazelnut praline in Basics)
90 g (3$^1/_4$ oz) almond paste (see Pistachio paste in Basics)
17 g ($^3/_5$ oz) unsalted butter
45 g (1$^3/_4$ oz) brown sugar crumble (see recipe above)
45 g (1$^3/_4$ oz) pailleté feuilletine (see Glossary)
17 g ($^3/_5$ oz) toasted slivered almonds, chopped
2 g ($^2/_{25}$ oz) sea salt flakes
Seeds scraped from $^1/_4$ vanilla bean

Preheat the oven to 200°C (400°F/Gas 6). Put the vanilla beans on a baking tray and bake for 30 minutes or until they look burnt and are dry and crisp. Cool, then put in a spice grinder and blend to a fine powder.

Melt the chocolate in a heatproof bowl over a saucepan of simmering water or in the microwave. Add the almond praline and almond paste and mix well.

Melt the butter in a small saucepan, then cook it until it is brown and nutty. Cool slightly.

Mix the crumble and pailleté feuilletine into the chocolate mixture, then fold through the burnt butter, vanilla bean dust, chopped almonds, salt and vanilla seeds. Spread evenly over the dacquoise and set aside.

vanilla chiffon cake

35 g (1$^1/_4$ oz) plain (all-purpose) flour, sifted
Seeds scraped from 4 vanilla beans
55 g (2 oz) egg yolks
10 g ($^1/_4$ oz) dark brown sugar
35 g (1$^1/_4$ oz) water
30 g (1 oz) canola oil
90 g (3$^1/_4$ oz) egg whites
45 g (1$^3/_4$ oz) caster (superfine) sugar
5 g ($^1/_8$ oz) rice flour

Preheat the oven to 160°C (315°F/Gas 2–3). Line a square 35 cm (14 inch) flat baking sheet with non-stick baking paper.

Put the plain flour, vanilla seeds, egg yolks, brown sugar, water and oil in a bowl and mix well. Put the egg whites in an electric mixer with a whisk attachment and whisk on medium speed until soft peaks form. Gradually add the sugar and rice flour, whisking well between each addition. Continue whisking until the whites have reached the consistency of a firm meringue. Gently fold a small amount of the meringue into the cake batter, then gently fold in the remaining meringue — try to retain the maximum amount of air in the mixture.

Spread the cake batter onto the lined tray to a thickness of 6 mm ($^1/_4$ inch) and bake for 15–20 minutes, until golden. Cool completely on the tray, then trim to make an 18 cm (7 inch) square.

white choc flower

700 g (1 lb 9 oz) white couverture chocolate, chopped or buttons, tempered (see Basics)
10 g ($^1/_4$ oz) titanium dioxide (see Glossary)
50 g (1$^3/_4$ oz) white couverture chocolate, chopped or buttons, tempered (see Basics), extra

Combine the tempered chocolate and titanium dioxide in a plastic bowl. Blitz with a stick mixer until combined and the chocolate is pure white.

Dampen the benchtop slightly with a moist cloth, then put a 30 x 40 cm (12 x 16 inch) acetate sheet (see Glossary) on it and use a clean dry cloth to smooth it out.

Use a crank-handled palette knife to spread 350 g (12 oz) of the chocolate mixture over the acetate until 2–3 mm ($\frac{1}{16}$–$\frac{1}{8}$ inch) thick. Holding opposite diagonal corners of the acetate, pull tight and shake gently to smooth out the chocolate. Repeat with another acetate sheet and the remaining chocolate.

While the second sheet is setting, the first sheet should be dry to the touch, yet still pliable. Using a ruler and the back of a paring knife, cut it into 5 cm (2 inch) squares, or 'tiles'. Cover with non-stick baking paper, then flip over and place a baking tray on top to prevent the chocolate bending as it crystallises and sets.

When the second sheet is dry to the touch, cut it into four 10 cm (4 inch) strips, then cut each strip into thin triangles. Do not separate them. Cover with non-stick baking paper and, starting at a corner, roll the acetate sheet around a rolling pin until it is all rolled up. Secure with adhesive tape and set aside to crystallise and set.

Unroll the acetate sheet — the triangles, or 'petals', will fall off. Using a chocolate tile as a base and small dots of the extra tempered chocolate to adhere the petals, start building the flower. Begin in the centre with 4 petals, then continue to build it up and out. Set aside.

water drops

300 g ($10\frac{1}{2}$ oz) sparkling mineral water
3 g ($\frac{1}{10}$ oz) algin (see Glossary)
18 g ($\frac{2}{3}$ oz) caster (superfine) sugar
500 g (1 lb 2 oz) sparkling mineral water, extra
3.5 g ($\frac{1}{8}$ oz) calcium carbonate (see Glossary)

Put the water, algin and sugar in a bowl and blitz with a stick mixer to combine. Refrigerate for 1 hour.

Place the extra water and calcium carbonate in a bowl and blitz with a stick mixer to combine. Use a large syringe to drop the algin mixture, 1 drop at a time, into the calcium carbonate mixture. Use a tea strainer to carefully scoop out the drops and then rinse them well under cold running water.

to assemble

Place a square 18 cm (7 inch) stainless-steel cake frame on a baking tray lined with non-stick baking paper. (You could also use a square 18 cm/7 inch cake tin.) Place the vanilla dacquoise covered with vanilla & almond crunch inside the frame.

Spread with a 1 cm ($\frac{1}{2}$ inch) thick layer of vanilla ganache, smoothing it with a small crank-handled palette knife. Place in the freezer until firm.

Lay the vanilla chiffon cake over the ganache and press down gently. Use a pastry brush to brush some vanilla syrup over the cake. Spread the toasted vanilla brûlée over the cake, using a crank-handled palette knife to smooth it out to the edges. Place the vanilla macaron over the brûlée, gently pressing it into place. Place the vanilla water gel over the macaron. Place in the freezer for 3 hours, until firm.

Place a square 20 cm (8 inch) stainless-steel cake frame on a baking tray lined with non-stick baking paper (or use a square 20 cm/8 inch cake tin, lined with acetate cut to fit each surface and adhered with a dab of water). Place the vanilla crème chantilly in an electric mixer with a whisk attachment and whisk on medium speed until soft peaks form. Use a piping (icing) bag with an 11 mm ($\frac{2}{5}$ inch) nozzle to pipe a 1 cm ($\frac{1}{2}$ inch) thick layer of chantilly into the frame. Use a palette knife to spread more chantilly over the sides, approximately 1 cm ($\frac{1}{2}$ inch) thick. Remove the assembled cake from the freezer. Use hot water and a cloth to rub the frame or tin until it releases the cake.

Carefully place the cake in the chantilly-lined frame or tin, with the gel layer on the bottom. Gently push the cake down — the chantilly should be pushed up the sides, leaving no gaps. The chantilly lining and dacquoise should be level. Freeze the cake for 3–4 hours to firm up.

Heat the vanilla glaze in the microwave on medium (50%) for 15 seconds, mix well and check the temperature. Repeat this process until the glaze reaches 30–35°C (86–95°F).

Place a wire rack over a large sheet of plastic wrap. Remove the cake from the freezer and invert it onto the wire rack, then use hot water and a cloth to remove the frame or tin. Remove the acetate. Pour the glaze over the cake, allowing it to run down the sides. Smooth the surface with a palette knife. Use the knife to dab glaze onto any bare spots. Set aside for a few minutes to allow the excess glaze to drip off. Carefully slide a large palette knife under the cake and transfer it to a serving plate.

Holding a tile in each hand, press them onto opposite sides of the cake. Pressing 2 tiles on at the same time will help you line them up neatly. Continue pressing on tiles, 2 at a time, until there are 4 tiles on each side of the cake. Arrange the chocolate flower and water drops on top of the cake. Allow the cake to defrost for at least 3 hours in the refrigerator before serving. **serves 16**

mustard crème anglaise

40 g (1½ oz) milk
112 g (3¾ oz) pouring (whipping) cream (35% fat)
Seeds scraped from 2 vanilla beans
48 g (1¾ oz) egg yolks
18 g (⅔ oz) lightly beaten egg
16 g (½ oz) caster (superfine) sugar
16 g (½ oz) honey (such as Tasmanian leatherwood)
12 g (⅖ oz) cocoa butter (see Glossary), finely chopped
30 g (1 oz) dijon mustard

Bring the milk, cream and vanilla seeds to the boil in a saucepan over medium heat. Whisk the egg yolks, egg, sugar and honey in a bowl until thick and pale. Pour over the hot cream mixture while mixing gently with a whisk. Transfer to a clean saucepan and stir continuously over medium heat until the mixture reaches 85°C (185°F) or is thick enough to coat the back of a spoon.

Meanwhile, melt the cocoa butter in a very small saucepan over low heat and cool to 32°C (90°F). Add to the anglaise with the mustard and whisk to combine. Strain into a chilled bowl. Cool slightly, then cover with plastic wrap, pressing it onto the surface to prevent a skin forming and refrigerate for 30 minutes or until chilled.

You will need twenty-four 2 cm (¾ inch) diameter demisphere flexipan silicone mould cavities, placed on a baking tray. Use a balloon whisk to whisk the anglaise until smooth, then use it to fill all the mould cavities. Freeze for 2 hours or until frozen.

dukkah

50 g (1¾ oz) sesame seeds
100 g (3½ oz) chopped pistachio nuts
10 g (¼ oz) ground coriander
5 g (⅛ oz) ground cumin
Pinch each of salt and freshly ground black pepper
Pinch of cayenne pepper

Place all the ingredients in a bowl and stir to combine.

dukkah pâte sablé a choux

150 g (5½ oz) dark brown sugar
150 g (5½ oz) unsalted butter, chopped and softened
1 g (1/25 oz) sea salt flakes
175 g (6 oz) plain (all-purpose) flour, sifted
20 g (¾ oz) dukkah (see recipe below left)

Put all the ingredients in an electric mixer with a beater attachment and beat on low to medium speed until the mixture comes together to form a paste. Wrap in plastic wrap, flatten to a 2 cm (¾ inch) disc and refrigerate for 1 hour or until the paste is firm.

Unwrap and roll out on non-stick baking paper to 3 mm (⅛ inch) thickness all over, then refrigerate again until firm. Use a round 6 cm (2½ inch) cutter to stamp out 12 discs. Place on a baking tray lined with non-stick baking paper and refrigerate until ready to use.

choux pastry

½ quantity choux pastry (see Croque-en-bouche recipe, page 164)
Plain (all-purpose) flour, for dipping cutter

Preheat the oven to 210°C (415°F/Gas 6–7). Lightly butter 2 large baking trays, then wipe off any excess with a paper towel.

Dip a round 6 cm (2½ inch) cutter into some plain flour, then stamp it on the trays to form 12 outlines, leaving a 3 cm (1¼ inch) gap between each to allow for spreading. Fill a piping (icing) bag with an 11 mm (⅖ inch) plain nozzle with the choux pastry. Hold the bag over the centre of a circle, about 2 cm (¾ inch) above the tray, and slowly but firmly pipe the mixture down, without moving the bag from this position. The pastry will spread towards the edge of the circle outline — stop just before it reaches the edge and turn the bag to 12 o'clock, then quickly swipe around and off at 6 o'clock. Lightly place a dukkah pâte sablé a choux disc on top of each choux round.

Bake for 20–25 minutes or until the puffs are golden. It is important not to open the oven door until the choux pastry has a good colour, otherwise you can halt the rising of the pastry, resulting in eventual collapse. Once the pastry is golden, reduce the oven temperature to 120°C (235°F/Gas ½) and cook for a further 10 minutes. This will extract any residual moisture in the choux so it stays nice and crisp. Choux pastry should always feel light when you lift it up — if it is heavy, it needs more cooking time. Cool the puffs on the trays.

alessia, i like big buns

[honey mustard/pistachio/raspberry]

pistachio crunchy

20 g (¾ oz) cocoa butter (see Glossary), finely chopped

90 g (3¼ oz) almond praline (see Hazelnut praline in Basics)

90 g (3¼ oz) pistachio praline (see Hazelnut praline in Basics)

60 g (2¼ oz) pailleté feuilletine (see Glossary)

11 g (²⁄₅ oz) pistachio nuts, finely chopped

Pinch of sea salt flakes

5 g (⅛ oz) freeze-dried passionfruit powder (see Glossary)

Melt the cocoa butter in a very small saucepan over low heat, then cool to 32°C (90°F). Put both the pralines in a bowl and mix in the cocoa butter, then the remaining ingredients. Tip the loose mixture onto a sheet of non-stick baking paper, then place another sheet on top and roll out to 4 mm (⅙ inch) thick. Transfer to a baking tray and refrigerate for 1 hour. Use a round 6 cm (2½ inch) cutter to stamp out 12 discs, then return to the refrigerator until ready to use.

pistachio mousseline

270 g (9½ oz) unsalted butter, chopped and softened

100 g (3½ oz) pistachio paste (see Basics)

730 g (1 lb 9¾ oz) crème pâtissiére (see Croque-en-bouche recipe, page 164, make ½ quantity and use the remainder in another recipe)

1–2 drops green food colouring (optional)

Cream the butter and pistachio paste in an electric mixer with a beater attachment for 3 minutes or until light and fluffy. Add the crème pâtissiére and mix to combine. If you choose to colour the mousseline, mix in the food colouring until an even light-green hue. Set aside until ready to use.

to assemble

84 fresh raspberries

80 g (2¾ oz) vanilla glaze (see V8 recipe, page 178)

A few drops of yellow food colouring

Carefully split the choux puffs in half to form a top and base. Fill a piping (icing) bag with a 9 mm (⅓ inch) plain nozzle with the pistachio mousseline and pipe an 8 mm (⅜ inch) layer onto the base of each puff. Place a pistachio crunchy disc on top of each. Pipe another 8 mm (⅜ inch) layer of mousselline to cover each disc. Arrange 7 raspberries around the circumference of the mousseline on each puff, ensuring they're evenly spaced.

Pop 2 demispheres of mustard anglaise out of the mould and sandwich the flat sides together (they will automatically stick together). Place in the very centre of the mousseline on one of the puffs. Hold the piping bag about 5 mm (¼ inch) above the anglaise sphere and pipe down, keeping the bag still until the mousseline is high enough to meet the height of the raspberries. Repeat with the remaining demispheres of mustard anglaise, piping mousseline over each. Cover each with a puff top.

Heat the vanilla glaze in a heatproof bowl over a saucepan of simmering water to 35°C (95°F), then colour with yellow food colouring. Use a small teaspoon to drop 8 dots of yellow vanilla glaze of random sizes on top of each puff. Allow to set for 10 minutes, then place on a serving platter or individual plates and serve.

makes 12

escape from a colombian rainforest

[cherry/cola/chocolate]

cherry cola jelly

7.5 g (¼ oz) gold gelatine leaves
45 g (1¾ oz) cold water
125 g (4½ oz) sieved cherry purée (see Basics)
250 g (9 oz) cola soft drink
6 pitted fresh cherries

Cut the gelatine leaves into small squares, place in a bowl with the cold water and set aside to soak.

Combine the cherry purée and cola. Put a quarter of the cola mixture in a saucepan and heat to 60°C (140°F). Add the gelatine and any soaking liquid and mix until the gelatine has dissolved. Add the remaining cola mixture.

You will need six 4 cm (1½ inch) diameter, 1.5 cm (⅝ inch deep) flexipan silicone mould cavities, placed on a baking tray. Fill the cavities with cherry cola jelly, right to the top, and press a cherry into the centre of each. Refrigerate for 1 hour to set, then transfer to the freezer for 3 hours or until frozen solid. Cut the jellies in half horizontally so you now have 12 discs of cherry jelly.

cola cherry slurp

130 g (4½ oz) cola
130 g (4½ oz) sieved cherry purée (see Basics)
5 g (⅛ oz) cola extract (see Glossary)
31 g (1 oz) caster (superfine) sugar
0.5 g (1/50 oz) iota (see Glossary)

Put all the ingredients in a saucepan and blitz with a stick mixer to combine. Bring to the boil over medium heat, then remove from the heat and set aside to cool.

flourless chocolate biscuits

90 g (3¼ oz) dark couverture chocolate (50%), chopped or buttons
75 g (2¾ oz) unsalted butter, chopped and softened
35 g (1¼ oz) pure icing (confectioners') sugar, sifted
5 g (⅛ oz) unsweetened cocoa powder, sifted
30 g (1 oz) lightly beaten egg
42 g (1½ oz) egg yolks
135 g (4¾ oz) egg whites
50 g (1¾ oz) caster (superfine) sugar

Preheat the oven to 170°C (325°F/Gas 3). Line a square 35 cm (14 inch) flat baking sheet with non-stick baking paper.

Melt the chocolate in a heatproof bowl over a saucepan of simmering water or in the microwave. Remove from the heat and cool to 40°C (104°F).

Cream the butter, icing sugar and cocoa in an electric mixer with a beater attachment for 2 minutes, until fluffy. Add the melted chocolate and mix well. Add the egg and eggs yolks a little at a time, mixing well between each addition. Transfer the mixture to a large bowl and clean the mixer bowl, ensuring you dry it thoroughly.

Put the egg whites in the mixer bowl and use the whisk attachment to whisk until foamy. Gradually add the sugar, whisking well between each addition. Continue whisking for 5 minutes or until the meringue has formed stiff, glossy peaks.

Fold a small amount of meringue into the chocolate mixture to lighten it, then gently fold in the remaining meringue, taking care not to beat out all the air.

Spoon the mixture onto the lined tray and use a crank-handled palette knife to smooth out to a thickness of 5 mm (¼ inch). Bake for 15–20 minutes or until set to the touch. Remove from the oven and allow to cool, then use a round 6 cm (2½ inch) cutter to stamp out 12 discs.

gassy fizzer discs

15 g (½ oz) bicarbonate of soda (baking soda)
20 g (¾ oz) citric acid (see Glossary)
500 g (1 lb 2 oz) dark couverture chocolate (64%), chopped or buttons, tempered (see Basics)

Line 2 baking trays with non-stick baking paper. Stir the bicarbonate of soda and citric acid through the tempered chocolate. Spread out on the lined trays to 1 mm (2/25 inch) thick. Leave at room temperature to set (if it is hot, you may need to use the refrigerator). Use a round 6 cm (2½ inch) cutter to stamp out 36 discs. Place in an airtight container, layered with non-stick baking paper, until required.

chocolate sabayon mousse

745 g (1 lb 10 oz) pouring (whipping) cream (35% fat)
365 g (12¾ oz) dark couverture chocolate (64%), chopped or buttons
165 g (5¾ oz) egg yolks
108 g (3¾ oz) caster (superfine) sugar
165 g (5¾ oz) pouring (whipping) cream (35% fat), extra

Whip the cream until soft peaks form, then cover and refrigerate. Melt the chocolate in a heatproof bowl over a saucepan of simmering water, then cool to 45°C (113°F). The chocolate needs to be at this temperature before it is added to the cold cream or it will either set too quickly (if cooler) or melt the cream (if too hot).

Meanwhile, put the egg yolks, sugar and extra cream in a heatproof bowl over a saucepan of simmering water and whisk constantly until the mixture reaches 82°C (180°F) and is aerated and thickened. Immediately transfer to an electric mixer with a whisk attachment and whisk for 3 minutes or until cool.

Working very quickly, add all the chocolate to the cold cream and immediately whisk to combine — it needs to look like a soft chocolate whipped cream with an even colour. Fold through the cooled sabayon.

to assemble

12 chocolate cups (3.5 x 1.5 cm/$1^2/_5$ x $^5/_8$ inch) (see Glossary)

300 g ($10^1/_2$ oz) cocoa butter (see Glossary), finely chopped

30 g (1 oz) red lipid-soluble food colouring (see Glossary)

Line a baking tray with non-stick baking paper and place twelve 7 cm ($2^3/_4$ inch) diameter, 4.5 cm ($1^3/_4$ inch) deep rings on the tray. Lightly spray the inside of each ring with cooking oil.

Place a biscuit disc in each ring. Fill a piping (icing) bag with a 9 mm ($^1/_3$ inch) plain nozzle with the chocolate sabayon mousse. Pipe a 1 cm ($^1/_2$ inch) layer of mousse onto the biscuit in each ring. Using a palette knife, push the mousse up the side of each ring so the inner surface of the ring is covered with mousse. Place a cherry cola jelly on the mousse in the base of each ring. Pipe another 1 cm ($^1/_2$ inch) layer of mousse so the jelly is covered. Place a gassy fizzer disc on the mousse and gently press it down. Pipe another 1 cm ($^1/_2$ inch) layer of mousse over the top. Place another gassy fizzer disc on top and gently press it down. Pipe a 1.5 cm ($^5/_8$ inch) layer of mousse on top. Press a chocolate cup into the mousse in each ring, they should sit snugly inside the mousse. Fill the cups with cooled cola cherry slurp. Pipe more mousse over the top so it rises 7 mm ($^3/_8$ inch) above each ring. Smooth the mousse with a palette knife so that the tops are flat. Gently run your finger around the edge of each ring, creating a small indent above the top. Place a gassy fizzer disc on top of the mousse in each ring. Place in the freezer for 4 hours or until frozen solid.

Soak a kitchen cloth in hot water and wring it out, then rub it in circular motions around each ring in order to melt the mousse slightly so you can carefully slide the rings off. Arrange the cakes in a single line on 2 baking trays, with a 5 cm (2 inch) gap between each.

Melt the cocoa butter in a saucepan over medium heat, then remove from the heat and add the colouring. Blitz with a stick mixer to combine, then cool to 32°C (90°F). Strain through a fine sieve into a wagner (see Glossary) and seal with the lid. Holding the spray gun 20 cm (8 inches) from the cakes, spray from left to right in an even fluid motion until coated all over, then turn and spray the other side, ensuring all the surfaces are sprayed. Freeze for 1 minute, then spray on one more coating of spray. Place in the refrigerator to defrost for approximately 2 hours before serving. **makes 12**

decoration (optional)

500 g (1 lb 2 oz) dark couverture chocolate (64%), chopped or buttons, tempered (see Basics)

Edible silver metallic dust (see Glossary)

Pour the tempered chocolate into 12 silicone can lid moulds and leave at room temperature to set. Pop the chocolates from the moulds and place on non-stick baking paper. Use a clean, dry paintbrush to brush the chocolates with silver metallic dust. Place on top of the sprayed cakes, then place on a serving platter or individual plates and serve.

what a great pear of...

[pear/apple/almond]

pâte sablé a choux

150 g (5½ oz) brown sugar

150 g (5½ oz) butter, chopped and softened

175 g (6 oz) plain (all-purpose) flour

4 g (⁴/₂₅ oz) leaf-green gel food colouring (see Glossary)

Place all the ingredients in an electric mixer with a beater attachment and begin mixing on low speed until just combined. Increase the speed to medium and mix for 2 minutes. Gather the dough together and place on a sheet of plastic wrap, then flatten to approximately 2 cm (¾ inch) thick. Wrap up and place in the refrigerator for 2 hours or until the dough has firmed up.

pear & vanilla crème pâtissiére

420 g (15 oz) sieved pear purée (see Basics)

420 g (15 oz) apple juice

Seeds scraped from ¼ vanilla bean

210 g (7½ oz) egg yolks

210 g (7½ oz) caster (superfine) sugar

105 g (3½ oz) cornflour (cornstarch)

125 g (4½ oz) butter, chopped and softened slightly

Put the pear purée, apple juice and vanilla seeds in a saucepan over medium heat and bring just to the boil, then remove from the heat. Whisk together the egg yolks, sugar and cornflour in a bowl until thick and pale, then gradually whisk in the hot pear mixture. Return the mixture to the pan and whisk continuously over medium heat until the mixture comes to the boil. Boil, still whisking, for 1 minute.

Place the crème pâtissiére in a bowl and cover with plastic wrap, pressing it onto the surface to prevent a skin forming. Cool to 50°C (122°F), then whisk in the butter, until smooth. Cover with plastic wrap as before and place in the refrigerator to cool completely.

pear gel

35 g (1¼ oz) sugar

335 g (11¾ oz) sieved pear purée (see Basics)

1 g (¹/₂₅ oz) gellan (see Glossary)

7 g (¼ oz) pectin NH (see Glossary)

Place 25 g (1 oz) of the sugar in a saucepan with the pear purée and gellan and blitz with a stick mixer until combined. Bring to 60°C (140°F) over medium heat. Combine the remaining sugar and the pectin, then add to the 60°C (140°F) pear purée and mix well. Bring to the boil and boil for 1 minute. Divide among twelve

4 cm (1½ inch) diameter, 1.5 cm (⁵/₈ inch) deep flexipan silicone mould cavities, placed on a baking tray, and then refrigerate to set.

almond crème puffs

100 g (3½ oz) almond crème (see Basics)

Preheat the oven to 180°C (350°F/Gas 4). Fill a piping (icing) bag with a 9 mm (⅓ inch) plain nozzle with the almond crème. Pipe the crème into twelve 2.5 cm (1 inch) diameter demisphere flexipan silicone mould cavities, placed on a baking tray, so the cavities are all three-quarters full. Bake in the oven for 10–12 minutes or until the puffs are golden brown. Set aside at room temperature to cool.

choux pastry

200 g (7 oz) unsalted butter, chopped

10 g (¼ oz) sugar

215 g (7½ oz) water

270 g (9½ oz) milk

10 g (¼ oz) salt

270 g (9½ oz) plain (all-purpose) flour,
    plus extra, for dipping cutter

366 g (13 oz) lightly beaten egg

1 g (¹/₂₅ oz) electric-green gel colouring

1 quantity pâte sablé a choux (see recipe above)

Preheat the oven to 210°C (415°F/Gas 6–7).

Combine the butter, sugar, water, milk and salt in a heavy-based saucepan and bring to the boil. Remove from the heat and quickly beat in the flour with a wooden spoon. Return the pan to the heat and continue beating until the mixture comes together and leaves the side of the pan. Beat over low heat for a further 1–2 minutes to cook the flour, then remove from the heat and allow to cool slightly.

Transfer the mixture to an electric mixer with a beater attachment and begin beating the mixture on medium speed to release some of the heat.

Add the egg gradually, beating between each addition until well incorporated. Add the colouring with the last amount of egg and continue beating until thick and glossy — a spoon should stand upright in it.

Lightly butter a baking tray, then wipe off any excess with a paper towel. Dip a round 6 cm (2½ inch) cutter in some flour, then stamp it on the tray to form 12 outlines, leaving a 3 cm (1¼ inch) gap between each to allow for spreading. Fill a piping (icing) bag with an 11 mm

(²/₅ inch) plain nozzle with the choux pastry. Hold the bag over the centre of a circle, about 2 cm (³/₄ inch) above the tray, and slowly but firmly pipe down, without moving the bag from this position. The pastry will spread towards the edge of the circle outline — stop just before it reaches the edge and turn the bag to 12 o'clock, then quickly swipe around and off at 6 o'clock.

Lightly butter another baking tray, wiping off the excess with a paper towel. Repeat the above process using a round 3.5 cm (1²/₅ inch) cutter, making 12 outlines and filling with choux pastry as before.

Remove the pâte sablé a choux from the refrigerator and roll out on a lightly floured benchtop or between 2 sheets of non-stick baking paper, to 3 mm (¹/₈ inches) thick. Using a round 6 cm (2¹/₂ inch) cutter, stamp out 12 discs, then use a round 3.5 cm (1²/₅ inch) cutter to stamp out 12 discs. Lightly place the discs on the choux pastry balls, the larger ones on the larger choux and the smaller ones on the smaller choux.

Bake for 20–25 minutes or until the puffs are golden. It is important not to open the oven door until the choux pastry has a good colour, otherwise you can halt the rising of the pastry, resulting in eventual collapse. Once the pastry is golden, reduce the oven temperature to 120°C (235°F/Gas ¹/₂) and cook for a further 10 minutes. This will extract any residual moisture in the choux so it stays nice and crisp. Choux pastry should always feel light when you lift it up — if it is heavy, it needs more cooking time. Cool the puffs on the trays.

almond crunch

48 g (1³/₄ oz) dark couverture chocolate (70%),
   chopped or buttons
24 g (⁹/₁₀ oz) unsalted butter, chopped
45 g (1³/₄ oz) almond praline (see Hazelnut praline
   in Basics)
210 g (7¹/₂ oz) streusel (see Basics)
45 g (1³/₄ oz) whole blanched almonds, crushed
Pinch of sea salt flakes

Melt the chocolate and butter in a bowl over a saucepan of simmering water, then remove from the heat and add the almond praline. Mix well, then add the remaining ingredients and mix until well combined.

Place twelve 7 cm (2³/₄ inch) diameter egg rings on a baking tray lined with non-stick baking paper. Press the mixture into the rings, smoothing the surface with the back of a spoon. Place in the refrigerator to set.

caramelised almonds

100 g (3¹/₂ oz) caster (superfine) sugar
20 g (³/₄ oz) water
15 toasted blanched almonds
1 g (¹/₂₅ oz) cocoa butter (see Glossary), finely chopped

Place the sugar and water in a small saucepan over medium heat and stir to combine. Bring to 121°C (250°F), then remove from the heat and add the almonds — the mixture will crystallise. Return to the heat and cook until caramelised, then add the cocoa butter and stir to combine. Spread on a baking tray lined with non-stick baking paper to cool.

green chocolate squares

6 g (¹/₅ oz) green lipid-soluble food colouring
   (see Glossary)
350 g (12 oz) white couverture chocolate,
   chopped or buttons, tempered (see Basics)

Add a small amount of green colouring to the tempered chocolate and mix well. Repeat until the colour is right.

Dampen the benchtop slightly with a moist cloth, then put a 30 x 40 cm (12 x 16 inch) acetate sheet (see Glossary) on it and use a clean dry cloth to smooth it out. Use a crank-handled palette knife to spread the chocolate mixture over the acetate until 2 mm (¹/₁₆ inch) thick. Holding opposite diagonal corners of the acetate, pull tight and shake gently to smooth out the chocolate.

When the chocolate is dry to the touch, yet still pliable, quickly mark into 5 cm (2 inch) squares using a paring knife and ruler. Cover with non-stick baking paper, then flip over and place a baking tray on top to prevent the chocolate bending as it crystallises. Leave to set completely.

green marzipan

300 g (10½ oz) marzipan
2 g (²/₂₅ oz) leaf-green gel food colouring (see Glossary)

Place the marzipan on the benchtop and add the colouring. Knead the marzipan until it is a uniform green (wear disposable gloves to stop your hands turning green). Roll out the marzipan between two sheets of non-stick baking paper to 2 mm (¹/₁₆ inch) thick, then use a round 6 cm (2½ inch) cutter to stamp out 12 discs.

pear mousse

660 g (1 lb 7 oz) pear & vanilla crème pâtissiére
    (see recipe on page 193)
400 g (14 oz) mascarpone cheese
240 g (8½ oz) pouring (whipping) cream (35% fat)

Place the crème pâtissiére and mascarpone in an electric mixer with a beater attachment and beat on medium speed until there are no lumps. Transfer to another bowl and clean the mixer bowl for the next step.
    Place the cream in the mixer bowl and use the whisk attachment to whisk until soft peaks form. Gently fold the whipped cream through the crème pâtissiére mixture, taking care not to beat out all the air.

to assemble

Pure icing (confectioners') sugar, to dust

Fill a piping (icing) bag with a 9 mm (¹/₃ inch) plain nozzle with the remaining pear & vanilla crème pâtissiére. Poke a small hole in the base of a small choux puff and fill it three-quarters full with pear & vanilla crème pâtissiére. Push an almond crème puff into the crème pâtissiére. Repeat to fill the remaining small choux puffs. Dust lightly with icing sugar.
    Fill a piping bag with a 9 mm (¹/₃ inch) plain nozzle with the pear mousse. Poke a small hole in the base of a large choux puff and fill three-quarters full with the mousse. Gently push a piece of pear gel into the mousse. Repeat to fill the remaining large choux puffs.
    Now, put the components together. Pipe a small ball of pear & vanilla crème pâtissiére between each component to attach them — it should not be visible. Place an almond crunch disc on a serving plate. Top with a large choux puff, then a green marzipan disc, a square of green chocolate, a small choux puff and finish with a caramelised almond. Place on a serving platter or individual plates and serve. **makes 12**

desserts

**team zumbo
gentlemen's
bowling league**

back row, from left: wagyu steak; cereal killa; no soup for you;
doggy style; gibbo & zumb's australian adventure; schnitzel
front row, from left: black rose; clancy, the rain's a comin'

Desserts are like an artist's palette, creating a movement or design of a memory on a plate. Colour, shape, flavour and design are key.

We don't sell desserts in the shop, but I make them for functions, demonstrations, competitions and master classes. Something I really love about desserts is that they're 'à la minute'. You plate them and people eat them straight away, giving you the freedom to use softer, more fragile textures that enhance the eating experience.

I've also made desserts for TOYS dinners. TOYS stands for Taste of Young Sydney, a group of young chefs I am part of. We have a dinner every three months or so, with the aim of promoting up-and-coming young chefs by giving them a chance to express their creativity to the public. Most of them work under more prominent chefs, so they're a bit hidden in their day-to-day jobs.

wagyu steak

wasabi pea crunch

25 g (1 oz) dark couverture chocolate (70%),
    chopped or buttons
5 g ($\frac{1}{8}$ oz) cocoa butter (see Glossary), finely chopped
10 g ($\frac{1}{4}$ oz) whole wasabi peas
2 g ($\frac{2}{25}$ oz) sesame seeds, toasted
35 g ($1\frac{1}{4}$ oz) chocolate-flavoured cereal
    (such as puffed rice or corn flakes)
4 g ($\frac{4}{25}$ oz) candied grapefruit peel (see Basics),
    very finely chopped
1 g ($\frac{1}{25}$ oz) sea salt flakes
150 g ($5\frac{1}{2}$ oz) isomalt (see Glossary)
15 g ($\frac{1}{2}$ oz) water

Line a baking tray with non-stick baking paper. Melt the chocolate and cocoa butter in a heatproof bowl over a saucepan of simmering water or in the microwave. Stir in the wasabi peas, sesame seeds, cereal, candied grapefruit and salt.

Put the isomalt and water in a saucepan and stir occasionally over medium heat until the isomalt has dissolved. Continue cooking until the mixture reaches 170°C (338°F). Remove from the heat and stir into the chocolate mixture. Pour over the lined tray and spread out using a spatula. Set aside to cool completely.

red wine caramel

50 g ($1\frac{3}{4}$ oz) liquid glucose
250 g (9 oz) caster (superfine) sugar
155 g ($5\frac{1}{2}$ oz) red wine
55 g (2 oz) pouring (whipping) cream (35% fat)
100 g ($3\frac{1}{2}$ oz) unsalted butter, chopped and softened
3 g ($\frac{1}{10}$ oz) agar-agar (see Glossary)
3 g ($\frac{1}{10}$ oz) xanthan gum (see Glossary)

Line a baking tray with non-stick baking paper. Place the glucose, sugar and 100 g ($3\frac{1}{2}$ oz) of the red wine in a saucepan over medium–high heat and stir until the sugar has dissolved. Boil for 10–12 minutes or until the mixture reaches 165°C (329°F) — it will start to smell like red wine toffee.

Meanwhile, put the cream, remaining red wine and butter in a separate saucepan and bring to the boil over medium heat. Remove from the heat, add the agar-agar and xanthan gum and blitz with a stick mixer until smooth. When the red wine caramel has reached 165°C (329°F), remove it from the heat and use a small whisk to slowly whisk in the warm cream mixture until well combined. Pour onto the lined tray and set aside to cool completely.

burnt wasabi mayonnaise brûlée

250 g (9 oz) pouring (whipping) cream (35% fat)
15 g ($\frac{1}{2}$ oz) wasabi powder (see Glossary)
Seeds scraped from $\frac{1}{4}$ vanilla bean
60 g ($2\frac{1}{4}$ oz) egg yolks
50 g ($1\frac{3}{4}$ oz) caster (superfine) sugar
125 g ($4\frac{1}{2}$ oz) Japanese mayonnaise (see Glossary)

Preheat the oven to 160°C (315°F/Gas 2–3). Put the cream, wasabi powder and vanilla seeds in a saucepan and bring to the boil over medium heat. Put the egg yolks and sugar in a bowl and mix with a small balloon whisk to just combine. Strain a little of the hot cream over the egg mixture and mix until smooth, then strain over the remaining hot cream, stirring until smooth. Pour into a square 15 cm (6 inch) cake tin and bake for 20 minutes or until set. Increase the oven temperature to 200°C (400°F/Gas 6) and cook for a further 8 minutes or until deep golden with a toasty aroma. Remove and cool to room temperature. Spoon the cooled brûlée into a food processor, add the mayonnaise and process until smooth.

suspended custard

200 g (7 oz) milk
10 g ($\frac{1}{4}$ oz) cornflour (cornstarch)
10 g ($\frac{1}{4}$ oz) full-cream milk powder
1.6 g ($\frac{1}{20}$ oz) xanthan gum (see Glossary)
5 g ($\frac{1}{8}$ oz) natural vanilla extract
20 g ($\frac{3}{4}$ oz) caster (superfine) sugar

Line a baking tray with non-stick baking paper. Put all the ingredients in a saucepan and blitz with a stick mixer until smooth, then stir continuously over medium heat until the mixture reaches 85°C (185°F) — it will be thick and gluggy. Remove from the heat. Spread half the mixture onto the lined tray to a thickness of 4 mm ($\frac{1}{6}$ inch) and set aside. Use the remaining mixture to fill a piping (icing) bag with a 2 mm ($\frac{1}{16}$ inch) plain nozzle. You will need twelve 4 cm ($1\frac{1}{2}$ inch) diameter, 3 cm ($1\frac{1}{4}$ inch) deep flexipan mould cavities, placed on a baking tray. Pipe abstract squiggles into each cavity, to resemble the marbling of fat through meat. Set aside.

blackcurrant sponge jelly

100 g (3½ oz) sieved blackcurrant purée (see Basics)

10 g (¼ oz) caster (superfine) sugar

2 g (²⁄₂₅ oz) gellan (see Glossary)

30 g (1 oz) chocolate flourless biscuit (see Tanzanie
    recipe, page 169), processed into crumbs

20 g (¾ oz) flourless almond & orange cake (see Celia's
    act recipe, page 134), processed into crumbs

100 g (3½ oz) sieved raspberry purée (see Basics)

Put the blackcurrant purée, sugar and gellan in a saucepan and stir over medium heat until the sugar has dissolved, then bring to the boil. Remove from the heat and fold through the biscuit and cake crumbs. Allow to cool to room temperature and set, then put the blackberry mixture in a food processor with the raspberry purée and process until smooth.

raspberry water

100 g (3½ oz) sieved raspberry purée (see Basics)

100 g (3½ oz) sparkling mineral water

Combine both ingredients and set aside.

to assemble

Fill a piping (icing) bag with a 9 mm (⅓ inch) plain nozzle with the blackcurrant sponge jelly. Pipe a walnut-sized ball over the 'fat' marbling in the moulds, ensuring each ball is centred over the base. Take a small palette knife and spread the sponge jelly from the centre outwards and up the side of the mould all the way around, forming a hollow in the centre but ensuring the base is covered.

Put a teaspoonful of red wine caramel into each hollow, then spoon in enough of the burnt wasabi mayonnaise brûlée to come almost to the top of the moulds. Break the wasabi pea crunch into pieces just big enough to fit in the top of the moulds and press down lightly so that it is level with the top edge of the sponge jelly. Freeze for 2 hours or until frozen through, then turn out of the moulds. Cut 3 x 12.5 cm (1¼ x 4¾ inch) strips of the suspended custard and wrap around the outside edge of each. Place a tablespoon of raspberry water on each serving plate and top with a piece of 'wagyu'. **makes 12**

doggy style

lemon & vanilla sorbet

50 g (1¾ oz) freshly squeezed and strained lemon juice

Seeds scraped from 1 vanilla bean

325 g (11½ oz) water

125 g (4½ oz) caster (superfine) sugar

1 g (¹⁄₂₅ oz) pectin NH (see Glossary)

1 g (¹⁄₂₅ oz) xanthan gum (see Glossary)

Put all the ingredients in a saucepan and stir over medium heat until the sugar has dissolved. Continue cooking until the mixture reaches 85°C (185°F), then remove from the heat and cool to room temperature. Churn in an ice-cream machine according to the manufacturer's instructions, then freeze until required.

chocolate isomalt bones

200 g (7 oz) isomalt (see Glossary)

20 g (¾ oz) water

20 g (¾ oz) cocoa mass (see Glossary)

Preheat the oven to 180°C (350°F/Gas 4). Line a baking tray with non-stick baking paper or Silpat (see Glossary).

Put the isomalt and water in a heavy-based saucepan over medium heat and stir occasionally until the isomalt has dissolved. Continue cooking until the isomalt syrup reaches 170°C (338°F), then add the cocoa mass and stir until the mixture is combined and smooth. Carefully pour onto the lined tray and set aside at room temperature to cool completely.

Take a piece of cardboard approximately 20 x 30 cm (8 x 12 inches) and trace around a bone-shaped cutter (4.5 cm/1¾ inches long x 2.5 cm/1 inch wide) 14 times, keeping the shapes evenly spaced. (You only need 12 but this allows for breakages.) Cut out the bone shapes using a box cutter or Stanley knife and discard. This will leave you with a template with 14 bone-shaped holes.

Break up the cooled isomalt mixture and place in a food processor. Process to a fine dust.

Grease a baking tray and line with non-stick baking paper or Silpat. Place the template over the lined tray and sift enough isomalt powder onto each bone-shaped hole to make an even layer, 2 mm (1/16 inch) thick. Carefully lift off the cardboard template.

Bake the isomalt bones for 10 minutes or until the powder melts and comes together — it will look shiny and smooth, like opaque chocolate glass. Remove from the oven and cool to room temperature. Line an airtight container with non-stick baking paper and carefully place the bones inside in single layers, layered with non-stick baking paper so they don't stick to one another. Seal with the lid until ready to serve. The isomalt bones will keep for up to 1 week when stored this way.

chocolate sablé

142 g (5 oz) chilled unsalted butter, cut into small dice
1 g (1/25 oz) sea salt flakes
155 g (5½ oz) plain (all-purpose) flour, sifted
30 g (1 oz) unsweetened cocoa powder
94 g (3⅓ oz) caster (superfine) sugar
25 g (1 oz) lightly beaten egg

Put the butter, salt, flour, cocoa and sugar in an electric mixer with a beater attachment and beat on medium speed until the mixture resembles coarse breadcrumbs. Add the egg and mix until just combined. Gather together into a ball, place on plastic wrap and pat down to a 2 cm (¾ inch) thick disc. Wrap up and refrigerate for 2 hours or until well chilled and firm.

Preheat the oven to 160°C (315°F/Gas 2–3). Line a baking tray with non-stick baking paper.

Roll out the dough between 2 sheets of non-stick baking paper to a thickness of 6 mm (¼ inch).

Use the bone-shaped cutter to stamp out bone shapes from the dough. Transfer to the lined tray and bake for 12–16 minutes or until dry to the touch. Pull a bone out, let it cool, snap it and then eat it — if it is not crisp to snap and does not have a short, melt-in-the-mouth texture when eaten, you will need to cook them for a minute or so more.

Leave the bones on the trays until cooled completely, then store in an airtight container until ready to use. (You will have more biscuits than you need, but they will keep for several days and can be eaten simply as they are.)

lemon meringue bones

50 g (1¾ oz) egg whites
50 g (1¾ oz) caster (superfine) sugar
50 g (1¾ oz) pure icing (confectioners') sugar, sifted
Finely grated zest of 1 lemon

Preheat the oven to 50°C (122°F). Spray 12 bone-shaped cutters (4.5 cm/1¾ inches long x 2.5 cm/1 inch wide) lightly with cooking oil and put on a square 35 cm (14 inch) baking sheet lined with non-stick baking paper.

Put the egg whites in an electric mixer with a whisk attachment and whisk on medium speed until foamy. Gradually add the sugar while whisking continuously. Continue to whisk for a further 2 minutes or until you have a shiny, firm meringue.

Remove the bowl from the mixer and use a rubber spatula to fold through the icing sugar and lemon zest. Fill a piping (icing) bag with a 3 mm (1/10 inch) plain nozzle with the meringue and pipe into each bone-shaped cutter to a depth of 8 mm (3/8 inch). Lift off the cutters.

Cook for 3–4 hours or until dry and crisp, but not coloured. Remove from the oven and cool completely. Transfer to an airtight container until ready to use.

coconut foam

5 g (⅛ oz) gold gelatine leaves
30 g (1 oz) cold water
500 g (1 lb 2 oz) UHT coconut cream (see Glossary)
50 g (1¾ oz) caster (superfine) sugar

Cut the gelatine leaves into small squares, place in a bowl with the water and set aside for 10 minutes to soak.

Meanwhile, put a quarter of the coconut cream and the sugar in a very small saucepan and stir over medium–low heat until the sugar has dissolved. Continue cooking until the mixture reaches 80°C (176°F), then remove from the heat. Add the gelatine and any soaking liquid and stir until the gelatine has dissolved. Stir into the remaining coconut cream, then place in the refrigerator until the mixture is completely cold.

Pour the mixture into a 500 ml (17 fl oz) cream canister (see Glossary) and charge with two N_2O bulbs. Refrigerate for at least 2 hours or until ready to use.

coconut & caramel kennels

500 g (1 lb 2 oz) dark couverture chocolate (70%), chopped or buttons, tempered (see Basics)
150 g (5½ oz) caster (superfine) sugar
60 g (2¼ oz) water
30 g (1 oz) liquid glucose
110 g (3¾ oz) UHT coconut cream (see Glossary)
10 g (¼ oz) coconut milk powder (see Glossary)
Pinch of sea salt

You will need twelve 3.2 cm (1²⁄₅ inch) diameter igloo-shaped polycarbonate mould cavities. Pour the tempered chocolate into the cavities and use a wide chocolate spatula to scrape off any excess from the top of the mould sheet in one quick, smooth movement. Tap the sheet on the bench to expel any excess air — you don't want tiny air bubbles in the chocolate. Then flip the mould sheet over a clean wide bowl, allowing the excess chocolate to spill into the bowl. Turn the sheet the right way up and scrape again with the spatula.

Lay two thin rods (such as chopsticks) parallel on a silicone mat. Turn the mould sheet upside down over the mat, laying it on the rods so it doesn't sit directly on the mat. Leave for 1 minute, then turn the sheet the right way up and use the spatula one final time to remove the last remnants of excess chocolate. Allow the chocolate to dry for 15 minutes.

Hold the mould sheet up to the light — if there are any see-through patches you will need to repeat the whole process again (on top of what you have already done). Gently reheat the tempered chocolate by directing a heat gun or hair dryer at the surface of the chocolate, stirring until it is just liquid again. When you're finished, leave the chocolate to set for 15 minutes as before. (Reserve the remaining chocolate for sealing the chocolates after they have been filled.)

Put the sugar, water and glucose in a deep saucepan over medium heat and stir until the sugar has dissolved. Continue cooking until the caramel reaches 200°C (400°F) and is dark amber in colour.

Meanwhile, put the coconut cream, coconut milk powder and salt in a heavy-based saucepan and bring to the boil over medium heat. When the caramel has reached 200°C (400°F), remove it from the heat and carefully whisk in the hot coconut cream mixture until smooth — watch out, it will spit and release a lot of heat.

Pour the caramel into a heatproof container and cool to room temperature. When cool, use it to fill a piping (icing) bag with a 5 mm (¼ inch) plain nozzle. Pipe the caramel into the chocolate-lined moulds, finishing 2 mm (¹⁄₁₆ inch) from the top of each. Set aside at room temperature overnight to allow a skin to form (if your kitchen is hot, place it in the refrigerator).

Gently reheat the tempered chocolate by directing a heat gun or hair dryer at the surface of the chocolate, stirring until it is just liquid again. Fill the top of the moulds with chocolate, ensuring you seal the chocolate completely. Scrape the top of the mould sheet with the chocolate spatula to remove the excess in one quick, smooth movement. Set aside until cool and the chocolate is dry to the touch.

warm coconut agar bones

250 g (9 oz) UHT coconut cream (see Glossary)
10 g (¼ oz) caster (superfine) sugar
1 g (¹⁄₂₅ oz) agar-agar (see Glossary)

Put the coconut cream, sugar and agar-agar in a saucepan and blitz with a stick mixer until smooth. Place over medium heat, stirring continuously until the mixture comes to the boil.

Put 12 bone-shaped cutters (4.5 cm/1¾ inches long x 2.5 cm/1 inch wide) on a baking tray lined with non-stick baking paper. Pour the coconut liquid into each to a depth of 8 mm (³⁄₈ inch). Leave at room temperature for 2 hours or until cooled and set, then lift off the cutters.

banana yogi

65 g (2¹⁄₃ oz) ripe banana
A few drops of lemon juice
250 g (9 oz) milk
5 g (¹⁄₈ oz) xanthan gum (see Glossary)

Mash the banana and lemon juice together in a bowl until smooth. Add the milk and xanthan gum and blitz with a stick mixer until smooth and thickened — the mixture will look like wobbly custard. Set aside at room temperature until ready to use.

chocolate sauce

100 g (3½ oz) dark couverture chocolate (64%),
    chopped or buttons
100 g (3½ oz) milk
100 g (3½ oz) pouring (whipping) cream (35% fat)
10 g (¼ oz) unsweetened cocoa powder, sifted

Put the chocolate in a bowl. Combine the milk, cream
and cocoa in a saucepan and place over medium heat,
mixing occasionally with a small whisk, until the mixture
comes to the boil. Pour the hot milk mixture over the
chocolate and stir until melted and smooth. Set aside
until ready to use.

chocolate fondant

20 g (¾ oz) butter, softened, for greasing
Unsweetened cocoa powder, sifted, for coating
150 g (5½ oz) dark couverture chocolate (70%),
    chopped or buttons
150 g (5½ oz) unsalted butter, chopped
155 g (5½ oz) lightly beaten egg
55 g (2 oz) egg yolks
85 g (3 oz) caster (superfine) sugar
13 g (⅖ oz) plain (all-purpose) flour, sifted

Preheat the oven to 200°C (400°F/Gas 6). Liberally
grease twelve 5.5 cm (2¼ inch) diameter, 4 cm (1½ inch)
deep mini ramekins with the softened butter. Tip in
some cocoa powder and turn the ramekins until evenly
coated with the cocoa. Tap out any excess and place the
ramekins on baking trays.

    Melt the chocolate and butter in a heatproof bowl
over a saucepan of simmering water.

    Put the egg, egg yolks and sugar in an electric mixer
with a whisk attachment and mix on medium speed for
6 minutes or until tripled in volume. Remove the bowl
from the mixer and gradually pour in the chocolate
mixture while stirring with a whisk until well combined.
Use a rubber spatula to fold through the flour.

    Fill a piping (icing) bag with a 7 mm (⅜ inch) plain
nozzle with fondant mixture and pipe into the ramekins,
filling them to 2 mm (1/16 inch) below the top edge.
Refrigerate for approximately 1 hour, until chilled.

    Bake the fondants for 8–10 minutes or until they
are just set on top, but still wobble in the middle when
you tap lightly on the side of the ramekins.

to assemble

Blackened vanilla bean dust (see Blackened vanilla
    bean macaron recipe, page 22, made using
    1 vanilla bean)

While the fondants are cooking, place the coconut
& caramel kennels in the refrigerator for a few minutes
to help release them from the moulds. Place a kennel
and a spoonful of chocolate sauce in the base of each
of 12 metal dog bowls. Arrange the meringue and sablé
bones around the bowl.

    Heat a saucepan of water to 60°C (140°F). Carefully
lower the coconut agar bones into the water for a few
seconds to warm through. Lift out with a slotted spoon.
Put a dollop of banana yogi next to the chocolate sauce.
Add the warm coconut agar bones and isomalt bones.

    When the fondants are ready, remove from the oven
and, working quickly but carefully, immediately turn out
and place one in each bowl. Use two tablespoons to form
quenelle shapes of sorbet and place one in each bowl.
Shake the cream canister and use it to pipe an amount
of foam the size of a golf ball into each bowl. Sprinkle
with blackened vanilla dust and serve. **serves 12**

cereal killa

milk anglaise

150 g (5½ oz) milk

200 g (7 oz) pouring (whipping) cream (35% fat)

30 g (1 oz) full-cream milk powder

Seeds scraped from 2 vanilla beans

80 g (2¾ oz) egg yolks

85 g (3 oz) caster (superfine) sugar

Put the milk, cream, milk powder and vanilla seeds in a saucepan and stir over medium heat until the milk powder has dissolved. Bring to the boil.

Meanwhile, put the egg yolks and sugar in a bowl and mix with a small balloon whisk until thick and pale. Gradually strain the hot milk mixture over the egg mixture while stirring continuously with the whisk. Return the mixture to the pan and stir continuously over medium heat for 2–3 minutes or until the mixture reaches 85°C (185°F) and easily coats the back of a spoon.

Remove from the heat, pour into a container and cover with plastic wrap, pressing it onto the surface to prevent a skin forming. Refrigerate for 3 hours or until completely cold.

milk crunchy

200 g (7 oz) plain sweet biscuits

300 g (10½ oz) cocoa butter (see Glossary), chopped

200 g (7 oz) honey and nut-flavoured cornflakes

Line a baking sheet with non-stick baking paper. Put the biscuits in a food processor and process until they are in roughly 5 mm (¼ inch) pieces. (Alternatively, bash them with a rolling pin.) Melt the cocoa butter in a saucepan over low heat, then when the temperature is at 32°C (90°F), combine it with the biscuits and cereal. Spread the mixture onto the tray and refrigerate for 1 hour or until firm.

condensed milk jelly

4 g ($^4/_{25}$ oz) gold gelatine leaves
24 g (1 oz) cold water
250 g (9 oz) milk
75 g (2$^3/_4$ oz) condensed milk

Cut the gelatine leaves into small squares, place in a bowl with the water and set aside for 15 minutes to soak.

Put a quarter of the milk in a saucepan and bring to the boil. Remove from the heat, add the gelatine and any soaking liquid and stir until dissolved. Add the remaining milk and condensed milk and stir until combined. Pour into a container and refrigerate for 3 hours or until set.

milk bottle chantilly

2 g ($^2/_{25}$ oz) gold gelatine leaves
12 g ($^2/_5$ oz) cold water
285 g (10 oz) pouring (whipping) cream (35% fat)
85 g (3 oz) milk bottle lollies

Cut the gelatine leaves into small squares, place in a bowl with the water and set aside for 15 minutes to soak.

Put the cream and milk bottles in a saucepan and bring to the boil. Stir until the milk bottles have dissolved. Remove from the heat and cool slightly, then add the gelatine and any soaking liquid. Strain into a bowl and chill for 2–3 hours or until completely cold.

cereal milk yolk balls

25 g (1 oz) gold gelatine leaves
25 g (1 oz) caster (superfine) sugar
250 g (9 oz) water
6 g ($^1/_5$ oz) titanium dioxide (see Glossary)
500 g (1 lb 2 oz) milk
100 g (3$^1/_2$ oz) honey and nut-flavoured cornflakes
4 g ($^4/_{25}$ oz) xanthan gum (see Glossary)

Cut the gelatine leaves into small squares and soak in a bowl of cold water for 5 minutes or until just softened and pliable. Remove from the water and squeeze out any excess. Discard the water.

Put the sugar and the 250 g (9 oz) water in a saucepan and stir over medium heat until the sugar has dissolved. Continue to cook until the mixture reaches 80°C (176°F), then remove from the heat, add the squeezed gelatine leaves and stir until they have dissolved. Add the titanium dioxide and blitz with a stick mixer until the mixture is consistently white.

Set aside at room temperature for about 3 hours or until the mixture has solidified.

Put the milk and cereal in a bowl and soak for 3 hours at room temperature to infuse the cereal flavour into the milk. (If your kitchen is hot, you will need to do this in the refrigerator and it will take a bit longer.) Strain into another bowl, pressing the cereal to extract all the milk. Add the xanthan gum to the strained milk and blitz with a stick mixer until smooth and thick.

You will need seventy 2 cm ($^3/_4$ inch) diameter demisphere flexipan silicone mould cavities, placed on a baking tray. Fill a piping (icing) bag with a 4 mm ($^1/_6$ inch) plain nozzle with the milk mixture and pipe into the cavities. Freeze for 3 hours or until frozen through.

Warm the solidified gelatine mixture to 28°C (82°F). Use toothpicks to lift the frozen demispheres out of the mould and sandwich them together to make circles. Dip them in the gelatine mixture to cover completely. Set aside on a baking tray lined with non-stick baking paper.

to assemble

Use a balloon whisk to whisk the milk anglaise until smooth, then pour into twelve 150 ml (5 fl oz) glasses, approximately 5–6 cm (2–2$^1/_2$ inches) in diameter, to make a 1.5 cm ($^5/_8$ inch) thick layer on the base.

Lightly whip the milk bottle chantilly and use to fill a piping (icing) bag with a 4 mm ($^1/_6$ inch) plain nozzle. Pipe the chantilly in a 1.5 cm ($^5/_8$ inch) layer around the edge of the glass so it sits on top of the anglaise. Break the milk crunchy into small pieces and add enough to each cup to form a 1.5 cm ($^5/_8$ inch) layer. Use a teaspoon to scoop condensed milk jelly from the container, adding enough to each glass to cover the milk crunchy layer.

Top with a few more pieces of the milk crunchy, then place 2–3 cereal milk yolk balls in each cup to cover the surface. Serve. **serves 12**

schnitzel

garlic & almond praline

1 large garlic bulb
45 g (1¾ oz) milk couverture chocolate,
    chopped or buttons
90 g (3¼ oz) almond praline (see Hazelnut praline
    in Basics)
Blackened vanilla bean dust (see Blackened
    vanilla bean macaron recipe, page 22,
    made using 2 vanilla beans)
90 g (3¼ oz) pailleté feuilletine (see Glossary)
20 g (¾ oz) whole blanched almonds, roasted and
    coarsely chopped
90 g (3¼ oz) almond paste (see Pistachio paste in Basics)
20 g (¾ oz) unsalted butter, melted

Preheat the oven to 180°C (350°F/Gas 4). Wrap the
bulb of garlic in a double layer of foil and roast for
2 hours. Squeeze out the flesh and mash with the back
of a fork to a smooth paste. Weigh out 20 g (¾ oz).

Melt the chocolate in a heatproof bowl over a
saucepan of simmering water or in the microwave.
Add the praline and mix well, then add the vanilla dust,
pailleté feuilletine, chopped almonds, almond paste and
20 g (¾ oz) garlic paste. Mix again until well combined,
then fold through the melted butter. Set aside.

coconut dacquoise

32 g (1 oz) ground almonds
40 g (1½ oz) pure icing (confectioners') sugar, sifted
32 g (1 oz) desiccated coconut
60 g (2¼ oz) egg whites
45 g (1¾ oz) caster (superfine) sugar
Pure icing (confectioners') sugar, extra, for dusting

Preheat the oven to 180°C (350°F/Gas 4). Line two
square 35 cm (14 inch) baking sheets with non-stick
baking paper.

Combine the ground almonds, icing sugar and
coconut in a bowl. Put the egg whites and sugar in an
electric mixer with a whisk attachment and whisk on
medium speed for 4 minutes or until the mixture forms
firm, glossy peaks. Remove the bowl from the mixer
and fold in the coconut mixture.

Divide the dacquoise mixture between the lined
trays, spreading out each to an even 7 mm (⅜ inch)
thickness. Dust with the extra icing sugar and bake for
10–12 minutes or until lightly golden. Remove from
the oven and cool completely on the trays.

apple purée

2 granny smith apples
40 g (1½ oz) water
20 g (¾ oz) caster (superfine) sugar
2 g (²⁄₂₅ oz) iota (see Glossary)

Peel and core the apples, then chop the flesh into rough
2 cm (¾ inch) squares. Place in a saucepan with the
water and cover with plastic wrap so it is airtight. Cook
over medium heat for 10 minutes or until the apple is
soft, but not breaking up. Remove from the heat and set
aside, still covered, for 10 minutes.

Blitz the apple with a stick mixer until smooth, then
set aside to cool. Place in the refrigerator for 1 hour to
chill. Blitz in the sugar and iota with a stick mixer until
combined. Bring to the boil over medium heat, stirring
continuously. Boil for 30 seconds to thicken slightly. Set
aside to cool completely, then refrigerate until required.

coconut crème

1.5 g (¹⁄₂₀ oz) iota (see Glossary)
160 g (5⅔ oz) lightly beaten egg
192 g (6¾ oz) caster (superfine) sugar
40 g (1½ oz) milk
88 g (3¼ oz) UHT coconut cream (see Glossary)
6 g (⅕ oz) coconut milk powder (see Glossary)
200 g (7 oz) unsalted butter, chopped and softened

Put the iota, egg, sugar, milk, coconut cream and
coconut milk powder in a bowl and blitz with a stick
mixer until smooth. Place in a saucepan over medium
heat and stir occasionally until the mixture reaches
85°C (185°F). Remove from the heat and cool to 50°C
(122°F), then blitz in the butter with a stick mixer until
smooth. Cover with plastic wrap, pressing it onto the
surface to prevent a skin forming. Refrigerate for 2 hours
or until completely cold.

rose & mandarin gel and sauce

1 g (¹⁄₂₅ oz) iota (see Glossary)
100 g (3½ oz) water
100 g (3½ oz) caster (superfine) sugar
50 g (1¾ oz) mandarin juice
50 g (1¾ oz) rosewater
2 g (²⁄₂₅ oz) xanthan gum (see Glossary)
100 g (3½ oz) mandarin juice, extra

Place the iota, water and sugar in a saucepan and blitz
with a stick mixer to combine. Bring to the boil, then

remove from the heat and add the mandarin juice, rosewater and xanthan gum. Blitz with a stick mixer again to combine well. Set aside to cool completely.

Place a quarter of the rose and mandarin gel in a small bowl, add the extra mandarin juice and stir to combine (this will make your sauce for serving). Set both mixtures aside, at room temperature, until required.

potato marshmallow mash

9 g (¼ oz) gold gelatine leaves
54 g (2 oz) cold water
165 g (5¾ oz) caster (superfine) sugar
40 g (1½ oz) inverted sugar (see Glossary)
25 g (1 oz) water, extra
30 g (1 oz) liquid glucose
43 g (1¾ oz) inverted sugar, extra
13 g (²/₅ oz) cocoa butter (see Glossary), finely chopped
200 g (7 oz) mashed cooked potato (no other
    ingredients added), pushed through a sieve,
    at room temperature
100 g (3½ oz) unsalted butter, chopped
150 g (5½ oz) pouring (whipping) cream (35% fat)
10 g (¼ oz) blackened vanilla bean dust (see Blackened
    vanilla bean macaron recipe, page 22, made using
    4 vanilla beans)

Cut the gelatine leaves into small squares, place in a bowl with the water and set aside for 10 minutes to soak.

Put the caster sugar, inverted sugar, extra water and glucose in a saucepan over medium heat and stir until all the sugar has dissolved. Cook until the mixture reaches 113°C (235°F). Melt the cocoa butter in a very small saucepan over low heat and cool to 32°C (90°F).

Place the extra inverted sugar in an electric mixer fitted with a whisk attachment. With the motor running on medium speed, slowly pour the 113°C (235°F) sugar mixture down the side of the bowl in a steady stream, mixing until the sugar has dissolved and the mixture is smooth. Add the gelatine and any soaking liquid. Continue to whisk on medium speed for 4 minutes or until light and fluffy.

When the mixture is around 40°C (104°F), slowly mix in the 32°C (90°F) melted cocoa butter. Remove the bowl from the mixer and then fold through the mashed cooked potato. Add the butter and cream and use a whisk to mix until smooth. Stir in the blackened vanilla bean dust until well combined. Set aside at room temperature until required.

thyme crumbs

200 g (7 oz) fresh white breadcrumbs
50 g (1¾ oz) caster (superfine) sugar
4 g (⁴/₂₅ oz) sea salt flakes
15 g (½ oz) thyme leaves, finely chopped
15 g (½ oz) rosemary leaves, finely chopped
Finely grated zest of 3 lemons
Seeds scraped from 1 vanilla bean

Put all the ingredients in a bowl and mix until well combined. Set aside.

to assemble

Olive oil, for shallow-frying

Draw a schnitzel shape, approximately 5 cm (2 inches) long and 4 cm (1½ inches) wide at the thickest part, on a piece of non-stick baking paper. Cut out the schnitzel shape and discard. This will leave you with a template with a schnitzel-shaped hole.

Spread a 5 mm (¼ inch) layer of garlic & almond praline over a sheet of dacquoise. Place the template on the other sheet of dacquoise and use a small sharp knife to cut out 12 schnitzel shapes. Repeat with the dacquoise coated in praline to make 12 more 'schnitzels'.

Fill a piping (icing) bag with a 7 mm (³/₈ inch) plain nozzle with coconut crème. Pipe a ring of coconut crème around the edge of each praline-coated schnitzel — it should be about 2 mm (¹/₁₆ inch) in from the outer edge of the dacquoise. Fill the middle of the ring with apple purée, then place the plain dacquoise schnitzels on top, pressing down lightly to adhere. Transfer to a tray and refrigerate for 2 hours or until cold.

Put the rose & mandarin gel in a bowl and place the thyme crumbs on a plate. Put these side by side on the benchtop. Dip a schnitzel in the gel to lightly coat all over, then transfer to the crumb plate and coat completely, patting the crumbs on lightly to help them adhere. Transfer to a tray and repeat to coat the remaining schnitzels.

Pour enough olive oil into a large non-stick frying pan to come 6 mm (¼ inch) up the side of the pan. Place over medium heat and when the oil is hot, cook the schnitzels, in batches, for 1 minute per side or until lightly golden. Transfer to paper towels to drain.

Put the potato marshmallow mash into a 500 ml (17 fl oz) cream canister (see Glossary) and charge with two N₂O bulbs. Pipe some mash onto each serving plate, add 2 schnitzels and drizzle with the rose & mandarin sauce to serve. **makes 12**

THE LAB

SUGAR PIES

INDUSTRY ARENA
THURSDAY APRIL 13TH 8 PM

ZUMBO

..VANILLA.CA
.TARTS.ECLA
RAMEL.PASTRIES
INS.BISCUITS.
LAIRS..MACARONS
RIES.MUFFINS.CAKES.SU
OLATE.VANILLA.TARTS.COOKIES.SWEETS
.CARAMEL.ECLAIRS.ALMON
.CARAMEL.SUGAR.CAKES.

MAGNETIC MUFFINS
FRIDAY 13th
THE LAB

SUGA PIES

INDUSTRY AR
THURSDAY APRIL 13

LV
E
UM
I LO
ZUMB
OVEZU
I LOVE

MACARONS LIVE FRI 21st

BAKE MORE CAKE

ZUMBO

clancy, the rain's a comin'

vanilla & saffron crème

500 g (1 lb 2 oz) pouring (whipping) cream (35% fat)
0.5 g (¹/₅₀ oz) saffron threads
Seeds scraped from 1 vanilla bean
130 g (4½ oz) egg yolks
100 g (3½ oz) caster (superfine) sugar

Preheat the oven to 120°C (235°F/Gas ½). Put the cream, saffron and vanilla seeds in a saucepan and bring to the boil over medium heat. Remove from the heat. Put the egg yolks and sugar in a bowl and mix together with a small balloon whisk. Strain the hot cream onto the egg mixture while stirring continuously to combine well. Pour into a square 25 cm (10 inch) cake tin and bake for 20 minutes or until set. Remove from the oven and allow to cool slightly, then refrigerate for 2–3 hours or until completely cold. Spoon into a food processor and process until smooth and shiny. Refrigerate until ready to use.

salt sablé

285 g (10 oz) chilled unsalted butter, cut into small dice
2 g (²/₂₅ oz) sea salt flakes
375 g (13 oz) plain (all-purpose) flour, sifted
188 g (6¾ oz) caster (superfine) sugar
50 g (1¾ oz) lightly beaten egg

Put the butter, salt, flour and sugar in an electric mixer with a beater attachment and beat on medium speed until the mixture resembles coarse breadcrumbs. Add the egg and mix until just combined. Gather into a ball, place on plastic wrap and pat down to a 2 cm (¾ inch) thick disc. Wrap and refrigerate for 2 hours, until firm.

Preheat the oven to 160°C (315°F/Gas 2–3) and line a baking tray with non-stick baking paper. Use a coarse grater to grate the cold dough over the paper to cover it evenly. Bake for 12–14 minutes or until light golden. Cool on the tray, then crumble into small pieces.

mango jelly

10 g (¼ oz) gold gelatine leaves
60 g (2¼ oz) cold water
500 g (1 lb 2 oz) sieved mango purée (see Basics)
70 g (2½ oz) caster (superfine) sugar

Cut the gelatine leaves into small squares, place in a bowl with the water and set aside for 10 minutes to soak.

Meanwhile, put a quarter of the mango purée and the sugar in a saucepan and stir over medium heat until the sugar has dissolved. Remove from the heat, stir in the gelatine and any soaking liquid and stir until the gelatine has dissolved. Stir into the remaining mango purée, then divide among twelve 150 ml (5 fl oz) glasses, approximately 5–6 cm (2–2½ inches) in diameter. Cover and refrigerate for 2 hours or until completely cold and set. You should have a layer about 1.5 cm (⅝ inch) thick in the base of each glass.

mango & corn salsa

2 mangoes
2 corn cobs (in their husks)
Finely grated zest of 1 lemon

Peel the mango and cut the flesh into 1 cm ($\frac{1}{2}$ inch) squares. Cook the corn cobs, still in the husks, in boiling water for 10 minutes or until the corn kernels are tender. Drain and when cool enough to handle, peel away the husks and slice the kernels from the cobs into a bowl of iced water. Set aside to cool completely, then drain well. Toss the mango, corn and lemon zest together. Cover and refrigerate for 2 hours or until ready to use.

pain d'épices

150 g ($5\frac{1}{2}$ oz) lightly beaten egg
25 g (1 oz) caster (superfine) sugar
250 g (9 oz) honey
50 g ($1\frac{3}{4}$ oz) dark brown sugar
150 g ($5\frac{1}{2}$ oz) rye flour
75 g ($2\frac{3}{4}$ oz) strong plain (all-purpose) flour
15 g ($\frac{1}{2}$ oz) baking powder
Pinch of fine salt
5 g ($\frac{1}{8}$ oz) ground cinnamon
5 g ($\frac{1}{8}$ oz) freshly grated nutmeg
5 g ($\frac{1}{8}$ oz) mixed spice
5 g ($\frac{1}{8}$ oz) ground star anise
5 g ($\frac{1}{8}$ oz) ground ginger
Finely grated zest of $\frac{1}{2}$ orange
Finely grated zest of $\frac{1}{2}$ lemon
112 g ($3\frac{3}{4}$ oz) milk

Preheat the oven to 160°C (315°F/Gas 2–3) and line two square 35 cm (14 inch) baking sheets with non-stick baking paper. Use a ruler and pencil to mark a 20 x 30 cm (8 x 12 inch) rectangle on each piece of paper and then turn them upside down.

Put the egg and caster sugar in an electric mixer with a whisk attachment and mix on low speed to just combine. Place the honey and brown sugar in a saucepan over medium heat and bring to roughly 75°C (167°F). With the motor running on medium speed, slowly pour the hot honey mixture down the side of the bowl. When it has all been added, continue to beat for 4 minutes or until pale and creamy, and 50°C (122°F). Replace the whisk attachment with a beater attachment.

Add the combined sifted flours, baking powder and spices, and the orange and lemon zest. Mix on medium speed to combine. Warm the milk in a saucepan over low heat to 38°C (100°F). With the motor still running,

gradually add the milk to the cake batter, mixing until just combined. Divide the batter between the lined trays, spreading it out to cover the marked rectangles. Bake for 15 minutes or until dry to the touch, and the top springs back when gently pressed with your fingertips. Remove from the oven and allow to cool on the trays. Trim the edges and cut into 6 mm ($\frac{1}{4}$ inch) cubes.

citron punch

150 g ($5\frac{1}{2}$ oz) freshly squeezed and strained lemon juice
100 g ($3\frac{1}{2}$ oz) caster (superfine) sugar
Seeds scraped from $\frac{1}{2}$ vanilla bean

Combine all the ingredients in a saucepan and stir over medium heat until the sugar has dissolved. Remove from the heat and cool to room temperature.

to assemble

Remove the glasses with the jelly from the refrigerator. Top with a 1 cm ($\frac{1}{2}$ inch) layer of the vanilla & saffron crème, followed by a layer of the crumbled salt sablé, then top with another 1 cm ($\frac{1}{2}$ inch) layer of the vanilla & saffron crème. Add an even layer of the pain d'épices cubes. Divide the mango & corn salsa over the top, then sprinkle with more pain d'épices. Fill 12 disposable pipettes (see Note) with the citron punch by dipping the tips into the syrup, squeezing the tops (holding tanks) and then releasing slowly in order for the syrup to be sucked into the top. Serve each dessert with a citron punch pipette for squeezing over.

note: Pipettes are small measuring instruments, commonly used for scientific purposes, that can be bought online. You can, of course, just pour a little citron punch over each dessert instead.

black rose

vanilla chantilly

4 g ($^4/_{25}$ oz) gold gelatine leaves
24 g (1 oz) cold water
590 g (1 lb 5 oz) pouring (whipping) cream (35% fat)
175 g (6 oz) caster (superfine) sugar
Seeds scraped from 2 vanilla beans

Cut the gelatine leaves into small squares, place in a bowl with the cold water and set aside for 15 minutes to soak.

Put the cream, sugar and vanilla seeds in a saucepan and stir over medium heat until the sugar has dissolved. Bring to the boil, then remove from the heat and cool to 75–80°C (167–176°F). Add the gelatine and any soaking liquid and stir until dissolved. Strain into a container and set aside to cool to room temperature. Cover and refrigerate overnight.

licorice gelato

500 g (1 lb 2 oz) milk
75 g (2¾ oz) pouring (whipping) cream (35% fat)
50 g (1¾ oz) soft licorice sticks (as fresh as possible),
    cut into 3 mm (⅛ inch) thick slices
310 g (11 oz) caster (superfine) sugar
10 g (¼ oz) liquid glucose
15 g (½ oz) skim milk powder
10 g (¼ oz) cornflour (cornstarch)

Put all the ingredients in a saucepan and stir over medium heat until the sugar has dissolved and the licorice has softened. Continue cooking until the mixture reaches 85°C (185°F), then remove from the heat and blitz with a stick mixer until smooth and the licorice is well incorporated. Strain through a sieve into a container and refrigerate until completely cold, stirring frequently to prevent a skin forming.

Churn in an ice-cream machine according to the manufacturer's instructions, then freeze in a covered container until ready to use.

raspberry gel

2 g ($^2/_{25}$ oz) gold gelatine leaves
12 g ($^2/_5$ oz) cold water
250 g (9 oz) sieved raspberry purée (see Basics)
20 g (¾ oz) caster (superfine) sugar

Cut the gelatine leaves into small squares, place in a bowl with the water and set aside for 5 minutes to soak.

Put a quarter of the raspberry purée and the sugar in a saucepan over medium heat and stir until the sugar has dissolved. Cook until the mixture reaches 80°C (176°F). Remove from the heat and stir in the gelatine until it has dissolved. Stir in the remaining purée. Pour into the bases of twelve 150 ml (5 fl oz) glasses, approximately 5–6 cm (2–2½ inches) in diameter, to make a layer 1 cm (½ inch) thick. Refrigerate for 1 hour or until you are ready to assemble and serve.

black sesame sponge

125 g (4½ oz) toasted black sesame seed paste
    (see Pistachio paste in Basics)
125 g (4½ oz) egg whites
85 g (3 oz) egg yolks
40 g (1½ oz) plain (all-purpose) flour, sifted
100 g (3½ oz) caster (superfine) sugar

Combine all the ingredients in a bowl, then spoon into a 500 ml (17 fl oz) cream canister (see Glossary) and charge with two N_2O bulbs. Place in the refrigerator for 10 minutes. Use scissors to cut three 2.5 cm (1 inch) long, evenly spaced slits in the side of each of 12 flexible plastic cups. Spray enough mixture from the canister to come a third of the way up the side of each cup, then microwave in batches on high (100%) for 55 seconds or until the mixture rises and stops. Transfer to the freezer.

brown sugar crumble

50 g (1¾ oz) unsalted butter, chopped
50 g (1¾ oz) ground almonds
50 g (1¾ oz) brown sugar
50 g (1¾ oz) plain (all-purpose) flour, sifted
1 g ($^1/_{25}$ oz) sea salt flakes

Preheat the oven to 170°C (325°F/Gas 3). Line a baking tray with non-stick baking paper.

Put all the ingredients in an electric mixer with a beater attachment and beat on medium speed until the mixture comes together in clumps. Scatter over the lined tray and bake for 12 minutes or until lightly golden. Remove from the heat and cool on the tray. When cool, break up the crumble into smaller pieces and process in a food processor until the mixture resembles coarse sand.

lychee caviar

125 g (4½ oz) sieved lychee purée (see Basics)
125 g (4½ oz) still mineral water
1.8 g (³⁄₅₀ oz) algin (see Glossary)
1.3 g (¹⁄₂₅ oz) calcic (see Glossary)
250 g (9 oz) still mineral water, extra

Combine the lychee purée, 125 g (4½ oz) water and algin in a bowl, then blitz with a stick mixer until the mixture starts to thicken. Combine the calcic and extra water in a separate bowl, then blitz with a stick mixer until the mixture is well combined and clear. Put both liquids in the refrigerator, still in separate bowls, for 2 hours or until well chilled.

Fill a large syringe with the lychee mixture, then add to the calcic mixture 1 droplet at a time — each droplet will set quickly into a small sphere and fall to the bottom of the bowl. Continue until you have used all the lychee mixture. Lift the lychee caviar out with a sieve and rinse under cold running water. Transfer to a plastic container, cover with cold water and refrigerate until ready to use.

raspberry & poprock chocolate

200 g (7 oz) white couverture chocolate, chopped or buttons, tempered (see Basics)
20 g (¾ oz) freeze-dried raspberries (see Glossary), crushed
40 g (1½ oz) plain poprocks (see Glossary)

Line a baking tray with non-stick baking paper. Combine the tempered chocolate with the raspberries and poprocks. Use a large spatula to spread the mixture onto the lined tray, to an even 2 mm (¹⁄₁₆ inch) thickness. (You will hear some of the poprocks popping as you spread it.) When the mixture has almost set, use a round 4 cm (1½ inch) cutter to stamp out discs.

rose emulsion

5 g (⅛ oz) powdered egg white (see Glossary)
200 g (7 oz) water
25 g (1 oz) caster (superfine) sugar
Seeds scraped from 1 vanilla bean
50 g (1¾ oz) pouring (whipping) cream (35% fat)
5 g (⅛ oz) rosewater
0.5 g (¹⁄₅₀ oz) xanthan gum (see Glossary)

Put the powdered egg white in a small bowl and mix in a small amount of the water (about 3 teaspoons), just enough to make a smooth paste. Put the sugar, remaining water, vanilla seeds, cream, rosewater and xanthan gum in another bowl and blitz with a stick mixer until smooth. Stir through the egg white paste. You can either blitz the emulsion with a stick mixer just before serving, or put it in a 500 ml (17 fl oz) cream canister (see Glossary) and charge with two N$_2$O bulbs. If doing this, fill the canister and refrigerate for 2 hours or until well chilled before using.

to assemble

36 fresh raspberries (optional)

Take the glasses with the raspberry gel out of the refrigerator. Whip the vanilla chantilly to soft peaks using electric beaters and use to fill a piping (icing) bag with a 5 mm (¼ inch) plain nozzle. Pipe a 1.5 cm (⅝ inch) layer on top of the raspberry gel in each glass, then top each with a raspberry & poprock chocolate disc. Sprinkle over enough brown sugar crumble to form a 1 cm (½ inch) layer over the chocolate discs. Top with the drained lychee caviar.

Pop the black sesame sponge out of the cups and break into small pieces — add enough to form a 1 cm (½ inch) layer over the lychee caviar. Use two teaspoons to make small quenelles of licorice gelato and place on top of the sponge layers. Top each dessert with 3 raspberries, if desired.

Blitz the rose emulsion and spoon onto each glass or use the canister to pipe an amount the size of a golf ball onto each glass. Serve. **makes 12**

note: You will have a lot of the black sesame sponge left over, but you need to make this amount in order to fill a canister. Keep the leftover sponge cups in the freezer for up to a month and serve with ice cream.

no soup for you

candied corn chips

300 g (10½ oz) water
300 g (10½ oz) caster (superfine) sugar
30 plain corn chips

Preheat the oven to 50°C (120°F/Gas ¼), or as low as you can get it. Line a square 35 cm (14 inch) baking sheet with non-stick baking paper.

Place the water and sugar in a saucepan over high heat and stir until the sugar has dissolved. Bring to the boil, then remove from the heat and set aside to cool to room temperature.

Dip 2 corn chips in the sugar syrup, then stick them together to create a larger chip with a fan effect and place on the lined tray. Repeat with the remaining chips. Bake for 1 hour, then dip them in the syrup again and return to the oven for 2–3 hours or until very crisp and shiny. It will look like they have been lightly lacquered.

vanilla risotto gelato

1050 g (2 lb 5¾ oz) milk
90 g (3¼ oz) arborio rice
Seeds scraped from 3 vanilla beans
750 g (1 lb 10 oz) milk, extra
112 g (3¾ oz) pouring (whipping) cream (35% fat)
15 g (½ oz) liquid glucose
38 g (1⅓ oz) cornflour (cornstarch)
22 g (¾ oz) milk powder

Put the 1050 g (2 lb 5¾ oz) milk, rice and vanilla seeds in a saucepan and cook over medium heat, stirring occasionally, for 20 minutes or until the rice is tender. Set aside to cool and then refrigerate until needed.

Put the extra milk, cream, liquid glucose, cornflour and milk powder in a separate saucepan over medium heat and stir until combined. Cook until the mixture reaches 85°C (185°F). Cool slightly, then refrigerate until cold. Churn in an ice-cream machine according to the manufacturer's instructions, then transfer to a bowl and stir through the cooked rice mixture. Cover and place in the freezer for 2 hours or until frozen through.

sweetcorn custard

3 corn cobs (in their husks)
300 g (10½ oz) milk
150 g (5½ oz) egg yolks
150 g (5½ oz) caster (superfine) sugar
90 g (3¼ oz) unsalted butter, chopped and softened

Cook the corn cobs, in the husks, in boiling water for 10 minutes or until the kernels are tender. Drain and allow to cool slightly, then peel away the husks and slice the kernels from the cobs into a bowl of iced water. Set aside until completely cool, then drain well and purée with a stick mixer until smooth. Strain into a saucepan, add the milk and bring to the boil over medium heat.

Meanwhile, put the egg yolks and sugar in a bowl and mix with a small whisk to combine. Strain a little hot milk mixture over the egg mixture and mix to combine. Strain the remaining milk mixture over the egg mixture while stirring continuously with a whisk until smooth and well combined. Pour into a clean saucepan, place over medium heat and cook, stirring continuously, for 2 minutes or until the mixture reaches 85°C (185°F) or is thick enough to coat the back of a spoon. Transfer to a bowl and cover with plastic wrap, pressing it onto the surface to prevent a skin forming. Cool the mixture to 50°C (122°F), then blitz in the butter with a stick mixer until smooth. Refrigerate until needed.

pine nut & saffron ganache

300 g (10½ oz) white couverture chocolate,
    chopped or buttons
60 g (2¼ oz) dark couverture chocolate (70%),
    chopped or buttons
180 g (6¼ oz) pouring (whipping) cream (35% fat)
1.5 g (¹⁄₂₀ oz) saffron threads
98 g (3½ oz) unsalted butter, chopped and softened
75 g (2¾ oz) pine nut paste (see Pistachio paste in Basics)
9 g (¼ oz) sea salt flakes

Place both the chocolates in a heatproof bowl. Put the cream and saffron in a saucepan and bring just to the boil over medium heat. Remove from the heat and set aside for 10 minutes to infuse. Return to the heat and bring just to the boil again, then pour over the chocolate and stir until the chocolate has melted and the mixture is smooth. When the mixture is at 50°C (122°F), blitz in the butter and pine nut paste with a stick mixer until well combined. Fold through the salt. Refrigerate for 1 hour or until firm, then roll into 2.5 cm (1 inch) balls and freeze on a tray for 1 hour, until frozen through.

lemon fluid gel

225 g (8 oz) freshly squeezed and strained lemon juice
225 g (8 oz) caster (superfine) sugar
225 g (8 oz) water
7.5 g (¼ oz) agar-agar (see Glossary)

Place all the ingredients in a saucepan and stir over medium heat until the sugar has dissolved. Bring to a rolling boil, then remove from the heat and set aside to cool to room temperature.

to assemble

150 g (5½ oz) panko breadcrumbs (see Glossary)
90 g (3¼ oz) ground almonds
3 g (¹⁄₁₀ oz) ground cinnamon
120 g (4¼ oz) egg whites, lightly beaten
Vegetable oil, for deep-frying
Roasted uncooked arborio rice, ground using a mortar
    and pestle or spice grinder, to garnish
Freeze-dried sweetcorn powder (see Glossary),
    to serve (optional)

Combine the panko crumbs, ground almonds and cinnamon and set aside. Dip a ganache ball in the egg white, allow any excess to drip off and then roll in the crumb mixture until well coated. Repeat with the remaining balls. Fill a deep saucepan one-third full of oil and heat to 190°C (374°F). Deep-fry the balls for 30 seconds or until lightly golden and then transfer to paper towels to drain.

Use the lemon fluid gel to fill a piping (icing) bag with a 9 mm (⅓ inch) plain nozzle. Pipe a 3 cm (1¼ inch) round of gel into the centre of a shallow bowl, approximately 14 cm (5½ inches) in diameter. Use the back of a spoon to smear the gel from the centre to the top of the outside edge of the bowl, and then again from the centre to the other edge.

Use a balloon whisk to whisk the sweetcorn custard until smooth. Pour enough sweetcorn custard into the bowl to come one-third of the way up the side. Place a candied corn chip directly opposite the lemon smear but sitting on top of the custard. Use two tablespoons to form quenelle shapes of gelato and place a quenelle on top of the corn chip. Place 3 deep-fried ganache balls in the middle of the bowl. Combine the ground arborio and sweetcorn powder, if using, and sprinkle over the custard next to the ganache balls. Serve. **serves 12**

gibbo & zumb's australian adventure

banana & passionfruit cream

85 g (3 oz) puréed banana

13 g ($^2/_5$ oz) passionfruit juice (strained fresh
    passionfruit pulp)

10 g ($^1/_4$ oz) freshly squeezed and strained lemon juice

125 g (4$^1/_2$ oz) caster (superfine) sugar

132 g (4$^2/_3$ oz) lightly beaten egg

200 g (7 oz) unsalted butter, chopped and softened

1 banana

20 g ($^3/_4$ oz) freshly squeezed and strained
    lemon juice, extra

Put the puréed banana, passionfruit juice, lemon juice, sugar and egg in a saucepan and stir over medium heat until the sugar has dissolved. Continue to cook, stirring occasionally, until the mixture reaches 85°C (185°F).

Remove from the heat and cool to 50°C (122°F), then blitz in the butter with a stick mixer until smooth. You will need twenty-four 2 cm ($^3/_4$ inch) diameter demisphere flexipan silicone mould cavities, placed on a baking tray. Fill a piping (icing) bag with a 5 mm ($^1/_4$ inch) plain nozzle with the mixture and pipe it into the cavities.

Cut 24 slices, 4 mm ($^1/_6$ inch) thick, from the banana and brush all over with the extra lemon juice. Put a slice of banana on top of the cream mixture in each mould cavity and freeze immediately for 6 hours or until set.

ginger ice cream

250 g (9 oz) pouring (whipping) cream (35% fat)

250 g (9 oz) rice milk

8 g ($^1/_4$ oz) peeled fresh ginger, finely chopped

83 g (3 oz) egg yolks

65 g (2$^1/_3$ oz) caster (superfine) sugar

Put the cream, rice milk and ginger in a saucepan over medium heat and bring to the boil. Remove from the heat and set aside for 15 minutes to infuse. Return the mixture to the heat and bring just to the boil again.

Meanwhile, put the egg yolks and sugar in a bowl and mix with a small balloon whisk until well combined. Gradually strain the hot cream mixture onto the egg mixture while mixing with the whisk to combine well. Return to the pan and cook, stirring continuously, over medium heat until the mixture reaches 85°C (185°F) or easily coats the back of a spoon. Pour into a bowl and cover with plastic wrap, pressing it onto the surface to prevent a skin forming. Cool to room temperature, then refrigerate for 2 hours or until completely cold.

Churn in an ice-cream machine according to the manufacturer's instructions. Freeze until ready to use.

lime marshmallow

22 g ($^3/_4$ oz) gold gelatine leaves

125 g (4$^1/_2$ oz) cold water

93 g (3$^1/_4$ oz) inverted sugar (see Glossary)

150 g (5$^1/_2$ oz) caster (superfine) sugar

58 g (2$^1/_4$ oz) water, extra

70 g (2$^1/_2$ oz) liquid glucose

30 g (1 oz) cocoa butter (see Glossary), finely chopped

58 g (2$^1/_4$ oz) freshly squeezed and strained lime juice

100 g (3$^1/_2$ oz) inverted sugar, extra

250 g (9 oz) desiccated coconut, for coating

You will need a 'dents de loup' triangular metal mould sheet, with 8 triangles measuring 30 cm (12 inches) long, 3.5 cm (1$^2/_5$ inches) wide and 3 cm (1$^1/_4$ inches) deep. Spray the sides of each triangle cavity with cooking oil. Measure out strips of baking paper the same width and length as the sides of the triangles, cut out and use to line the sides of each cavity. Set aside.

Cut the gelatine leaves into small squares, place in a bowl with the cold water and set aside to soak.

Put the inverted sugar, caster sugar, extra water and glucose in a saucepan and stir over medium heat until the sugar has dissolved. Continue to cook until the mixture reaches 113°C (235°F).

Meanwhile, melt the cocoa butter and cool to 50°C (122°F). In a separate, very small saucepan gently warm the lime juice to 50°C (122°F). Keep an eye on both liquids and maintain their temperature as the sugar syrup is getting close to 113°C (235°F).

Place the extra inverted sugar in an electric mixer with a whisk attachment. When the syrup has reached 113°C (235°F), slowly pour it down the side of the mixer bowl, with the motor running on medium speed. When all the syrup has been added, continue to mix for 30–60 seconds to dissolve the inverted sugar.

Immediately mix in the gelatine and any soaking liquid — it is important that the sugar mixture is still quite warm when the gelatine is added so the gelatine fully dissolves. Allow to cool to 50°C (122°F).

With the motor still running on medium speed, gradually add the 50°C (122°F) cocoa butter and the lime juice (it is important that these components are all at the 50°C/122°F mark when they are combined). Once all the ingredients are combined, continue to mix on medium speed for up to 13 minutes or until the mixture is light and fluffy.

Fill a piping (icing) bag with a 17 mm ($^2/_3$ inch) plain nozzle with the mixture and pipe into the lined triangle cavities, filling them all the way to the top. Tap the mould sheet lightly so the tops settle evenly.

remove from the heat, add the gelatine and any soaking liquid and stir until the gelatine has dissolved. Pour into the lined container and refrigerate for 2 hours or until set.

note: Use wild strawberries in the purée if possible, as they are more aromatic and flavoursome.

sablé sand

120 g (4¼ oz) chilled unsalted butter, chopped
80 g (2¾ oz) caster (superfine) sugar
158 g (5²⁄₃ oz) plain (all-purpose) flour, sifted
Seeds scraped from 2 vanilla beans
Salt and pepper, to taste
25 g (1 oz) lightly beaten egg

Put the butter, sugar, flour, vanilla seeds, salt and pepper in an electric mixer with a beater attachment and beat on medium speed until the mixture resembles coarse breadcrumbs. Add the egg and mix until just combined. Gather together into a ball, place on plastic wrap and pat down to a 2 cm (¾ inch) thick disc. Wrap up and refrigerate for 2 hours or until well chilled and firm.

Preheat the oven to 160°C (315°F/Gas 2–3) and line a baking tray with non-stick baking paper. Use a coarse grater to grate the cold dough over the lined tray to cover the paper evenly. Bake for 12–14 minutes or until lightly golden. Cool on the tray, then break up and process in a food processor until it resembles sand.

pistachio & polenta tuile

21 g (¾ oz) pouring (whipping) cream (35% fat)
50 g (1¾ oz) unsalted butter, chopped
21 g (¾ oz) liquid glucose
0.8 g (¹⁄₅₀ oz) yellow pectin (see Glossary)
62 g (2¹⁄₅ oz) caster (superfine) sugar
58 g (2 oz) polenta
40 g (1½ oz) pistachio nuts, finely chopped

Put the cream, butter and glucose in a small saucepan over medium–low heat and stir until the mixture reaches 60°C (140°F). Combine the pectin and sugar, then stir into the cream mixture until combined. Continue to stir until the mixture emulsifies. Add the polenta and stir to combine. Remove from the heat, transfer to a bowl and refrigerate for 2 hours or until completely cold.

Roll the mixture out between two sheets of non-stick baking paper until 2 mm (¹⁄₁₆ inch) thick. Place on a baking tray and freeze for 30 minutes, until frozen solid.

Set aside at room temperature for 1½ hours or until the mixture has set and feels like a spongy marshmallow. Cover a tray with a thick layer of coconut. Turn the marshmallows out of the moulds and gently peel away the paper. Gently touch each side of the long marshmallow triangles on the coconut to coat. Set aside.

strawberry jelly

3.5 g (⅛ oz) gold gelatine leaves
21 g (¾ oz) cold water
104 g (3½ oz) sieved strawberry purée
   (see Basics and Note)
17 g (³⁄₅ oz) caster (superfine) sugar
0.5 g (¹⁄₅₀ oz) agar-agar (see Glossary)

Cut the gelatine leaves into small squares, place in a bowl with the water and set aside for 15 minutes to soak.

Meanwhile, line a square 12 cm (4½ inch) container with plastic wrap. Put the strawberry purée in a saucepan with the sugar and agar-agar and stir over medium heat until the sugar has dissolved. Bring to the boil, then

Preheat the oven to 170°C (325°F/Gas 3). Remove the tray from the freezer and peel away the top layer of paper. Sprinkle the chopped pistachios evenly over the top and bake for 11 minutes or until golden. Set aside to cool on the tray.

pistachio crème anglaise

105 g (3½ oz) milk
32 g (1¼ oz) egg yolks
32 g (1¼ oz) caster (superfine) sugar
0.8 g (¹⁄₅₀ oz) xanthan gum (see Glossary)
10 g (¼ oz) pistachio paste (see Basics)

Put the milk in a saucepan over medium heat and bring to the boil, then remove from the heat.

Meanwhile, mix the egg yolks and sugar in a bowl with a small balloon whisk until well combined. Gradually strain the hot milk onto the egg mixture while stirring continuously with the whisk. Return to the pan, place over medium heat and stir continuously until the mixture reaches 85°C (185°F) or easily coats the back of a spoon. Remove from the heat, add the xanthan gum and pistachio paste and blitz with a stick mixer until combined. Strain into a bowl and cover with plastic wrap, pressing it onto the surface to prevent a skin forming. Cool to room temperature, then refrigerate for 2 hours or until completely cold.

sous-vide strawberries

48 small strawberries, hulled
4 vanilla beans, split lengthways
100 g (3½ oz) caster (superfine) sugar

Fill a large, deep saucepan with water and heat to 60°C (140°F). Ensure the temperature stays consistent throughout the following process.

Divide the strawberries, vanilla beans and sugar evenly among 4 square 15 cm (6 inch) snaplock bags. Seal the bags, leaving one end of each slightly open for the moment. Holding a bag at the top, slowly dip it in the 60°C (140°F) water — the bag will start to cling to the contents. Just before the top of the bag reaches water level, squeeze any excess air out through the open edge, then seal and let the bag sit in the water. Working quickly, repeat with the other bags until they are all sitting in the water. Leave them in the water, ensuring the temperature remains consistent at 60°C (140°F), for 10–15 minutes or until the strawberries are tender, but still whole. They should not change colour or texture in any noticeable way. Remove from the pan and set aside, in the bags, to cool completely. Drain the strawberries from the liquid.

to assemble

Use a sharp knife dipped in hot water and dried thoroughly to cut thirty-six 1 cm (½ inch) thick slices from the marshmallow triangles. Set aside.

Use a balloon whisk to whisk the pistachio crème anglaise until smooth. Fill a piping (icing) bag with a 2 mm (²⁄₂₅ inch) plain nozzle with the anglaise.

Cut the strawberry jelly into 1 cm (½ inch) pieces. Break the pistachio & polenta tuile into shards.

Pop the frozen banana & passionfruit demispheres out of the moulds and roll in the sablé sand.

Starting about 2 cm (¾ inch) in from the edge of a serving plate, and curving out towards the opposite edge of the plate, pipe 4 dots of the pistachio crème anglaise in decreasing size, from around 1 cm (½ inch) down to 2 mm (²⁄₂₅ inch). Repeat on the opposite side of the plate.

Arrange 3 sablé-coated demispheres, banana side down, on the plate, following the anglaise curve. Arrange a marshmallow triangle, drained sous-vide strawberry and tuile shard next to each demisphere. Use two tablespoons to make 2 quenelles of ginger ice cream and arrange them on the plate, then add some strawberry jelly cubes. Serve immediately. **makes 12**

basics

sweet success

In order to get the best results from these recipes, there are some important things to note. Firstly, the recipes in this book use very specific quantities of ingredients and some of these are too small to weigh on regular kitchen scales, so you will need a set of mini digital scales. These are most often sold at tobacconists.

A digital thermometer is another essential piece of equipment required for making these recipes. You can also get small metal clips that help hold them onto the side of the pan. Both are available from speciality kitchenware stores.

Small piping (icing) bags can be bought at supermarkets or you can find a variety of sizes at speciality kitchenware or cake decorating stores. You can use disposable bags, where you simply snip off the tip once filled and discard when finished, or you can buy a piping set that will include a reusable bag and nozzles in various shapes and sizes. Nozzles are also sold separately from cake decorating stores.

As small amounts of egg are called for, whole egg quantities are measured by cracking the eggs into a bowl, beating to combine and then weighing. Egg whites and egg yolks are also measured this way.

You will also find that some of the recipes make more of a certain component than you need. This is because it is not practical to reduce the quantities any further — it may compromise the results. Keep any extra quantities to use as you see fit.

All the recipes in this book have been tested in a standard oven, so if your oven is fan-forced you will need to lower the temperature by 20°C (35°F) as a general guide.

tempering chocolate

Tempering is the term used to describe the technique of heating and cooling chocolate to specific temperatures to ensure it sets hard, snaps cleanly when broken and has a professional glossy shine. It also gives the chocolate a higher melting point, which is important when making chocolates and chocolate decorations.

Tempered chocolate is used whenever chocolate is going to be visible in the finished product. If chocolate is going to be melted and then incorporated into a mixture, there's no need to temper it. You must use couverture chocolate for tempering, and follow the seeding or tabling methods detailed below.

seeding method

500 g (1 lb 2 oz) couverture chocolate (dark, milk or white), chopped or buttons

Melt three-quarters of the chocolate in a clean, dry heatproof bowl over a saucepan of just-simmering water. The water should not touch the base of the bowl. As the chocolate starts to melt, stir gently with a spatula so that the chocolate melts evenly and monitor the temperature with a digital thermometer. When the chocolate reaches 45–48°C (113–118°F) for dark chocolate or 40–45°C (104–113°F) for milk or white chocolate, remove the bowl from the pan. This is the temperature where the cocoa butter crystals in the chocolate will have melted.

Immediately add the remaining chocolate to the bowl and stir until the temperature drops to 27°C (80°F) and all the pieces of chocolate have melted.

Return the bowl to the saucepan of just-simmering water and reheat the chocolate to its ideal working temperature. This is 31–32°C (88–90°F) for dark chocolate and 29–30°C (84–86°F) for milk chocolate and white chocolate. Stir gently and use the chocolate as soon as it reaches the correct temperature.

To test if the chocolate has been correctly tempered, dip the end of a clean palette knife in it. The chocolate should harden, with no streaks, in approximately 3 minutes. (This is at a room temperature of around 20°C/68°F.)

If the temperature drops while you are working with the tempered chocolate, use a heat gun or a hair dryer to gently reheat it to the ideal working temperature.

tabling method (marble benchtop required)

Melt all the chocolate in a clean, dry heatproof bowl over a saucepan of just-simmering water. The water should not touch the base of the bowl. As the chocolate starts to melt, stir gently with a spatula so that the chocolate melts evenly and monitor the temperature with a digital thermometer. When the chocolate reaches 45–48°C (113–118°F) for dark chocolate or 40–45°C (104–113°F) for milk or white chocolate, remove the bowl from the pan. This is the temperature where the cocoa butter crystals in the chocolate will have melted.

Pour two-thirds of the chocolate onto the marble and spread out with a large spatula or chocolate scraper. Use the spatula or scraper to push the chocolate into the centre, then spread it out again. Continue until the chocolate thickens slightly.

Scrape the thickened chocolate back into the bowl with the remaining warm chocolate and stir until it reaches 27°C (80°F). Gently heat the chocolate to its ideal working temperature, as listed above.

fruit purées

These can be bought from speciality food stores and speciality pastry suppliers, often in Tetrapaks or frozen. Buying them is actually more economical and convenient than making your own, however if you prefer to make your own purée it is a simple process. For fruits such as lychee, apricot, cherry, blackcurrant, raspberry, strawberry, mango, peach and passionfruit, first peel if necessary, then remove any pits, stones or stalks. Process the fruit in a food processor to a purée and then press through a fine sieve (discarding any pulp). You will lose some of the weight of the fruit as you are sieving it, so keep that in mind when purchasing the fruit. Store in the refrigerator or freezer.

pear purée Use well-ripened beurre bosc pears, peeled and cored.

rhubarb purée Purée the stewed rhubarb (see recipe below) and then press through a sieve.

candied grapefruit peel

150 g (5½ oz) water
100 g (3½ oz) caster (superfine) sugar
2 long strips grapefruit rind, pith removed

Put the water and sugar in a medium saucepan and bring to the boil over medium heat. Add the grapefruit rind and simmer for 10 minutes. Use a slotted spoon to remove the rind from the syrup and place it on a wire rack to cool completely. Store in an airtight container.

stewed rhubarb

400 g (14 oz) trimmed and washed rhubarb, cut into 1 cm (½ inch) long pieces
133 g (4¾ oz) raw (demerara) sugar

Preheat the oven to 210°C (415°F/Gas 6–7). Place the rhubarb in a roasting tin and sprinkle with the sugar. Cook for 15 minutes or until the rhubarb is tender to the touch and almost falling apart. Cool to room temperature. Store in an airtight container in the refrigerator.

roasted rhubarb pieces

300 g (10½ oz) trimmed large rhubarb stalks
65 g (2⅓ oz) raw sugar

Preheat the oven to 160°C (315°F/Gas 2–3). Wash the rhubarb and cut into 10 cm (4 inch) long pieces. You should have about 20 pieces. Place in a ceramic ovenproof dish large enough to hold the rhubarb snugly in one layer. Sprinkle with the sugar and bake for 10 minutes. Check if the rhubarb is cooked — you only want it to be just tender and remember it will continue to cook slightly once removed from the oven. Cook for a further 2–5 minutes if required.

Remove from the oven and cool to room temperature. Gently turn the rhubarb pieces in the syrup and then place in a single layer in an airtight container. Store in an airtight container in the refrigerator.

simple sugar syrup

250 g (9 oz) caster (superfine) sugar
250 g (9 oz) water

Put the sugar and water in a small saucepan over medium heat and stir until the sugar has dissolved. Bring to the boil, then remove from the heat and cool completely. Store in an airtight container in the refrigerator.

hazelnut praline

250 g (9 oz) hazelnuts
250 g (9 oz) caster (superfine) sugar

Preheat the oven to 180°C (350°F/Gas 4). Line a baking tray with non-stick baking paper. Spread the hazelnuts over the lined tray and roast for 10–12 minutes or until lightly golden. Remove the skins while the nuts are still warm by rubbing the nuts in a tea towel (dish towel). Caramelise the sugar in a saucepan over medium–low heat, shaking the pan occasionally and rolling the sugar around the pan as it melts. Cook until a dark-amber colour, then quickly add the hazelnuts and stir with a heatproof spatula to coat each nut. Spread onto the lined tray. Allow to cool, then break into pieces and process in a food processor until finely chopped. Store in an airtight container.

almond praline Replace the hazelnuts with 250 g (9 oz) roasted blanched almonds. There is no need to rub the roasted nuts in a tea towel.

pistachio praline Replace the hazelnuts with 250 g (9 oz) roasted pistachio nuts. There is no need to rub the roasted nuts in a tea towel.

pistachio paste

250 g (9 oz) pistachio nuts
30 g (1 oz) vegetable oil

Preheat the oven to 180°C (350°F/Gas 4). Line a baking tray with non-stick baking paper. Spread the pistachios over the lined tray and roast for 10–12 minutes or until lightly golden. Cool slightly, then transfer to a food processor and process to a fine paste. Add up to 30 g (1 oz) oil, with the motor running, if needed.

almond paste Replace the pistachios with 250 g (9 oz) blanched almonds.

hazelnut paste Replace the pistachios with hazelnuts. Remove the skins while the nuts are still warm by rubbing them in a tea towel (dish towel).

macadamia paste Replace the pistachios with 200 g (7 oz) macadamia nuts and do not add the oil.

pine nut paste Replace the pistachios with 250 g (9 oz) pine nuts, roasted for 7–10 minutes, and do not add the oil.

toasted black sesame seed paste Replace the pistachios with 125 g (4½ oz) toasted black sesame seeds (there's no need to roast them) and use sesame oil.

almond crème

75 g (2¾ oz) unsalted butter, chopped and softened
75 g (2¾ oz) pure icing (confectioners') sugar, sifted
75 g (2¾ oz) almond meal
7.5 g (¼ oz) cornflour (cornstarch)
82 g (2¾ oz) lightly beaten egg
97 g (3½ oz) crème pâtissiére (see Croque-en-bouche recipe, page 164,
    make ½ quantity and use the remainder in another recipe)

Put the butter, sugar, almond meal and cornflour in a bowl. Use hand-held electric beaters to beat until lightly creamed. Add the egg and beat until incorporated. Fold through the crème pâtissiére until smooth, cover with plastic wrap and refrigerate for 1¼ hours before using.

clear neutral glaze

250 g (9 oz) water
10 g (¼ oz) pectin NH (see Glossary)
265 g (9⅓ oz) caster (superfine) sugar
20 g (¾ oz) liquid glucose

Place the water in a saucepan and bring to 60°C (140°F). Mix the pectin with 65 g (2⅓ oz) of the sugar, add to the water and stir to combine. Bring to the boil and add the remaining sugar. Return to the boil and add the glucose. Remove from the heat and allow to cool completely. Store in an airtight container in the refrigerator. To use, reheat to 35°C (95°F) in a heatproof bowl over a saucepan of simmering water or in the microwave.

chocolate mirror glaze

100 g (3½ oz) water
180 g (6¼ oz) caster (superfine) sugar
50 g (1¾ oz) liquid glucose
150 g (5½ oz) pouring (whipping) cream (35% fat)
100 g (3½ oz) unsweetened cocoa powder, sifted
12.5 g (²⁄₅ oz) gold gelatine leaves
62 g (2⅕ oz) cold water
182 g (6¼ oz) clear neutral glaze (see recipe on page 243), heated to 35°C (95°F)

Put the water, sugar, glucose, cream and cocoa in a saucepan over medium heat and mix with a heatproof spatula (not a whisk), stirring the whole time to ensure the mixture doesn't catch on the base or side of the pan. Heat to 103°C (217°F), then remove from the heat and cool to 50°C (122°F).

Cut the gelatine leaves into small squares, place in a bowl with the cold water and set aside to soak.

When the chocolate mixture reaches 50°C (122°F), mix in the gelatine and any soaking liquid. Add the clear neutral glaze and blitz with a stick mixer until combined. Transfer to a heatproof bowl and place in the refrigerator until completely set. To use, reheat to 35°C (95°F) in a heatproof bowl over a saucepan of simmering water or in the microwave.

milk chocolate glaze

20 g (¾ oz) gold gelatine leaves
120 g (4¼ oz) cold water
75 g (2¾ oz) water, extra
150 g (5½ oz) caster (superfine) sugar
150 g (5½ oz) liquid glucose
100 g (3½ oz) condensed milk
150 g (5½ oz) milk couverture chocolate, chopped or buttons

Cut the gelatine leaves into small squares, place in a bowl with the cold water and set aside to soak. Put the extra water, sugar and glucose in a small saucepan over medium heat, stirring until the sugar has dissolved. Heat the syrup until it reaches 105°C (221°F). Stir in the gelatine and any soaking liquid, as well as the condensed milk. Put the chocolate in a heatproof bowl. Pour over the hot condensed milk mixture and stir until smooth. Allow to cool, then cover with plastic wrap and refrigerate until set. To use, reheat to 35°C (95°F) in a heatproof bowl over a saucepan of simmering water or in the microwave.

caramel maison

220 g (7¾ oz) pouring (whipping) cream (35% fat)
1 vanilla bean, split and seeds scraped
120 g (4¼ oz) water
300 g (10½ oz) caster (superfine) sugar
60 g (2¼ oz) liquid glucose

Put the cream and vanilla seeds and bean in a saucepan over medium heat. Bring to the boil, then remove from the heat and remove the vanilla bean.

Meanwhile, put the water, sugar and glucose in a heavy-based saucepan over medium–low heat and cook, stirring occasionally, until the sugar and glucose have dissolved. Brush down the side of the pan with a clean pastry brush dipped in water to avoid any crystallisation. Increase the heat to medium and cook the sugar mixture until it becomes a dark-amber colour. Carefully stir the hot cream mixture into the caramel to deglaze — watch out, it will spit and release a lot of heat. Stir until smooth. Transfer to a bowl and cool to room temperature, then cover with plastic wrap and store in the refrigerator.

italian meringue

250 g (9 oz) egg whites
150 g (5½ oz) water
450 g (1 lb) caster (superfine) sugar

Put the egg whites in an electric mixer with a whisk attachment. Put the water and sugar in a heavy-based saucepan over medium–low heat and cook, stirring occasionally, until the sugar has dissolved. Brush down the side of the pan with a clean pastry brush dipped in water to avoid any crystallisation. Increase the heat to medium and bring the sugar syrup to 121°C (250°F). With the motor running on medium speed, pour the sugar syrup down the side of the mixer bowl in a slow steady stream. Continue to mix until the temperature drops to 50°C (122°F), stopping the mixer whenever you check the temperature. Use as directed. (Make as needed, as it doesn't store well.)

streusel

250 g (9 oz) chilled unsalted butter, chopped
250 g (9 oz) brown sugar
375 g (13 oz) almond meal
250 g (9 oz) plain (all-purpose) flour
10 g (¼ oz) salt

Preheat the oven to 180°C (350°F/Gas 4). Put all the ingredients in an electric mixer with a beater attachment and beat on medium speed until the ingredients start to bind and form lumps. Spread over 2 baking trays lined with non-stick baking paper and bake for 15 minutes or until golden. Cool and break up into small pieces. Store in an airtight container at room temperature.

lavender sugar

200 g (7 oz) caster (superfine) sugar
50 g (1¾ oz) dried lavender

Put the sugar and lavender in a spice grinder and grind to a fine powder. (You may need to do this in batches, depending on the size of your spice grinder.) Store in an airtight container.

citric acid solution

50 g (1¾ oz) warm water
50 g (1¾ oz) citric acid (see Glossary)

Put the water in a bowl, add the citric acid and stir until it has dissolved. Store in an airtight container at room temperature.

egg wash

150 g (5½ oz) lightly beaten egg
25 g (1 oz) pouring (whipping) cream (35% fat)
5 g (⅛ oz) salt

Lightly whisk together, then use as directed.

glossary

Acetate sheets are available from art supply stores.

Agar-agar is a setting agent derived from seaweed that has strong gelling properties. We use it in powdered form. It is available from selected health food stores, Asian grocers and online.

Algin is a brand of sodium alginate, a natural gelling agent derived from brown seaweed. It is used for thickening and emulsifying, and is available from selected speciality food stores and online.

Bergamot essential oil is available from health food stores.

Calcic is a brand of calcium chloride, a calcium salt commonly used in the food industry. It is an essential ingredient in the reaction with algin that produces spherification. Calcic is available from selected speciality food stores and online.

Calcium carbonate is combined with water to enable spherification. It is available from selected speciality food stores and online.

Chocolate cups are available from speciality food stores and some supermarkets.

Citric acid is available from supermarkets.

Cocoa nibs, cocoa mass and cocoa butter:
When cocoa beans are cleaned and separated from their shells, cocoa nibs (the edible part of the bean) are produced. The nibs are then roasted, crushed and processed into premium-quality cocoa mass, cocoa butter or cocoa powder.
Cocoa mass is the most important ingredient in the manufacture of chocolate.
Cocoa butter is solid and has no taste, but it helps produce shine and gives harder cracking properties to tempered chocolate. Available from speciality food stores, speciality pastry suppliers and online.

Coconut milk powder is available from Asian grocers.

Cola extract is often used to make cola drinks with carbonated water. It can be found at stores that sell machines and supplies for making your own carbonated drinks, and may be called cola concentrate.

Cream canisters are used to aerate liquids (not just cream). Small bulbs of nitrous oxide (N_2O) are used to charge the canisters. The canisters and bulbs are available from kitchenware stores.

Dark couverture chocolate Tanzanie is available from speciality pastry suppliers. It is fragrant and floral with only a trace of sweetness and has 75% cocoa solids.

Date molasses is available from Middle Eastern grocery stores.

Dipping forks (for chocolate) are available from speciality kitchenware stores.

Edible gold leaf is thin, delicate sheets of pure edible gold. It is available from speciality food stores and cake decorating stores.

Edible silver and bronze metallic (for dusting macarons) is available from cake decorating stores.

Fresh yeast is available from selected speciality food stores and delicatessens.

Freeze-dried fruit/vegetables are sold at speciality food stores and pastry suppliers. They are available whole and/or powdered, depending on the fruit or vegetable.

Gel food colourings are available from cake decorating stores.

Gelatine leaves are available in different strengths, so instead of stating the number of leaves to use we have given gram measurements so you can adapt the recipes for the various types of leaf gelatine available. They are available from speciality food stores.

Gellan is a gelling agent that is obtained from the fermentation of *sphingomonas elodea* bacteria. It is available from selected speciality food stores and online.

Hickory chips are used to impart a strong smoky flavour and are available from barbecue supply shops.

Inverted sugar is a syrup made by heating and adding an acid (such as citric acid) to a simple sugar syrup. It retains moisture, so is used in baked goods to help prevent them drying out. As it doesn't crystallise, it is also helpful to prevent ice or crystals forming in ice creams, sorbets and glazes. It is available from speciality pastry suppliers.

Iota is a gelling agent extracted from a type of red algae found on the coasts of the north Atlantic, as well as in the Philippine and Indonesian seas. It is available from selected speciality food stores and online.

Isomalt is a sugar made from the natural sugar in beetroot. It has half the calories of cane sugar and unlike regular sucrose, it can be heated up to 190°C (375°F) without changing colour and can be used to create virtually any shape. It is available from speciality pastry suppliers and online.

Japanese mayonnaise has a unique taste that goes well with Japanese flavours. It is available from Asian grocers.

Lecithin is a powder extracted from soy beans that is used as an emulsifier, stabiliser and thickener. It is available from speciality food stores and online.

Lightly salted corn kernels are also referred to as corn crunch. Available from selected health food stores.

Lipid-soluble food colourings are fat-soluble food colourings, available from speciality pastry suppliers.

Maltodextrin is a modified starch that can be made from corn, potato, tapioca, wheat and rice. It is used as a carrier for flavours, and also as a thickening agent and sweetener. We use maltodextrin powder from tapioca. Available from speciality food stores and online.

Natural violet extract or oil is available from selected health food stores or naturopaths.

Pailleté feuilletine is made from crushed wafers or crepes (gavottes) and is used by pastry chefs to add texture. It is available from speciality food stores and speciality pastry suppliers.

Pandan leaves and extract are taken from an aromatic member of the pandanus family and are widely used in Asian cooking. The leaves are long and thin. Available from Asian grocers.

Panko breadcrumbs are flaky Japanese breadcrumbs that are available from Asian grocers.

Pearl sugar is a coarse, opaque white sugar that resembles rock salt in appearance. It adds both sweetness and texture to a dish. It is available from speciality food stores.

Pectin is a natural product that can be found in the cell wall of all plants. Most commercial pectin is extracted under mildly acidic conditions from citrus peel or apple pomace (the pulp that is left after apples are squeezed and juiced). There are a number of pectins available, all with specific characteristics.
Yellow pectin, also called pectin jaune, and *pectin NH* are available from speciality pastry suppliers and online.

Pomegranate molasses is available from selected delicatessens and Middle Eastern food stores.

Poprocks are available from speciality pastry suppliers and some lolly (candy) shops. Be sure to buy the plain variety, not the flavoured ones.

Powdered egg white is available at speciality food stores.

Ready-to-roll icing is available from selected supermarkets, speciality food stores and cake decorating suppliers.

Silpat is a non-stick baking mat made of fibreglass and silicone that is available from speciality kitchenware stores and online.

Solid coconut oil is available from Asian grocers and selected health food stores.

Titanium dioxide is a food-grade white pigment in powder form that is used to create a bright white colour in foods. Available from wholesale pastry suppliers.

Tonka beans are native to South America and are used in a similar way to a vanilla bean, however the beans are finely grated like nutmeg. Only a little is used as tonka beans contain coumarin, which is an anti-coagulant and in high doses can thin out the blood to dangerous levels. Available from speciality spice stores and online.

Tonkatsu sauce is a popular Japanese condiment available from Japanese or Asian grocers.

UHT coconut cream is available from selected Asian grocers. (The Kara brand is nearly all coconut, so I find it gives the best results.)

Wagners are airless spray gun canisters, available from hardware stores. Buy a new one to use only in cooking.

Wasabi powder is available from Asian grocers.

Xanthan gum is produced by fermenting corn starch and is used extensively in the food industry as a thickener. It is gluten free and available from health food stores and selected supermarkets.

Yuzu is the Japanese name for a yellow citrus fruit with a distinctive sharp taste. The bottled juice is available from good Japanese food stores.

index

acknowledgements

The team at Murdoch Books: Kylie, Livia, Hugh, Brett, Matt, Sonia and Anna. Thanks! Your hard work has made this book amazing, you are all so talented.

Jane Lawson: Thanks for sitting there, listening to me trying to explain recipes while you typed and for getting this opportunity for me.

My Mum and Dad (Little Franky and Nancy): I wouldn't be in this position, with these opportunities, without your help. You supported me from the start, even though you thought I was wasting my time when I first began cooking, but I opened your eyes. I know you are both so proud of me from all of your love and support. Thank you, I love you both.

My sister Rosie (Rosalba): You got me through my apprenticeship and now we work together. You have helped me so much - a great partnership for many years to come. Thank you and I love you.

Trisha (my other sister), my bro H, and Jeremey, Hunter and Dakota (my nieces and nephews): Your love and support is priceless.

Dean Gibson: You have been a massive mentor since I met you in 2000 as a second-year apprentice. I cherish the love for good product that you showed me when you were my boss. You are an important part of baking and pastry in Australia, and your passion is bringing everyone in the industry together.

My team: Dean, Charlie, Tash, Chelsea, Wah-Wah, Alessia, Stacey, Rhian, Phoebe and the rest of you, so many to name. Thanks for all the prep, photo shoots, your talent and hard work. This wouldn't be possible without you.

The customers, fans and supporters of Adriano Zumbo Patissier: Thank you. Your support and love of great patisserie is the fuel in the fire that keeps me going.

Pierre Hermé, Ramon Morató, Philippe Conticini, Christophe Adam, Christophe Michalak, the Adrià brothers, Heston Blumenthal, Willy Wonka: I thank you for what you have done for pastry worldwide and the inspiration, fantasy and imagination you have brought into my world. Keep leading the way!

Gary Willis: Thanks for being a great supporter of my career, and pastry and chocolate in Australia.

The producers, suppliers and ingredient specialists: These products are possible due to your great ingredients, support and focus on quality.

My angels who watch over me every day and guide me on my journey: I don't know who you are, but thank you.

Everyone out there who loves patisserie, chocolates and baking: We've only just begun.

eat sweet & keep baking!

Published in 2011 by Murdoch Books Pty Limited

Murdoch Books Australia
Pier 8/9
23 Hickson Road
Millers Point NSW 2000
Phone: +61 (0) 2 8220 2000
Fax: +61 (0) 2 8220 2558
www.murdochbooks.com.au
info@murdochbooks.com.au

Murdoch Books UK Limited
Erico House, 6th Floor
93–99 Upper Richmond Road
Putney, London SW15 2TG
Phone: +44 (0) 20 8785 5995
Fax: +44 (0) 20 8785 5985
www.murdochbooks.co.uk
info@murdochbooks.co.uk

For Corporate Orders & Custom Publishing contact Noel Hammond, National Business Development Manager

Publisher: Kylie Walker
Designer: Hugh Ford
Photographer: Brett Stevens
Stylist: Matt Page
Project Manager: Livia Caiazzo
Food Editor: Sonia Greig
Editor: Anna Scobie
Production Controller: Alexandra Gonzalez

National Library of Australia Cataloguing-in-Publication entry
Author: Zumbo, Adriano.
Title: Zumbo : Adriano Zumbo's fantastical kitchen of other-worldly
delights / Adriano Zumbo.
ISBN: 9781741968040 (hbk.)
Notes: Includes index.
Subjects: Confectionery.
Cooking.
Dewey Number: 641.86
A catalogue record for this book is available from the British Library.

Printed by 1010 Printing International Limited, China
Reprinted 2011.

The Publisher and stylist would like to thank Dinosaur Designs for lending equipment for use and photography.

IMPORTANT: Those who might be at risk from the effects of salmonella poisoning (the elderly, pregnant women, young children and those suffering from immune deficiency diseases) should consult their doctor with any concerns about eating raw eggs.

OVEN GUIDE: You may find cooking times vary depending on the oven you are using. For fan-forced ovens, as a general rule, set the oven temperature to 20°C (35°F) lower than indicated in the recipe.